ISBN 978-1-334-02888-5
PIBN 10573530

1 MONTH OF
FREE
READING

at

www.ForgottenBooks.com

By purchasing this book you are eligible for one month membership to ForgottenBooks.com, giving you unlimited access to our entire collection of over 700,000 titles via our web site and mobile apps.

To claim your free month visit:
www.forgottenbooks.com/free573530

English
Français
Deutsche
Italiano
Español
Português

www.forgottenbooks.com

Mythology Photography **Fiction**
Fishing Christianity **Art** Cooking
Essays Buddhism Freemasonry
Medicine **Biology** Music **Ancient**
Egypt Evolution Carpentry Physics
Dance Geology **Mathematics** Fitness
Shakespeare **Folklore** Yoga Marketing
Confidence Immortality Biographies
Poetry **Psychology** Witchcraft
Electronics Chemistry History **Law**
Accounting **Philosophy** Anthropology
Alchemy Drama Quantum Mechanics
Atheism Sexual Health **Ancient History**
Entrepreneurship Languages Sport
Paleontology Needlework Islam
Metaphysics Investment Archaeology
Parenting Statistics Criminology
Motivational

TRUE

MANHOOD

A MANUAL FOR YOUNG MEN.

A GUIDE TO PHYSICAL STRENGTH, MORAL EXCELLENCE, FORCE OF CHARACTER, AND MANLY PURITY.

A SPECIAL PHYSIOLOGY,

BY

E. R. SHEPHERD,

Noted Author and Physiologist.

ALSO

THE WHITE CROSS:

Its Origin and Progress.

BY B. F. DE COSTA, D. D.

---

*" My strength is as the strength of ten,
Because my heart is pure."*
—TENNYSON.

EIGHTH EDITION.
REVISED AND ILLUSTRATED.

CHICAGO.
A. B. STOCKHAM & CO.,
1891.

DEDICATION.

TRUE MANHOOD

Is Respectfully Inscribed

to

DR. C. B. WINSLOW,

A Pioneer in Purity Reform,

For many years President of the

Moral Education Society, of Washington, D. C.,

To whose inspiration more than to any other source

The Young men of America are indebted

for the instruction in

these pages.

PUBLISHER'S NOTICE.

The manuscript of MANHOOD was sub-mitted for examination, with reference to its anatomical and physiological details to Dr. D. S. Lamb, A. A. Surgeon, U. S. A., and Pro-fessor of Anatomy of Howard Medical College, and is published as approved by him. Recom-mended by prominent ministers, philanthro-pists, physicians, and physiologists. Endorsed by leading journals of the country.

CONTENTS.

INTRODUCTORY; TO PARENTS.

PART I.

CHAPTER I.

LIFE FROM SEEDS AND EGGS.

CHAPTER II.

HUMAN LIFE.

CHAPTER III.

THE FATHER PART OF PLANT LIFE.

CHAPTER IV.

ABOUT ANIMALS.

CHAPTER V.

THE HUMAN TREE OF LIFE.

CHAPTER VI.

WHEN I'M A MAN.

CHAPTER VII.

THE SCIENCE OF THE HUMAN BODY.

CHAPTER VIII.

WHAT CELLS DO.

CHAPTER IX.

GLANDS.

CHAPTER X.

THE LIVER GLAND.

PART II.

CHAPTER I.

SPECIAL PHYSIOLOGY OF MAN.

CHAPTER II.

MANHOOD ABUSED.

CHAPTER III.

SECRETION VS. ABSORPTION.

CHAPTER IV.

VIRILITY.

CHAPTER V.

PROCREATION.

CHAPTER VI.

POWER OF THOUGHT.

CHAPTER VII.

CONSCIOUS AND UNCONSCIOUS THOUGHT.

CONTENTS.

ILLUSTRATIONS.

PHYSICAL CULTURE.

INTRODUCTORY.

TO PARENTS.

The earliest truth impressed by reverent parents upon the little one is, that God made all things. The child comprehends that although toys, furniture and the like are made by men out of wood from trees, that man cannot make trees; that men build houses of stone, but cannot make rocks; that the moon, stars and clouds are upheld by some greater Power than man. He sees no reason to doubt the assertion, when he is told that God made man; that God made him.

When later he inquires, "Where did I come from?" or, "Where did you get the baby?" he already believes that God made him. It is not that he may be continually reminded of this, that he repeats the question, and it as much of an insult to rebuff him with that reply as it would be were you to be told, "God made it," or, "You must not ask questions," when you inquire where a specimen of a plant or animal was found.

It is of the process of formation and growth he would learn, and his parent knows very well that it is. If you do not tell now what his little mind can grasp, what will satisfy his present desires, he will not forget and give up the search, but in the street some luckless day he may pick up an answer. There are no debasing thoughts in his mind now, and if he is told the truth with that same devout reminder that God is the author of all about which he is learning, he will continue free from them. His questions should not be evaded with scorn, shame, ridicule or falsehood.

Just *what* answer you should give depends on circumstances. No set rule can be laid down as to what knowledge must come first, or in what manner given; this must be decided by the questions the child asks, and his ability to comprehend. Some are more precocious than others.

If a child of six or seven years manifests no curiosity and you are *very sure* that no associate has initiated him into the mysteries of sex, do not hasten to arouse his inquisitiveness. Meanwhile be storing in his mind facts and experiences to draw from when the questions do come.

Cultivate a few flowers or vegetables, allowing him to assist you in gathering and planting the seeds. Keep some fowls if possible, or a bird or two; also a kitten and dog. By pictures and books give him some idea of the numerous other plants and animals in the world.

Meet square questions with fair truth. For instance, it is easy to say the egg of the hen is formed in her body, but it is more delicate and distasteful to say that kittens grew in the mother cat's body, yet it *should be said*, and once the ice is broken, smooth sailing follows.

Conquer your prudery. Remember it is all in your own mind, and not at all in his. Yours came from wrong education. Realize the truth, and show in all your talk with your child your belief that *there is nothing in God's works of which to be ashamed.* The shame is made by man. Your boy will listen with wide open eyes, with no tell-tale blush or hanging of the head, if he is as yet untainted with false shame.

It should be made clear to him that there are certain times and occasions when these topics should be avoided. Examples are obvious which could be used in illustration; as the use of injections in sickness, or the cleaning of finger nails, etc., which are proper when necessary, in private or in the presence of parents, but to which the attention of strangers should not be attracted. He may be taught the beauty of modesty in better ways than the old fashioned one of crying shame upon innocent queries.

To a very young child the facts herein stated must be given orally, enlarged upon and illustrated at your

2

option. In that case the book becomes to you only an outline, a guide, to be expanded as much as you please. It may require several months or years to impart, piecemeal, these truths.

A few simple rules will safely guide in every case.

1. *Tell nothing but the truth.*

2. Tell no more at a time than the child is prepared to receive.

3. When the questions are too advanced, impress upon his mind that he is too young to understand everything, but must wait till he is older. Make him feel he may get all he desires to know from you. Then he will not seek information from others. That child is safe whose parents are his confidants; to whom all the sayings and doings of playmates are reported.

Your boy, when old enough, should be encouraged to read aloud to you such chapters as you may select. This reading should always be mingled with familiar comments and the free interchange of questions and answers. It will bind him to you for life. Call his attention to the organic formation of the domestic animals. Remind him that these are God's works. This will aid to throw around him that safeguard of reverence which is most invulnerable to impurity of thought and life. For this knowledge is hallowed through being brought to him by a beloved and re-vered parent. Make of the reading a pleasant task, not a frivolous recreation. When the day's chapter is completed put the book away, as it is better for him to read it with your explanations. Yet do not be seriously alarmed should this volume fall into the hands of a child not thus specially prepared for the reception of its truths.

Do not shrink before the subject of masturbation. It is not enough to lay down a command and threaten punishment. Painstaking explanation is what is needed. Reasoning and proofs will do more than rods to save the child. Even little ones four and five years old are not too young to contract the habit, and should be warned. An only child nearly ruined himself before puberty with this habit. Yet he had been so carefully shielded from evil influences that he had read nothing of this vice, been told nothing, never slept with any one, nor played with any other child except in the presence of one of his parents. He had originated the practice himself.

"My own impression once was," writes a parent, "that it would be a pity to poison the mind of a high-spirited lad with any cautions about such debasing practices; but that opinion has been altered. I now believe a parent should at least hint to his son that he may very possibly have occasion to witness unclean practices, and warn him at once to manfully resist them, pointing out at the same time the consequences to which they tend."

You must of course discriminate delicately between what instruction is needed by a little boy and the fuller enlightenment which you must give your son upon his entrance into puberty. The warning given in early childhood will not suffice to meet the temptations of youth and the lessons in impurity which may be thrown in his way. This is the critical time which Part II. was written to meet. Have it read aloud to you by your boy, as before, and thus still maintain the bond of sympathy between you, so that he may say, "I can say *anything* to father or mother."

But if the boy has arrived at this age before the book comes into your hands, and a reserve already exists between you, place it in his hands to read by himself. Talk with him if you can, but if you are too timid, let the book do its good work in silence.

If a boy should remark a difference between the practices of men and the advice given, tell him just as you do when he finds that he knows more of grammar or geography than his parents, that people are constantly finding out more and more, because there are greater educational advantages now than in your young days.

You may perhaps judge that some of the chapters of this book, as, The Rights of Others, and Marriage and Parenthood, are too advanced for your son, and should be reserved for married men. But not so. Would you have him take "a leap into the dark" when he enters the marriage relation? You instruct him as to his relations to a life beyond this world, you prepare him for death. Do you not know that life is more solemn than death? That the entrance into a married life involves the eternal welfare of not only himself but others? Can you risk the health, happiness and spiritual development of your beloved son and of his future wife and children for an unwise fastidiousness? Do you not know that the prevalent spirit of the age, in its self-indulgence and lack of continence, teaches that the marriage altar is the open door to unbridled indulgence in the animal passions; that physical intercourse rather than spiritual and mental communion is the purpose and design of wedlock? Do you not realize, mothers, and you fathers, more especially, that your silence is giving sanction to this debasing view of life in what should be its most holy relation?

The infant mortality of our civilization; the birth of idiotic, deformed, diseased or vicious children; the breaking up of what ought to be and might be happy and beneficent homes; these are largely the results of ignorance on the part of those who enter the marriage relation. The policy of silence will never dispel that ignorance.

It is early instruction in facts; it is teaching the young to trace effect back to cause; to use their reasoning powers, and to observe, which is to do this essential service for humanity. It is to place before them an exalted standard of purity that is to lead them to a higher life.

The way to save a nation is to save the individual, and this work must *begin with the young.* A youth who is awakened to the value of all seed, and to rightly conserve his own; who asks what is right and seeks to do the right with regard to it, will not go far astray in other directions; but if he errs here we tremble for his future.

It is "the *seed* of Abraham," "the *seed* of David," "the *seed* of the righteous," " and the fruit (containing the seed) of the tree of life," which forms the burden of God's solicitude concerning the human race, as revealed in the Bible. Once the *seed* of man is consecrated to the service of the Divine, all will be well.

My heart glows with the exulting thought that MANHOOD may be the means by which thousands of young men may preserve health for themselves, and transmit it to whole generations of strong, wise and happy beings; that it may be one of the instrumentalities of a real physical redemption for mankind, out of which will be developed all moral excellence, intellectual elevation, social harmony and individual and general happiness.

For encouragement, these admirable words by Dr. C. B. Winslow are quoted: "Happy and twice blessed are those parents who possess sufficient strength of character to say to their children, 'Through ignorance of nature's laws or by foolish weakness, did I receive this physical injury ; let me warn you of life's quicksands in this direction—in that did I blunt my intellectual perceptions ; in this manner did I acquire such and such imperfections which have been trans- mitted to you ; let me assist you in overcoming them, and implore you to avoid their continued transmis- sion. The pre-natal influences attending you were so inharmonious that such and such characteristics have been entailed upon you ; let us together come to an intelligent understanding of their extent, and en- deavor to overcome their evil influences. Through my ignorance did this come to you ; my only repara- tion is in giving you an understanding of the causes, hoping to enable you to resist them, at least prevent you from extending them.' In this way (never under the iron rule of command and obedience, deigning no explanation, no instruction) can parent and child work together as companion and friend."

Let me urge upon parents a thorough and serious study of this book. You will thus be enabled to dis- criminate as to each boy, whether he is prepared to benefit by the reading of this volume in its entirety, or whether certain selections should be made for him. You will be better fitted to lead his mind in the right channels, and also to judge of the book on its merits, and to decide as to the truth and importance of the principles herein inculcated. All may not be thus convinced at first reading. I beg of you to lay aside prejudice and to re-read and re-examine in the light of reason, science and Christianity, all doubtful points. Remembering that "to the pure all things are pure," and that when God saw everything that He had made He saw that "it was very good," will you aid your dear boys to obey the injunction, "Know Thyself"?

E. R. SHEPHERD.

Hillhurst, Washington Territory.

TRUE MANHOOD.

PART I.

CHAPTER I.

LIFE FROM SEEDS AND EGGS.

Most boys, by the time they are eight years old, know that all plants and all animals can produce more plants and animals like the old ones. This is a rule or law to which there are no exceptions. It is true of everything that has life. There are many things in the world that have no life, such as rocks, crystals, soil, air, water. These having no life, cannot produce more objects like themselves.

Every plant has seeds which grow in its body or stalk, and more plants may grow, or, we might say, be born out of their seeds. Like all plants, so do all animals produce seeds in the bodies of the old ones which may grow, or be born, into more animals.

There is a little place in the body of every plant and of every animal where these seeds are formed. Plant seeds must drop out of the stalk, and be covered with warm, moist earth for awhile before they can be born into young plants. But animal seeds have different ways of being born. We may class them under two principal methods of birth:

First: Those that like plant seeds must pass away from the mother's body before they can be born, as the seeds of the hen, the bird, the fish, the bee, the spider, and many other insects.

Animal Seeds are Called Eggs.

The eggs of these animals must be laid *outside* the body of the mother, after which if they are kept warm in some sheltered place, the yelk and white inside the shell will turn into a little animal like its parent. When this little animal has grown large and strong enough to be born, it bursts the shell and comes out into the air where we can see it.

Second: Those that, unlike plant seeds, remain within the body of the mother animal until they have grown large and strong enough to be born. Probably there is not a boy eight years old (and some learn much younger) who does not know the names of many animals that bring forth young out of their own bodies, all ready to breathe, to eat, and some of them, to walk. They know that cats have kittens born out of the body of the mother cat, and that colts and calves are born in the same way—out of the body of the mother horse, and cow. Perhaps but few of these boys knew before that kittens, colts, calves and many other young animals were first seeds or eggs formed in the bodies of the old ones; yet this is the truth.

All things that have life may be arranged in three divisions:

a.   Plants having seeds born outside the parent stalk.

b.   Animals having eggs born outside the parent's body; as birds, fisbes, insects.

c. Animals whose young are made ready for birth inside the parent's body ; as colts and calves.

Which Know the Most ?

Plants do not know anything, and cannot be taught anything; they have life, but not intelligence.

Animals know more than plants ; they have life and intelligence.

The least intelligent among them can search for food, and where it is necessary, can love and care for and fight for their young, and that is more than plants know and can do. Because of this, animals are said to be of a higher order than plants.

While all animals possess life and intelligence, some know more, or are more intelligent than others. Some can be taught more than others. Some can be taught nothing whatever ; what they know comes to them by nature, just as their eyes, ears and feet were given them by nature. Thus nature taught birds to build nests, and gophers to dig holes in the ground. This may be called *natural intelligence*, or instinct. Other animals can be taught by man many things they do not know by nature. This may be called *acquired intelligence*.

Elephants can be trained to perform many wonderful feats in a circus. Dogs are taught to do many curious tricks, to watch the sheep, to bring home the cows, and to become useful to their masters in other ways. Horses are capable of much training ; can be broken to the saddle and harness; taught to work, to come at their master's call, to be gentle and patient, and are exceedingly valuable creatures, both by nature and by teaching.

Animals that know the most, and can be taught the most, belong to the highest class.

Judged by their intelligence, we may also arrange living things in three divisions:

1.   Plants that have life, but not intelligence.

2.   Animals that have life and natural intelligence.

3.   Animals that have life, natural intelligence, and are capable of being taught many things by man, or are capable of acquired intelligence.

It is a curious fact that those animals which are the most useful to man as servants, that possess the most natural intelligence, and that may acquire the most added knowledge, and hence belong to division 3, retain their eggs within the mother's body until birth, and hence also belong to class c, as described on page 35.

Baby Life.

Of course every boy knows that men and women were once babies, knows that a baby is a small human being, which, if it lives, will grow up to be large and to resemble its parents.

Even little boys, of four or five years old, know that babies have mothers, as they know that baby calves, baby colts, and baby chickens have mothers. Children who live in the country very frequently hear it said, " There goes a little baby colt," or " baby calf," sometimes "baby chicken," and "baby bird," and the old ones are called the mothers of them. And occasionally plant buds are spoken of in the same way, as " baby rosebud," " baby lily," " baby violet," or whatever kind of flower bud it is, and it would likewise be proper to speak of the " mother bush."

To which class does a baby belong, to plants or animals?

"Oh, to animals," replies every boy. Yes, right. A baby is an animal, not a plant.

. How do we know that it is an animal, not a plant? One boy says, "Because it can creep about and walk." Another, "Because it can cry, and laugh, and talk." "Because it can see, and hear, and breathe, and eat," says a third. And so the boys go on giving the differences between plants and animals, but none have yet guessed the most important one. Try again. Think a moment of what you have read in chapter I. Babies have teeth to eat with, tongues to talk with, feet to walk with, and hands to play with. How can they tell which things to eat? what to say? when to cry or laugh? where to go with their feet? what to do with their hands?

"They see what others do, and do the same."

"Their mothers show them, and after that they know," answer the boys.

Very true. But what do babies have yet more, besides the eyes, ears, hands and feet, in order that they may do as others do, and learn and remember?

At last the answer, "They have intelligence," "They have minds," comes from boys in every direction. And this is correct. It is intelligence which most distinguishes animals from plants.

A baby is better or higher than a plant because it knows more; has a mind and intelligence, while plants have none.

Plants which know nothing and can be taught nothing, are born from seeds which fall on the ground.

But babies, that have minds and can learn are not born like plants.

We have already learned that all animals come from seeds or eggs. A baby is also born from an egg.

We also learned that there were two classes of animals. One born outside the body of its mother, the other formed before birth inside the body of its mother. We also learned that the animals which had the most intelligence, the most mind, and could be taught the most, were formed within, and born out of the mother's body.

Knowing these facts we can easily understand that the animal of highest organization, which is to develop into a being capable of knowing, loving and serving its Creator, is provided for in the best way before birth, that is by development within the body of the mother.

CHAPTER II.

HUMAN LIFE.

The method described in the first chapter by which human beings are produced and the earth kept full of intelligent, valuable lives, is *the most beautiful arrangement of anything in all the world.* Just think of it. We plant seeds in the ground, but thousands of them never grow. They perish with too much cold, or too much heat, or too much rain; sometimes the squirrels and birds dig them out and eat them. Often the farmer loses whole crops by having the seeds destroyed before they can be born into more plants.

And then too, the eggs of those animals that lay them outside the parent's body before birth are destroyed by hundreds, and are never born. The eggs of hens, birds and fisbes, and all other species, are liable to be destroyed with cold or heat, and to be eaten by other animals.

But the eggs of the highest class of animals, that are the most valuable because they are the most intelligent, cannot possibly be destroyed in these ways.

We would expect to find the most precious, noble and costly things in nature the best protected during their forming period—while they are small, weak and helpless. And this is precisely what we do find.

As long as the mother of the unborn kitten, and calf, or colt is alive, nothing can harm the little one.

No cold, nor heat, nor storm, nor fierce wolf or bear can destroy it, for it is safely sheltered, nice, warm and comfortable, growing within its mother's body until large enough to take some care of itself.

We would expect that the human animal, the baby, the precious little brother or sister that is to grow into a grand, wonderful man or woman, the most priceless creation on the earth, ought to be the best protected from danger, while it is weak and helpless and getting ready to be born. And so it is.

Can you think of any better or more appropriate place, more safe, more comfortable and nice every way than this beautiful arrangement that the Creator planned, by which the baby that the mother loves best, and the mother that the baby loves best, should be thus kept together during the time that the little one needs to be the best loved, cared for and shielded in all its existence?

Boys having read thus far are full of all sorts of questions about the human egg, and so in order to teach them certain laws of health, which they ought to know, it will be necessary to explain this subject fully. Their curiosity will be satisfied, and at the same time the knowledge so extremely necessary to a boy's health and growth will be gained.

The Ovum.

Very small boys have seen seeds in plenty; such as apple, orange and cherry seeds, and know that seeds are of different colors and shapes, and also of various sizes, from the tiny grass, portulacca and mustard seeds to the large horse-chestnut or buckeye, butter-nut and cocoanut.

How about the inside of seeds? How many small boys have examined this part of them? Perhaps many of you suppose that the inside is alike all through—a hard, white substance.

To prove that this idea is a mistake, and to see what else may be found, just soak a few beans, or grains of corn, or any seed (the larger kinds show the best to the naked eye), three or four days in water, or until so soft that they may be readily opened with a knife, and there in the "eye" end will be seen a little white lump or spot, which looks different from the rest of the seed.

Left in the water a few days longer this part increases in size, and plainly shows its true nature. There will be seen one or two white leaves and a stem formed out of the lump; in fact, the little spot consisted of the leaves and stem— very small, folded into a mere dot (as may be

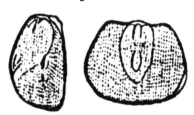

Fig. I.   Seeds, showing parts inside.

seen at first with a microscope), but which have opened and increased in size, under the influence of warmth and moisture.

Blossom buds are often called "baby buds," but that is only by comparison with the full-grown flower. It is the baby age of the blossom, but the baby of the *whole plant* is this little germ, which every perfect seed contains, and which may grow and expand to largest size, and make a vine many feet in length, a

3

wide, low shrub, or a tree over three hundred feet high, according to the kind of seed it is.

This little lump of leaves and stem is the true baby plant, and before it begins to grow it is called a *germ*. The remainder of the inside is called the *albumen* or white, and the outside covering is called the *envelope*.

Very small boys have also seen eggs, as birds', hens', and turkeys' eggs, and know that eggs are of different colors, shapes and sizes. They are all the way in size from the tiniest insect eggs, that can scarcely be seen, up to the eggs of the ostrich, a single one of which is as large as twenty-four hens' eggs put together, and weighs three pounds.

And boys also know something of the inside of eggs. Eggs are all made on the same plan, and contain the same parts, so that a figure of one will give an idea of all.

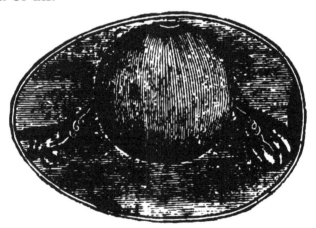

Fig. II. Hen's egg—Natural size.

The eggs of animals correspond to the seeds of plants. That is to say, it is the part in both from which the new life springs, and their inside contents are alike in many respects.

The egg contains a germ, a little spot from which starts the young chick. It does not contain the form and shape of the chicken, as the plant germ contains the form of the plant—they are unlike in this respect —but the germ is the point at which the change begins which turns the egg into a little animal like its parent. Both the seed and the egg have the albumen or white, but the latter has a yolk or yellow, and the former has none. And both are inclosed in an outside covering, shell or envelope.

But the boys are most interested just now in human seeds or eggs, from which babies are born, and we will pass on to a description of them.

It is usually the case in nature that the smallest plants and animals produce the smallest seeds and eggs, and the largest sizes, the largest seeds and eggs, but this is not so with human beings. Although the parents are so large, their eggs are very small indeed, not being larger than the point of a needle, scarcely discernible with the naked eye.

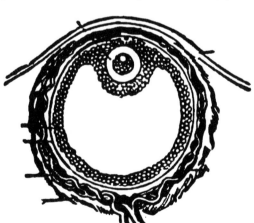

It requires the aid of a good magnifying glass to get a distinct view of them. With this instrument they are seen to be built on the same general plan as the eggs of all animals—having a thin, soft, transparent covering or envelope, containing a yellow yolk, and a germ, and in shape to be round like a ball.

Fig. III. Human Ovum, magnified many times.

The proper name for the human seed or egg, and the one which will be used in future pages, is *ovum.* More than one is *ova.*

It requires about one hundred and thirty ova, lying side by side, to make a row an inch long. It would take hundreds of them to fill an egg shell— yet every man was once an ovum, no larger than the point of a needle—or a mere dot.

An ovum is very tender, delicate, and easily destroyed, so that it requires the safest and best place which nature can provide for it to remain during the earliest stages of its preparation for life. And though we may try, over and over again, to think of the very best place where it might stay, so that no blows or rough treatment could reach it to harm its thin covering, neither heat nor cold to destroy it, we should conclude every time that we could not contrive anything better than the mother's body.

The Plant Ovary.

In plants the seeds grow in a pod. The correct name for pod is *ovary.* Pea and bean pods are familiar examples of the ovary. To say pea ovary and bean ovary would be as proper as to say pea pod and bean pod. Rose seeds grow in a pod at the lower side of the blossom, which when ripe is of a scarlet color. That pod is the ovary of the rose. When the rose leaves or petals fall off, the bright red ovary is left standing alone, and full of seeds which in their turn fall to the ground by the bursting of the ovary.

There are various sizes and shapes of ovaries as well as of seeds, and a full description of them is given in the science of Botany, which is a very in-

Fig. IV. Seed Pod or Ovary.

teresting study. We must leave that for the reader to study, and pass on to a description of

The Animal Ovary,

or place where the eggs of animals are formed.

One or two kinds may be represented in order to show the similarity between them and plant ovaries, and explain some things about them necessary to our

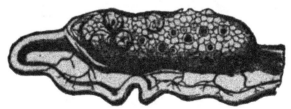

Fig. V. Ovarium of the Rabbit showing Ova in various stages of growth.

present purpose. In animals they are called ovaria. A single one is ovarium.

The young of rabbits are first grown inside the body

of the mother rabbit. Figure V. shows the ovarium full of eggs, which in animals belonging to division c, chapter I., are also called ova. In this class the ova form inside the ovarium, like plant seeds. As soon as an ovum becomes large enough it separates from the ovarium and passes through the tube where it reaches another part, the uterus.

Fig. VI. Ovarium of a Hen.

This cut shows the ovarium of the hen in which the part itself is entirely hidden by the multitude of eggs which form upon the outside, instead of in the inside of it, like the plant ovary. We recollect that the young of the hen is hatched outside the mother's body. Sometimes when a hen is being dressed for cooking you can easily examine the ovaries or unde-veloped eggs.

The different parts of animals and plants are called *organs*, and this word will be used hereafter, mean-ing parts.

The proper name of the organ represented in the picture below is uterus. It may be compared to a nest, basket or cradle, where the young rabbit lies forming and growing, ready for birth.   Plants do not

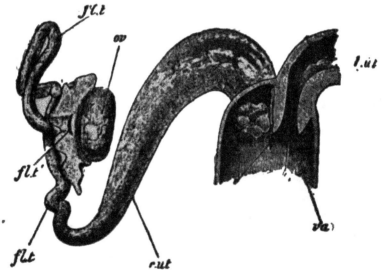

*Fig. VII.   Uterus of a Rabbit.   Va., vagina ; r. ut., right uterus ;
l. ut., left uterus ; ov., ovary ; fl. t., fallopian tube.*

require a uterus because the ground answers the same purpose. And with animals belonging to divi-sions b, chap. I., the nest made of leaves and sticks by the bird mother, and covered by her warm body ; or, in the case of fisbcs, the warm rays of the sun falling upon the spawn laid in the sand ; or in the case of insects, the cocoon spun around the larvæ, are all different arrangements having the same end in view; viz., shelter, warmth and protection of the eggs until they have grown sufficiently large to be born out of the shell.

This class does not require and therefore does not possess a special organ. But it will readily be seen that in animals of the highest class, in order to prevent the ovum from passing into the wrong place in the body, and thus getting lost and destroyed, a special provision is necessary. Hence we find in all these a uterus or womb. Some butchering time the reader may perhaps persuade his father to show him these parts of a pig or cow.

These are all very wise arrangements of the Creator, and show how much interest and affection He must have had for everything He made; even the most insignificant of them being planned by Him, and taking a share of his attention.

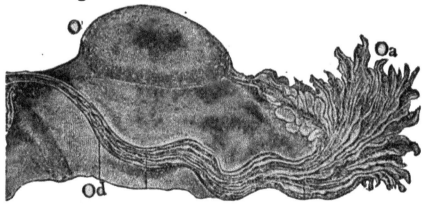

Fig. VIII. Human Ovary. O., Ovary; Oa., fingerlike extremity of the oviduct; Od., oviduct or fallopian tube.

The above cut shows very clearly the fingerlike ends of the oviduct, which grasp the ovum and convey it to the uterus.

The Uterus.

A muscular organ situated in the inferior portion of the pelvis, between the bladder and rectum. It is less than three inches in length and two inches in width, and one in thickness. It is pear shaped, the cervix pointing to the coccyx.

The Oviducts or Fallopian Tubes.

Minute cylindrical openings from the superior and lateral portion of the uterus, about three inches in length and terminating in fimbriated or finger-like extremeties. The latter are minute muscular bodies, which grasp the ovum as it bursts through the membranes of the ovary, and convey it into the oviduct on its way to the uterus. The ovum is less than $\frac{1}{110}$ of an inch in diameter, and the cavity of the oviduct is so small that it would scarcely allow the entrance of a hog's bristle.

Divine love and skill reached its highest triumph in the creation of the human ovaries and uterus.

The ovary is here entire, but if the outer envelope was removed it would resemble the inside of that of the rabbit. The ovaries are in the broad ligaments at the right and left of the uterus. The ova are very small indeed. On maturity they separate from the ovarium, pass into the tube, shown most plainly at the left of the uterus, and through it reach that organ.

This organ is commonly called the womb. The word means hidden, mysterious. Sometimes you will hear speakers use it; as, "the womb of morning," the "womb of thought," it refers to wonderful operations, performed in secret and impenetrable ways and places.

In the mother's body the womb is placed under her ribs, beneath her heart, upon a soft, warm mattress among the intestines, and there hidden from sight and from danger, in some strange and mysterious way that the wisest man has never yet learned, the ovum becomes a baby boy or girl.

CHAPTER III.

THE "FATHER" PART OF PLANT LIFE.

We have so far been learning only of the mothers of plants, animals and babies. Nothing has yet been said about the fathers of them. But children have a father as well as a mother, as all children know. Also every plant and every animal must have a father as well as mother, which many children never knew before.

The part the father contributes in the formation of a new life is exceedingly important, and holds true of all created life; plant, animal, and man. There are some things that *young* boys could not understand, if it was explained to them, until older, just as in Botany and other studies, but there are many things they may learn.

Let us begin with plants. The seeds are the children of plants, or rather the cradle containing the babies—the little germs in them are the true children. On page 37 we said it would be proper to speak of "mother bush," "mother branch," "mother tree." It would be equally proper to call the same parts of the plant "father bush," "father branch," "father tree," because they are just as much father as they are mother of the baby germs.

There is, however, one particular part of the plant which is the true mother and nothing else, and also

(51)

brown and yellow things that stand in the center of the blossom are the fathers and mothers.

Some plants have the father in one blossom all by themselves, and the mothers in another blossom all by themselves, yet on the same stalk. Others are separated not only in the blossom but are on different stalks also, while still others live together in the same blossom.

The latter remind us most of our own homes, where fathers, mothers and children live all together in one dwelling, so we will confiue our attention to these and leave the other kinds for you to examine at some future time when you take up the study of Botany.

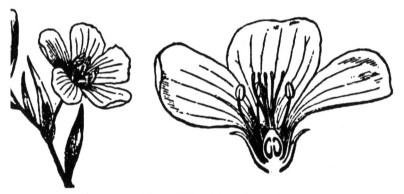

Fig. XI. Hawthorn Blossom.

We have here in the first cut a representation of a Hawthorn blossom, with the fathers, mothers and children all together in their pretty house built of flower leaves or petals.

In the second cut a part of the blossom is taken away to show the ovary containing the seeds or children. The mother part of the blossom is divided into five stalks, which grow in the center close to the children. The father part, divided into three . stalks, stand in a circle around the mother. The third part shows the full grown seeds or children.

Flowers have different arrangements of these parts in each different sort or species. Thus, the ovaries are not all shaped like this one, and some have more, others less, father and mother stalks. And then the petals are of a great variety of forms and colors, or else, in a few cases, entirely lacking, but all of them *do* have the father, mother, and seed parts in some shape and place.

Fig. XII. is the father part of the plant. *Stamen* is his scientific name. The top or head is called the *anther*. The little dots upon and around the anther are called the *pollen*. The stem or stalk upon which the anther is placed is called the *filament*.

Fig. XIII. is the mother part of the plant. *Pistil* is her scientific name. The top or head is called the *stigma*. The stem or stalk on which the stigma is placed is called the *style*, and at the base is the ovary or seed pod.

Fig. xii. Stamen.
Fig. xiii. Pistil.

Half Seeds and Whole Seeds.

A seed to be perfect and able to grow a new plant, or able to have a germ composed of leaves and stem, must be formed of material from both the father and mother part of the plant, or, using the scientific names, the stamen and pistil.

The pollen (see Fig. XII.) is the part which the sta-men contributes toward making the seed perfect. It is made in the anther, and when fully ripe the anther bursts and it falls out, covering the surface. It looks like bright colored dust, and is what rubs off on your face when in smelling a flower you put your nose too deep among the petals, and what insects get on their wings when they fly into the cup after the honey and the dew.

It would astonish you to look at these dots or specks of pollen dust through a microscope. You could hardly believe that what you then see would be like one of the figures below, or some others quite as surprising ; but it is true. Different plants produce differently shaped pollen grains.

Fig. XIV.   Pollen magnified two hundred times as large as nature.

The inside of the grains would appear equally as-tonishing. They are filled with a watery fluid in which float an immense number of grains or *granules*, and how very small they must be as compared with the pollen grain itself.

If you will pull a blossom to pieces and look in the ovary very soon after it spreads its petals and before any pollen comes on the anther, you will see some very small spots or beginnings of seeds. They will continue to increase in size as the flower blooms, but unless they receive this pollen they will not ripen and be able to sprout. While young and soft and before the pollen reaches them, they are called *ovules*.

The wind that is constantly bending the flowers shakes the ripe pollen upon the stigmas, which under the magnifying lens is seen to be full of little openings just adapted to receive the grains—differently shaped in various flowers, to correspond with the differently made pollen. It slides down the style and lodges among the ovules in the ovary, and in some mysterious way, not fully understood, the ovules are changed into seeds.

Thus we see the two kinds of life in plants; the mother life and the father life. The ovules are full of the mother life, and the pollen full of the father life of the plant, and a seed contains them both. Ovules are half seeds, and pollen grains are half seeds, and it takes them both to make a whole seed.

Or, putting it another way, pollen dust is seed; alone considered, it is the whole seed of the father stamen, and ovules are likewise seeds; the whole seed of the mother pistil. But considered as parts of the *whole plant* we must regard them as only half seeds, until by union in the ovary they become whole seeds of the *entire plant*.

When the stamens and pistils grow on separate stalks, as is the case with some species, the bees and other insects carry the pollen over to the pistils on their wings, or the breezes waft it to them through the air.

We have now learned about that little place in the body of every plant, mentioned on page 33, where their seeds are formed, and we have examined the

seeds themselves, and found that it requires two **half**
seeds, one from the mother life, and one from **the**
father life of the plant, to be united in that little place
in order to produce whole seeds.

The Fruit of the Tree.

Every species of plant is capable of producing fruit
or seed.   The fruit of the vine, the fruit of the shrub,
the fruit of the herb is the seed, or contains the seed.

In common conversation we make a distinction between fruit and seed.   We speak of fruits, meaning
those seeds which are surrounded with a rich, juicy,
eatable pulp or meat, as apples, cherries, plums, nuts,
while those not so surrounded we call simply seeds,
as wheat, oats, rye, corn.   In reality both are fruits.

We may understand this better if we inquire into
the use of the albumen, which surrounds the germ
(see Fig. I.).   When the leaves and stem of the germ
commence to sprout and expand under the influence
of heat and moisture, they must, like a growing boy,
have something to eat, in order that they may continue to grow larger and larger.   And this is what
the albumen is for.   It furnishes food to the baby
germ—the new plant.

Its leaves and stem soak up or draw into themselves the soft, moist particles of albumen until it has
taken up the entire grain, and by that time, and sometimes sooner, the baby germ has grown large enough
to be born out of the shell or envelope (see Fig. I.),
and push its leafy head out of the ground and fasten
its little feet of roots into the soil.   And now having
eaten the albumen of the seed it begins to take in
air and sunlight with its leaves, and to absorb water

and other elements of the soil with its roots, and it lives and grows upon them, as in Fig. XV.

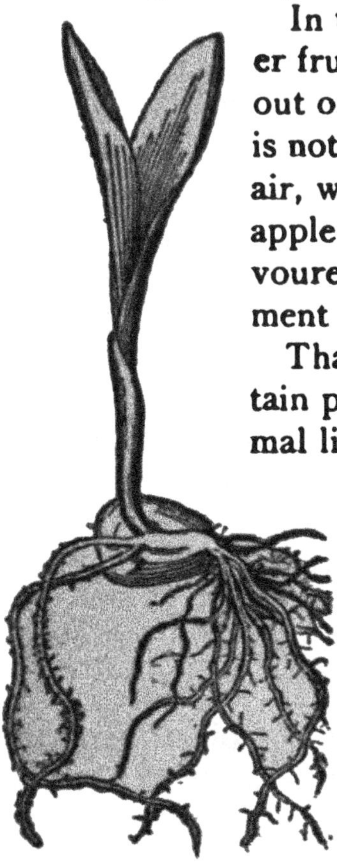

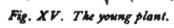

In the case of apples, nuts and other fruits, when the baby germ is born out of the envelope of the seed, if it is not yet strong enough to subsist on air, water and soil, it begins to eat the apple or nut. By the time that is devoured it is able to obtain nourishment from other sources.

That seed or fruit which can sustain plant germs can also sustain animal life, and seeds and fruits are eaten for that purpose very freely. In fact bread, which is made of grain seeds, is called "the staff of life."

We may call the seed and the fruit, which contains the seed, the most important part of the plant. Of course there could be no fruit without root, stem and leaves, and these parts are very important. Some roots are good for food, as beets, onions, potatoes. Some leaves and stems are also eaten, especially by animals, as grass, clover, hay; but when we would select for food *the most* valuable and important part of all, we choose the fruit or seed.

Fig. XV. The young plant.

1. Because it is capable of producing or giving birth to more plants.

2. Because it is capable of sustaining its own life to a certain extent, and of maintaining animal life.

4

CHAPTER IV.

ABOUT ANIMALS.

Wise and beautiful as are the arrangements of father and mother germs by which plants give birth to young plants so that there shall be no decrease in any kind, we find the plan for the increase of animals no less wise and even more beautiful. For animals know more than plants. Plants do not recognize each other; animals do. Plants have no feeling of love for their young; animals have. Plants cannot care for and feed their young; animals can.

What sight more charming than a pair of birds in the early springtime, together building in the leafy bough a cunning little nest—such as no one can imitate.

While the mother bird for many days sits patiently on her nest, the father bird hops around on the limbs of the tree keeping her company, singing wonderful songs—such as no human voice or musical instrument can imitate—cheering her spirits and anon taking his turn to brood the eggs while she comes off to eat her dinner.

When the eggs are hatched he rejoices with her, and stopping his singing goes right to work flying all day, back and forth, sometimes going long distances, bringing bugs and worms for the young to eat.

When they are full fledged he gives them lessons

in flying and hunting, and as the cold winter draws near he introduces them to other families of birds, which·they join, and the whole flock migrate to a warmer climate.

Boys who rob birds' nests do not consider this beautiful home life of birds; do not stop to watch them and study their affectionate habits; if they did they would not be so cruel and thoughtless. If we break off the buds of a plant the old bush does not care and mourn. But if a nest is robbed and the brood broken up, the old birds will try to fight, and fly in the face and dart at the eyes of the invader, and sometimes make sad cries and calls for days after.

There is scarcely a prettier thing in all nature than a downy chicken, nor a more beautiful sight than to see the mother hen gathering her brood under her wings, or to watch with what patience and interest she scratches and clucks, scratches and clucks all day long when her chicks are not resting their little tired feet and taking their baby naps among her warm feathers.

Fig. XVI. A Family Scene.

We hardly know which to admire most, the delicate forms, colors and family arrangements of plant

life, or the affection, intelligence and family arrangements of animal life.

"*Male and Female Created He Them.*"

The stamens and pistils of plants are not called father and mother in books and in conversation, but
are spoken of as *male* and *female* organs. They were
however, so called in previous pages, in order that
young readers might get a clear idea of their nature.

All things that have life are divided into two classes, of male and female, and are set in pairs—the male
for the father, and the female for the mother.

In many *plants* with which we are most familiar,
they are united in the same stalk, but some grow in
separate plants, while the male and female *animals*
are in two distinct individuals—except in a few of the
lower orders, where they are united in one form.

Boys, especially those who live in the country,
know this about the domestic animals, and can give
the names of the males and females, as roosters are
the males of the hen kind, and fathers of little chickens; bulls are the males of the cow kind, and fathers
of calves; rams are the males among sheep, and stallions among horses. Mother horses are called mares,
and mother sheep, ewes.

We have seen that stamens and pistils, or male and
female organs of *plants*, differ from each other; so
also male and female *animals* have different organs.

A few pages back we read that the female has the
ovarium, in which is formed the ovum, egg or seed,
and the higher species have the uterus. Males have
not these, but other organs, with forms and uses peculiar to themselves.

We have yet to learn of that place in the body where grows the male seed or egg, corresponding to the pollen, or male seed of plants ; of its name and formation, and how it is carried to the mother to meet the ovum or egg ; how united, it grows in her body until it is ready to be born.

Human Father Life.

The semen contains the male sperm or father part of human life. This corresponds to the pollen or male seed of plants, and this is supplied by the father to the ovum that is within the body of the mother, so that human life may be perpetuated. Semen is secreted in the organs peculiar to the male. It is not a dust like pollen, but a liquid, thickish and of a yellow white color.

We know that flowers do not have pollen when first in bloom, and it requires many days, and in some species, many weeks, for it to form and ripen in the anther, before it is ready to appear on the outside of the anther and be carried to the ovules. In the same way it takes many years for human male seed or semen to grow and mature before it can be really called seed, or before it can make its appearance, even, as a distinct production.

Hence, boys and youths do not have semen. A man must be full grown before *perfect* semen forms. There may be a secretion before maturity, but it is unlike that which comes in manhood. It may be compared to apples, melons, etc., which contain unripe, soft patterns of seeds, while the fruit is green, but which do not become complete until the fruit has well ripened : fruit and its seed develop together.

The most important part of the semen may
called the germ of the drops, as it corresponds in
nature to the germ of the ova, and also to the ge
of plant ovules. It is from these germs in all ca
that a new life begins.

In manhood they become completely formed.

These germs, or sperm as they are called, are
ceedingly small. It takes about seven hundred
them to make a row an inch long.

It is not until sperm has matured that it is able
do its part toward forming a new human being.

Boys have doubtless noticed that people do n
become fathers and mothers until they have gro
tall, large and strong, and now they know at le
one reason for it. They also understand that peo
need to be large and strong, so as to work hard a
build homes for their families, and to earn food a
clothing ior them. They need to get an educatio
that they may teach their children. This takes tin
and makes all come out right together.

CHAPTER V.

THE HUMAN TREE OF LIFE.

Sperm is man's seed—his whole seed. Ova is woman's seed—her whole seed. And the two are half-seeds of the human tree of life. This tree, like all plant trees, bears "its seed in itself," and like them it requires that both the male and the female seed, or the mother and father seed, shall be united and diffuse their life elements in order to produce another tree of life—a little child.

The two half seeds unite and become a whole seed—a baby—in some mysterious way that nobody understands to-day, any more than they did in ancient Bible times, when it was written, "Thou knowest not what is the way of the spirit (life), nor how the bones do grow in the womb of her that is with child."

It is only the sperm of the semen, and the germ of the ovum that unite and form the child. The remainder of the ovum, the yolk, becomes food for the new human being in a similar way as the plant germ feeds upon the albumen of the seed, described in chapter III.

When that is all used up there is a way provided, by which the mother's blood supplies food and nourishment. The mother eats and drinks to make plenty of blood for the child as well as for herself; she

breathes for it ; she keeps it warm and comfortal
protects it from danger ; its life is a part of her
It requires nine months for the two tiny germs
grow to the size of a baby, fully formed and strc

When it is able it pushes its way out of the :
rounding cavity, out into the world, as a little pl
comes out of the ground. Milk now becomes
food, which is supplied for it in the mother's bre
and is made out of what she eats and drinks. Th
because it has no teeth at first ; but in a year or (
the teeth grow out, and then it may take other fi
and no longer depend upon its mother's milk.

The father, for his part, now provides food, cli
ing, school-books and other necessaries, for the cl
is still small, weak, ignorant, and unable to work.

It is thus you and every one else that has e
lived were formed and born.

Your mother has often told you that you w
once a little baby like this one or that one, or sc
other one that you have seen, so that is no news
you. You knew that before. But probably you h
never before received a true description of the pi
ess by which the father part and the mother par
that life from which we all proceed is united int
new life and is carried on to completion.

The Bible says, "Honor thy father and thy mi
er," and "Children obey your parents, for this
right." All that children are and have came fi
their parents. The most constant and tender gr
tude can never repay the debt due to those who h
thus given life, love, and protecting care.

If children are obedient, minding promptly, w
out whining and fretting, parents feel well paid

all their trouble, and are thankful for the presence and company of their sons and daughters.

Try then to act so that your father and mother will be proud of you. Follow their advice cheerfully, even when you would prefer to have your own way, for they know more than you, and love you too well to advise you to do anything that will lead to harm.

It is the disobedient ones who, thinking their way is the best, and following it against the wishes of the parents, get into danger and trouble; their lives are *not* " long in the land."

Closing Advice.

Thus we have given plain, square facts to honest boys, curious to know the truth. Still more important truths in regard to their bodies remain to be told, for better reasons than curiosity.

There are laws or rules which must be obeyed i. the body is kept well, and if boys would become strong, well-developed, healthy men. The reader has doubtless many questions to ask. Yet he is too young to understand all these things, even if they were explained. He is not expected to know the principles of steam engines, or the mysteries of chemistry. As he waits patiently to grow old enough to study these deeper questions he must likewise follow the instructions of wise and good parents and friends, as to the mysterious laws of his being.

There is one very important truth that the smallest boys may understand and should know, and that is. that the *sexual* organs should never be handled, nor even touched, except in bathing, or when necessary in passing water.

5

Self-abuse is very wrong. It is harmful in the first place because too much blood flows to this part, making the organs feverish. A finger or any other part often becomes swollen and irritated by repeated rubbing. When a great deal too much blood is drawn to one part some other parts must have too little, and thus become pale and weak. This practice continued, a boy will become weak and unable to go to school, or run and play. The head will ache, the face look sallow, the eyes dull, the lips and ears lose their bright red color. He will look more like a corpse than a living boy. His face and complexion show it, his walk shows it, and he suffers with pains in the back. He has a downcast, sheepish look and. manner. He is sullen, irritable,.and too tired to work. If he catches cold or gets sick in other ways, he will have so little strength that he will be apt to die, when otherwise he might have easily recovered.

He will stop growing, and never make as large or vigorous a man as he should, even if he lives to grow· up. The life seeds will never ripen. How could pollen grow in anthers, if any one was handling and tossing the flowers about? Only blossoms that are let alone to grow undisturbed bear seeds and fruit. Children, too, often die as flowers die, when thus disturbed. These organs need quiet and rest to properly grow and develop.

Other reasons why this practice is injurious you will understand as you get older. For the present, remember that what I have told you is all true.

If you were playing near a dangerous precipice would you not thank me to warn you against the danger of going near it? If you were rowing a little boat on a great river, and I knew that there were frightful falls just below you, of which you were unaware, would you not think me your friend if I told you your nearness to them, and showed you how to keep your boat out of the current that would surely carry you over?

Just that do I do for you in these pages.

Let me add another word of caution. Never have secrets from your father or mother. Never say or do anything you would be afraid or ashamed to have them know. Never listen to vulgar stories, nor to any stories that you cannot tell your parents, for if you shrink from telling them anything, you may be sure your minds will be misled by listening to it.

Every one admires the strong, robust, self-reliant boy. His frank manners, his light step, his innocent face, his rollicking mirth, his helpful ways, his confidence in his parents, all win him friends. He is at once his father's pride and his mother's joy.

Therefore engage in healthful games and sports, together with brothers, sisters and schoolmates. Also remember the golden, rule, "Do unto others as you would have others do unto you." Do not indulge in selfishness, unkindness, or rudeness.

When the time for study and work comes, do it with might and main. Study as hard as you play; work with a hearty good will.

> " All work and no play
> Makes Jack a dull boy,
> But all play and no work
> Makes Jack a dull shirk.
> So work while you work, play while you play,
> For that is the way to be happy and gay."

CHAPTER VI.

WHEN I'M A MAN.

Every boy looks forward eagerly to the time when he shall become a man. He enjoys boyhood heartily, yet would not always be a boy. Oh, no! The hope of future manhood inspires him with patience in the faithful performance of disagreeable tasks. He earnestly trains his clumsy fingers to manage the delicate pen, and patiently overcomes the difficulties of arithmetic because he knows that to be successful in business one must be a good penman and accurate in figures. A lazy boy makes an idle man, who can never expect to prosper. It is industry which brings wealth. One learns to work when young, in order that he may succeed in life.

And so the wood is cut, the coal brought in, the cows milked, the errands done, the ground plowed, the corn husked and much hard work performed. He knows that many men now rich and prosperous worked when boys, and he cheerfully completes his task before seeking recreation. Duty first, pleasure afterward.

Meanwhile the boy pictures to his imagination the man he would be. It is the image of

A Healthy, Vigorous Man.

Whatever the business or profession to which he

looks forward, be it farming, merchandise, the minis-
try, the law—whether his tastes incline him to philan-
thropy, to literature or to business—one and the same
picture rises before his mind.

No boy wishes to be a pale, thin, stoop-shouldered,
whiskerless, weak-voiced, nervous, sickly, sauntering
man. He would be tall, erect, broad-chested, heavily
bearded and deep voiced, having well developed
muscles and a strong, enduring frame. He would be
able to move with agility and vigor, the embodiment
of manly power and strength. This is the vision
which rises in his mind when the word *man* is spoken.

Moral Laws.

Boys know that there is no need for swearing, lying,
stealing, cheating, idleness, disobedience, gambling
and other evil ways which are called sins.

As he grows older he becomes convinced that for
business success, under-handed, selfish, dishonest
methods are not necessary.

All his conduct must be carefully governed by

The Golden Rule,

which embraces all moral laws. Breaking this rule
invariably causes suffering. No good ever comes
from wrong doing. It always leads to pain, shame
and sorrow.

There are also laws or rules for the different members, or organs of the human body. These are called

Physical Laws.

The breaking of these causes pain and sickness. If
they were obeyed the different parts of the body

would work in harmony ; there would be no suffering, no disease. None would die young—unless destroyed by accident—all would live to hearty old age.

Sickness is as Needless as Sin.

More than that, it is as wicked as sin. It is wrong because God made these laws, and He made them to be obeyed, not to be broken. They are just as binding as the moral laws. It is true that many people have been sick who violated these laws through ignorance. But in these days there is no excuse for ignorance.

If boys would grow to be vigorous, well-developed, healthy men, free from bodily weakness and suffering, they can do so. All that is necessary is a *knowledge of physical laws and a cheerful and faithful observance thereof.*

> When I'm a man, a man,
> I'll have good health, if I can, *and I can.*
> With a temper that's even and cheery and glad,
> I'll shun impure talk and thoughts that are bad;
> From wine and tobacco I'll keep myself free,
> From morning till night I will work cheerily;
> My muscles will train and labor with zest,
> Striving hard to do always the things that are best,
> For the health of a man.

CHAPTER VII.

THE SCIENCE OF THE HUMAN BODY.

The science of the Human Body embraces Anatomy, Physiology and Hygiene.

Anatomy describes the different organs or parts of the body.

Physiology describes the uses of the organs.

Hygiene describes the laws for the preservation of health.

Physiology is a general term for the science of the body, and the two other departments are commonly included when this word is used.

Many think physiology a complicated and difficult study. This idea is largely imaginary, and arises from the frequent use of foreign words in naming the organs. In the following pages these are so simplified and explained as to be easily comprehended, and readily remembered.

The body, with all its seemingly complex structure is built on the following simple plan:

1. Cells.		3. Force.	
2. Tubes.		4. Substance.	

These and their combinations will be considered to the extent demanded by our subject.*

---

* "The Man Wonderful in the House Beautiful," is recommended as a juvenile physiology. It is both fascinating and instructive.

Cells.

The solid parts of the body, such as muscle, fat, cartilage, bone, nails, teeth, brain, lungs, liver, spleen, kidneys, and skin, are chiefly composed of cells. Cells also enter into the formation of tubes, and of some of the fluids of the body as blood and chyle.

Cells may be compared to little bladders, or drops. The cells of the body are very minute and can only be seen by the aid of the microscope.

Their Number.

We may obtain some idea of how very, very small they are, when we know that it takes two hundred vesicles or air cells of the lungs lying side by side to make a row an inch long; that it takes three thousand, five hundred corpuscles or blood cells to make a row an inch long.

It is estimated that there are at least six hundred million air cells in the lungs, and nine hundred million nerve cells in the brain; and that the nerve cells in the rest of the body would number more than as many again as those in the brain; so there are some two billions nerve cells in the body and brain together. The whole amount of blood corpuscles has been estimated as high as 65,750,000,000,000. And then think of the billions, trillions, quadrillions of other cells; those which make up the muscles, those of the liver, those of the bones (which comprise a tenth of the body's weight); and those composing a large bulk of the other organs!

Some idle, rainy day, sit down and see how far you can count in an hour, and you will get a faint idea of the magnitude of these numbers. The mind cannot comprehend them and we can only compare the cells in the body to the sands on the seashore, or to the stars in the sky, which cannot be numbered.

Next, with a pen, trace on paper a line an inch long, and directly underneath it make a dotted line containing 3,500 dots—the number of blood cells in an inch. Can it be done so that each dot may be seen separately?

Cells are finer than sand; we may see the latter with the naked eye, but not the former; with a micro-scope of sufficient power each cell may be separately distinguished and counted. We are at a loss which to admire the more, the body with its infinitude of cells, or the instrument that reveals them. God has a never slumbering eye; a microscopic eye so powerful that it takes cognizance every moment of each little cell that He has fashioned and made.

Their Parts.

The microscope assists the eye, not only in distinguishing each individual cell, but it shows also that it is composed of three parts. •

1. *The nucleus*, a tiny grain or granule found in the interior of the cell. It is the kernel or germ, and is thicker and darker in hue than the other parts. Surrounding this is

2. *The envelope*, a thin, colorless, transparent covering. This part is sometimes wanting.

3. *The protoplasm* forms the main body or substance of the cell, and furnishes nutriment as the yolk of the ovum nourishes the germ.

Besides these three parts, the lens also shows that every cell lies in a network which is as delicate as

5

the fiuest silken lace, and is called a *plexus.* This plexus is composed of tubes crossing each other in every direction, like the threads of lace. Of these tubes there are three kinds: Capillaries, joining the veins and arteries, absorbents and nerves.

Cells are of various shapes ; some round like drops, some very long and narrow, some six-sided, others oblong. Some have two, three or more tails or appendages, others are star-shaped. Still others are thin, flat scales or plates and lap over each other like shingles.

Tubes.

Tubes or pipes traverse the solid parts of the body, as roads run across the fields, or as streams divide the land. Some may be seen with the naked eye ; others only with the microscope.

Among important tubes of the body, we may enumerate the following :

The *alimentary canal* is a large tube, consisting of the mouth, esophagus, stomach and intestines.

The *arteries* begin in the heart and dividing and subdividing, like the branches of a tree, reach every part of the body.

The *veins* begin where the arteries end, in the minute *capillaries,* and likewise run throughout the body and terminate in the heart.

The *perspiratory ducts* are placed just underneath the outer skin.

Some tubes are hollow, as hair, allowing the free passage of liquids ; others are filled with semi-liquids, still others with solid material.

Their Length.

Some interesting estimates have been made by anatomists of the length of tubes. The perspiratory ducts of an adult are computed to be about twenty-eight miles in length.

The intestines measure some twenty-five feet and are lined with a membrane laid in folds that if straightened out would be fifty feet long.

If the six hundred thousand air vesicles of the lungs were spread out over a flat surface, they would cover ten or twelve rooms fifteen by sixteen feet. This membrane is thickly covered with four kinds of tubes; namely arteries and veins joined as capillaries, nerves, and absorbents. There are three thousand capillaries lying side by side in a space an inch wide.

It would form an interesting problem to ascertain how many miles of capillary tubing would cover ten rooms, fifteen by sixteen feet. This result multiplied by three would give the approximate number of miles of nerves and absorbents.

The two billions of nerve cells have a plexus of capillaries that if laid out in a line like the irons of the railroad track, would extend many miles. Each cell of the liver, spleen, kidneys, and of all the muscles, is placed in a network of capillaries, absorbents and nerves, which if laid out in one straight line would measure hundreds of miles.

By counting the hairs in a square inch of the human head, and calculating the number of square inches in the scalp, an estimate has been formed that there is an average of one hundred and twenty thousand hairs on the head. If each hair measured twelve inches in length, this would give over twenty-three miles of hair. We thus see that the minuteness and multitude of cells is fully matched by the length of this wonderful tubing.

We are again filled with amazement at this display of God's creative power, and overwhelmed with a sense of the majesty of infinite minuteness.

Force.

Force is the third element in the plan on which the system is constructed. It cannot be seen, either with the naked eye or with the microscope. We cannot number or measure it as we did cells and tubes, yet we may describe its effects and tell what it does.

Hands and feet, muscles and bones, cannot move themselves. Force moves them. One cannot make a movement of any kind without using force. In walking, the foot must be lifted with *force*. Next it is put down with *force*. Running is using more force than walking. Kicking is still more force than either. A gentle kick is a little force applied to the foot; in a hard kick a great deal of force is used.

Sometimes the words strength, power, energy, vitality, spirit, life, are used to denote force.

When a man drives a nail, builds a house, plows the ground, reads aloud, laughs, groans or does anything whatever, he does it by means of his strength, energy, force.

Force does not occupy a space or organ by itself, but it fills all the material of which the system is composed.

Force keeps the tubes open and vigorous. Force operates on the cells making them plump and lively.

Force holds the body together. When it departs, death occurs. The parts of the body gradually separate and decay because force or life has left them.

This vital force has various manifestations. By its means our food is digested, assimilated and appropriated. This marvelous power controls the rythmic human heart beat. It insures the purification of the blood through the action of the lungs.

Our personal supervision over these movements is not needed. Sleeping or waking, busy or idle, their action is unceasing. Thus the unconscious mind presides over all the involuntary functions.

Substance.

Substance, the fourth element in the plan on which the human system is built, comes into the body from the outside. It feeds nerves, canals, arteries, veins, capillaries, absorbents, and all the other tubes. *It feeds all the cells.*

Food, water and air unite to form the substance of the body. Food furnishes the solids. Seven-eighths of the body-substance is water. From 3,000 to 5,000 gallons of air pass through the lungs every twenty-four hours to supply gases. The outside or walls of tubes and envelopes of cells are likewise made of what we eat, drink and breathe. Thus membrane, muscles, bone, liver and heart, once existed in other external forms. Force takes them into the body and appropriates them in a marvelous way to the carrying on of the life process.

CHAPTER VIII.

WHAT CELLS DO.

The word cell means *to hide, to conceal.* The name is very appropriate, for it is in these little hidden chambers that force so completely conceals its most important operations, that man never has been and probably never will be, able to penetrate its mysteries.

He may know *what* is done in them but not *how* it is done. He cannot construct such cells nor produce what is produced in them.

Force in the cell makes for himself a little home in which to live and work.

The protoplasm by the aid of this force takes up liquids and gases. Sometimes it will soak up matter from the outside and pass it to the contents inside; sometimes it allows the inside matter to pass out. Sometimes both processes are going on at the same time as illustrated by the following experiment:

Fill a glass with milk; tie tightly over the top a fresh bladder and thrust it into a jar of water. The water will soon become milky and the milk watery, showing that the water and milk are passing through the bladder at the same time. This process is called *osmosis.* Thus gases may pass through membranes.

We remember there is a network or plexus of tubes surrounding each cell filled with substance obtained from food, water and air. It is from these tubes, under the guidance of force, that the cells unerringly absorb what they need. They do not take everything that comes along, but each select the appropriate particles and allow the remainder to pass on.

The protoplasm, like a living thing full of vitality or life, or force, holds its existence against surrounding elements. These are as lifeless, inert material over which it exerts living, acting power. It is like a child that can eat apples, potatoes and bread, but apples, potatoes and bread cannot eat the child. ·

Cells never take the wrong kind of food unless forced to do so. Then they instinctively make the best of a bad case and use the most appropriate food furnished.

The life force of the cell, by some mysterious alchemy

Creates a New Substance.

This alchemy is not merely that of the chemist, by action of the elements and heat, for in addition vital force is exerted. This no chemist is wise enough or powerful enough to handle. By its aid the cell transforms dead matter into living, vital, growing substance.

We have now seen that cells can absorb outside matter and appropriate it; that they are endowed with an *instinct* what to select from the tubing, and what to omit; that they *transform* these selections into entirely different substances, which become living, growing parts of the human body.

Multiplication of Cells.

The human body grows by the multiplication of

cells. Force first splits the cell nucleus or germ in two, forming two germs. Next, it moves them to opposite sides of the protoplasm, one in each side or end, and then proceeds to split the protoplasm itself into two parts, so that one of the germs will lie in each part. Thus two complete cells appear where only one was before. These two cells are divided, making four. Out of these four eight are produced, and out of eight sixteen and so on and on, until the original cell is full of segments, having the appearance of a mulberry.

Thus the human body is formed out of the ovum or egg of the mother. The germ of the ovum and the sperm of the semen unite, forming a new cell. Immediately the process of division begins, whereby the cells multiply, and growth is carried on.

After birth, cells still constitute the organs and tissues. They are incessantly forming, accomplishing their work, and dying. Millions die or are destroyed daily. Some live days, others weeks or months, but sooner or later each cell reaches the end of existence, is swept away and is then replaced by others. Finger nail cells live four months in summer and five in winter, while brain, blood and other kinds are probably renewed every few days.

"The outer surface of our body is covered by layers of cells in loose connection; they are cells in old age. The friction of our clothing daily removes immense numbers of them. A cleanly person who uses sponge and towel energetically every day, rubs off still greater quantities. The mucous membrane of the mouth is covered with a thick layer of cells. Here, also, many thousand senile or worn out cells are rubbed off daily. We swallow ; our tongue acts in speaking ; drink and food pass this entrance of the digestive apparatus. Every one knows this. That which began at the entrance is continued through the entire canal. An excess of cells is thus lost daily."—*Frey*.

This is why we must eat, drink and breathe constantly ; so that there may be an abundance of material in the tubes for new cell making. In each organ may be found simultaneously cells in various stages of growth ; those that are old or mature just ready to be swept away ; others half grown, and the remainder young, new ones. Only the latter are engaged in the work of multiplication by division. Cells do not seem to retain this power during the whole term of their existence. Their first power of growth is expended in splitting themselves up into more cells, and next this growth is turned to becoming larger in size and in manufacturing new substances ; when the work of division ceases.

As they grow, they move forward to find room or are pushed out of the way by the newer multiplying cells behind them. They ripen or mature as they grow, occupying all their time and force in chemico-vital creations of new matter.

When this new creation is all finished, these marvelous cells have power to dispose of it in various ways, according to its nature and the nature of the organs containing the cells which produced it, and which will be described each in its proper place. We have also to consider how the old cells are removed, and the nature and use of the new substances or elements they have created.

CHAPTER IX.

GLANDS.

A gland is a collection of cells, which, together with their duct (or canal), are inclosed in a strong membrane.

Glands are among the solid organs of the body. There are numerous glands, as the liver, pancreas, spleen and kidneys. Each one produces by means of its cells a secretion peculiar to itself. The secretion turned out by one gland is a bitter juice; by another sweet; by still another saltish, yet it is all taken from the blood.

The nucleus of all gland cells is covered with an envelope, and the protoplasm of some kinds is also surrounded by the same, while others are devoid of covering, and hence called membraneless.

Glands are composed of cells in all stages of formation. The new young cells, engaged in multiplication, are situated nearest the inclosing membrane; then come the half-grown cells which have moved forward as they grew; and finally the oldest and ripest ones, full as they can hold, crowd upon the ducts, their term of life completed, their work finished. Their walls burst, and the cells are no more forever.

They pour into the duct, tipped out protoplasm (now called secretion) and broken envelopes in a heap together. The next oldest cells then crowd forward and in their turn meet the same fate.

The Salivary Glands.

There are six of these placed in the flesh around the mouth ; three on each side.

Saliva is a colorless liquid which pours into the mouth and moistens the food while it is being chewed.

Creative force residing in salivary cells chooses certain particles from the blood (which is made from the food we eat) as it courses by in the plexus, draws it into the body of the cell by osmosis and with the help of the protoplasm manufactures it into

Fig. XVII represents the cells of one gland with the tube plexus removed, and the cells attached to the duct.

a new kind of juice—the salivary secretion or saliva. This contains some constituents found nowhere else in the body.

When a boy begins to eat his dinner, he fills his mouth with food ; sets his teeth into the mouthful and masticates it, moving his jaws up and

Fig. XVIII shows the plexus without the cells. The darker spots represent vacant spaces from which the cells were removed.

down and from side to side, with a great deal of *force*.

This breaks the cells and spills out all the juice. There are hundreds of these cells bursting at the same time during meals. They fill the ducts, which, beginning very fine and small like the twigs of a tree, unite and re-unite, forming larger and larger branches until they all join in one large canal, out of which the saliva is poured into the mouth. (See Fig. XVII).

There is another strong force able to affect the cells and to destroy them and discharge their juices.

It Is the Force of Thought.

A familiar example of this is observed when the mouth " waters " at the *thought* of savory food. The wish or thought, beginning in the brain, goes down the nerve tubes, which also begin in the brain and form part of the plexus. Nerves are made for the special use of thought. They contain a liquid a trifle thicker than water, through which thought passes as light, sound, heat and electricity pass through air and water.

In this case nerve force roused by the thought of luscious food, goes straight to the ripest cells, bursts their envelopes, and the secretion comes pouring into the mouth.

And this too, when the person is not thinking of his mouth at all ; perhaps does not know anything of the process of saliva making. His thoughts are all centered upon the coveted dainty of the palate, imagining how good it would taste, wishing he had some, possibly planning how to get it. Yet the result of these thoughts is acting upon the glands, breaking the cells and wasting their contents.

If a boy continues to think about and greedily desire some imaginary luxury of the appetite, after the ripe cells are all destroyed, what next? Then, thought force will still go on acting upon nerves lying deeper in the gland, attacking the next ripest cells, and breaking them up before their protoplasm is completed. Having destroyed these it next grasps the undeveloped cells while they are engaged in the work of division, and destroys them.

And if the boy does not stop fretting and pining after the sweet morsel, if he does not quit his vain and useless longing, his thought force will go right on thwarting nature, so that it not only cannot build up any more cells, but will *eventually destroy the gland forever*. This condition is called *atrophy* of the gland. This, thought force can do. It can influence secretions and destroy glands.

Then when meal-time comes bringing the usual plain and common fare, or even the savory dainty so ardently desired, he finds himself unable to enjoy it. Appetite gone, and no saliva, the morsel is dry and tasteless in his mouth.

Cannot one prevent his mouth "watering" and the cells from premature destruction by will, by a command of thought? Not while he continues to fret and dream over the forbidden or unattainable morsel.

There is only one way he can stop it—and it is a very easy way. •

He Must Stop the Thought.

Let him take his thought force away from the tempting article of food, put it upon some other object, and it will leave the gland. Atrophy of the salivary gland is not common, *but hundreds of men have destroyed other glands in precisely this way.*

We may now gather from the preceding study of

the salivary glands two physical laws which govern them, God's golden laws, because God made the gland. These laws apply to all the other glands as well.

Thought Influences Secretions.

Bad Thoughts May Destroy Glands.

In India advantage is taken of the first of these laws to aid in detecting thieves. All suspected parties, as for example, the servants of a family, are obliged by the judge to hold a certain quantity of rice in the mouth for a few minutes; then the one whose rice is dry is convicted as the thief. The superstitious belief is, that the gods will preserve from moisture the rice in the mouth of the guilty one. Under this belief fear takes strong hold of his mind, and this thought of fear influences the gland so forcibly as to prevent the escape of saliva.

The gland is prostrated or paralyzed for the time being with the force of fear. And it is quite possible that this temporary paralysis could be carried so far as to become permanent and entirely destroy the gland. Other glands have been paralyzed by the mind. Despair, grief, disappointment and fright have been known to dry up the salivary secretions.

On the other hand, happiness, peace, contentment shed over the gland such benign influences that it turns out an abundant, healthful secretion, from which fact we know that

Good Thoughts Preserve Glands.

Bad thoughts are death dealing. Good thoughts give harmony, health and life.

The Lachrymal Glands.

· These glands are so called because tears are secreted by them. They are quite similar in construction to the salivary glands and lie above the outer angle of each eye.

Fig. XIX. Lachrymal Gland and Nasal Canal.

The gland can be seen in the cut at the left hand upper corner of the eyeball. The tiny ducts run from it carrying the fluid which moistens the eye. From the opposite corner the nasal canal conducts the overflow or waste to the nose. The lachrymal secretion is distinguished from others in being a salt-ish fluid. It is being constantly produced, usually very slowly. It oozes drop by drop through the ducts, of which there are from six to twelve. All day these drops fall upon the eyeball keeping it smooth and moist, as oil lubricates the moving parts of a machine. How important and useful a secretion this is! Can you realize how often in a day the eye-ball moves in every direction?

This is the ordinary action of this gland.

Strong emotions such as grief, disappointment and sometimes anger, prove that *thought affects secretion.*

The force of mental emotion acts upon the cells,

pressing out the tears with great rapidity. These course through the ducts and fill the eye faster than the nasal canal can carry them away. Of course they must overflow upon the face. This we call crying.

In excessive weeping, cell force works very fast and very hard to create tears for the occasion. If this is long continued, the material is exhausted, the young cells are destroyed, the tubes become emptied of substance, and there is nothing more of which to make tears.

Then poor bankrupt force knows not what to do; the situation grows critical; force in the brain is calling for more tears which the gland cannot supply. Force searches the eyeball, the lids and surrounding flesh, trying to extract from them something for the purpose, but they have no material to spare, and thus are robbed and injured. This makes them burn, smart and become dry, and inflammation follows.

Excessive weeping has in some cases destroyed not only the gland, but the eyesight as well.

Joyful and happy emotions are so intense sometimes as to break gland cells, yet these are less liable than depressing thoughts to result seriously.

Then again, some very sudden and violent grief may dry up the tears before they are shed. The mental force itself may be said to be in a fever in the brain, and it reacts upon the gland inflaming it almost instantly. It dries up the tears as water is evaporated when dropped on a red hot stove. In such a case as this, if the thought fever is not soon cooled after destroying all the cells, it will affect the surrounding tissues. Hence we see that

Thought Influences Secretion in Two Ways.

1. By rousing the gland to unusual action, tending to inflammation.

2. By checking its action, tending to paralysis.

In either way death of the gland may ensue.

The Remedy.

Those who would preserve this gland (and also eyesight itself) must learn the laws by which mental force may be controlled. The sovereign law is expressed in three words.

Change the Thought.

Self-pity will never check the excessive flow of tears. Neither will reasoning upon the matter nor even an effort at *direct* self-control avail much. A new impulse must be given to thought. Imaginary troubles may be dissipated by a resolute turning of the mind upon real issues, and engaging in something of absorbing interest; even a naughty, whining child fiuds help in drying his tears under the stimulus of deserved but unexpected punishment.

Use Self-Control.

This exercise of will-power is not brought to bear directly upon the gland. The mind is controlled, and the result of this control acts through the nerves upon the gland.

To illustrate: A wee toddler, in climbing stairs and chairs has mishaps often, and as often cries. When he is a little older, the hammer, in his awkward hands, the knife in his untrained eager fingers, frequently induce vigorous and tearful outbursts. The older

6

brothers nickname him "cry-baby." But his wise mother appeals to his incipient manliness, and by rousing his aspirations, changes the thought from his momentary annoyance to a noble resolution.

She often suggests: "That cut is not so *very* bad. Papa wouldn't cry .for it. Brother does not cry every time he pounds his fingers. Babies cry; but you are not a baby. Be a man like papa."

A higher ideal begins to fill his mind, though perhaps silently and almost unconsciously. He contrasts his childish whimper with the brave self-control of a man suffering pain, danger and grief. He determines to cry less, and soon notices an encouraging improvement; he finds he can repress all his accustomed howlings, and yet suffer no more than formerly. He takes new courage; restrains even tears, and with every victory gains a new, brave feeling of manliness, and soon has outgrown the name of "cry-baby." The tear gland is now seldom called upon for service, and as he matures, there is no lachrymal waste except when under the heaviest affliction, or affected by the tenderest sympathy.

What the mind thus does for one gland it can do for all.

Inherent force under the influence of a cheerful mind is the true remedy for disordered action.

CHAPTER X.

GLANDS—CONTINUED.

The Liver Gland.

This gland is somewhat differently constructed from those already described. A large number of cells with their ducts and plexus are formed into a separate bunch, called a Lobule. Each lobule is covered with a membrane, and has another plexus of tubing in this.

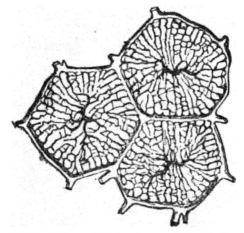

Fig. XX. Three lobules from a lobe of the liver.

The lobules are laid side by side in rows and piles in such a way as to form five great divisions called Lobes. These make up the entire liver.

The liver produces an intensely bitter secretion called bile. There is nothing in the blood that is

(91)

bitter like bile, yet bile is made from the substance
in the plexus—and from the very same substance is

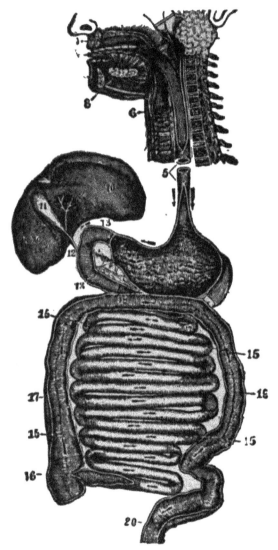

Fig. XXI. *The Alimentary Canal. 10, liver; 11, gall bladder;
12, its duct; 8, salivary gland; 5, esophagus; 6, trachea; 9, stomach;
13, duodenum; 15, small intestines; 17, 18, 19, colon; 20, rectum.*

manufactured by the liver a sugar also. This is in
some points unlike the sugar we eat.

Bile is stored in the gall bladder—see cut—until needed for use.

Thought influences the secretions of the liver gland. Bitter thoughts like a benumbing influence act upon the cells preventing them from their work of separating out the bitter element. Thus it remains in the blood, clogging and poisoning it. The complexion takes on a yellow hue, the eye a greenish cast.

Long continued anxiety or fright, or other depressing emotions have in some instances changed the complexion from a clear white to a dull yellow in a few hours.

A brisk, cheerful, contented mind brings to the liver health and vigor to pursue its busy life-work of purification.

Thus unwittingly the physical reveals the state of the spiritual man.

Disturbances of the liver are also caused by other undesirable mental conditions. Lack of reasonable self-control, with an indolent habit of life, leads to over eating. This gives the gland too much work to do; more food substance than power of assimilation. The system becomes clogged, and all the powers correspondingly inert.

The popular diet of our present civilization tends especially to overload this organ. All preparations of bolted or fine white flour; as bread, biscuit, cakes, puddings and pie crust, carry to the liver more starch than that much abused gland finds itself able to manufacture into sugar.

God made wheat, but not white flour. Fats, gravies, sugars and syrups increase the difficulty; also salt, pepper, spices, and all other condiments.

A simple diet of wheat, oats, and other grains, cracked, crushed, or ground coarse and not bolted ; vegetables fresh, and simply cooked, and ripe fruit eaten at the table only—never between meals—will furnish plenty of sugar making material, and lessen the danger of overloading the liver.

Hard workers commit the opposite error of not taking sufficient time to eat. A grasping mind, over-reaching to get much of this world's goods, or a business-driven, fretted, anxious state reacts with paralytic tendencies upon this gland.

In either case the cure to be effectual must begin in the mind. It is useless to irritate the delicate tissues of this gland with drugs. Tonic thought must cleanse the mind of its bilious thought forces, and then physical treatment applied on hygienic principles will restore the normal action of the liver.

The greedy eater must be made willing to "eat to live" rather than to "live to eat" as he now does. The greedy worker must be made willing to "take no thought for the morrow." The true physician is physician of the soul first.

People sometimes die of liver disease, as a result of their bitter, low-spirited, lazy, idle, or anxious thoughts.

We may now add two more immutable truths to those already demonstrated :

Bad Thoughts Poison Secretions.

Good Thoughts Preserve Secretions.

"He that ruleth his spirit (thoughts) is better than he that taketh a city."

The Mammary Glands.

The breasts, or mammary glands, secrete a milk that is much like goat's or cow's milk. This is provided by the mother half of the human family only when there is a new life to be nourished, and continues until the little one's teeth are developed, and the general system is adapted to demand other food. Milk is made out of the blood supplied by the plexus, the same substance that furnishes material for the salt of the tears, the sugar and bile of the liver.

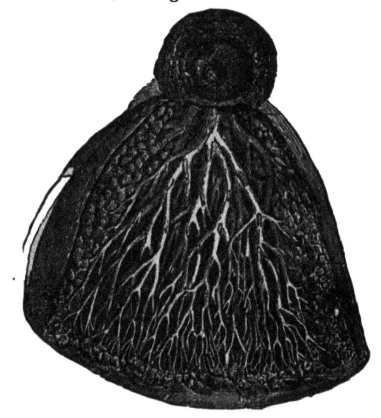

Fig. XXII. Inside View of Breast.

These glands are constructed much like the salivary glands. The pressure of the infant's lips in the act of nursing is the force that bursts the gland cells, filling the ducts, which pour their contents directly into the mouth of the little one.

This gland is particularly susceptible to thought force. Sir A. Cooper, who wrote a valuable treatise on the breast, assures us that "the secretion of .milk proceeds best in a *tranquil state of mind* and with a cheerful temper; then the milk is regularly abundant, and agrees well with the child. On the contrary, a *fretful temper* lessens the quantity of milk, and makes it thin and serous. *Fits of anger* may produce a very irritating milk. *Grief* or anxiety has a great influence on lactation, and consequently upon the child. The loss of a near and dear relative, or a change of fortune, will often so much diminish the secretion of milk as to render other food necessary for the support of the child. The reception of a letter, which leaves the mind in anxious suspense, lessens the draught, and may cause the breast to become empty for the time being. *Fear* and terror have a powerful influence on the secretion of milk ; the apprehension of the brutal conduct of a drunken husband will put a stop for a time to the secretion."

Bad Thoughts May Cause Death.
Good Thoughts Preserve Life.

These truths are more fully proved by the same author: "A carpenter fell into a quarrel with a soldier billeted in his house, and was set upon by the latter with his drawn sword. The wife of the carpenter at first trembled from fear and terror, and then suddenly threw herself furiously between the combatants, wrested the sword from the soldier's hand, broke it into pieces, and threw it away. During the tumult some neighbors came in and separated the men. While in this state of strong excitement the mother took up her child, who was in the most perfect health, gave it the breast, and in so doing, sealed its fate. In a few minutes the infant became restless, panted, and sank dead upon its mother's bosom."

"Another mother fell into a violent passion, and her babe, being nursed, soon afterward died in convulsion. One babe went into convulsions after taking the breast of one who had been severely reprimanded. Another infant was seized with convulsions and paralysis upon nursing after its mother had met with some distressing occurrence."

" *The iniquity of the fathers (and mothers) is visited upon the children unto the third and fourth generation.*"

Thus the law of heredity enforces, through nature, the voice of Scripture, and warns both fathers and mothers that heart and mind must be kept at peace, lest harm and death result to the helpless.

The Gastric Glands.

The walls of the stomach have a lining called *mucous* membrane, similar to that which lines the mouth. Within this are situated numerous small glands with ducts opening into the stomach. These are called *gastric* glands, and produce *gastric juice.*

Without gastric juice there can be no digestion of food. It is an intensely sour secretion. The elements peculiar to it are hydrochloric acid and pepsin.

The mucous lining lies in folds when the stomach is empty ; these stretch out and increase the size of the cavity to accommodate the amount of food put into it.

The outer coat of the stomach is smooth and highly polished, and is. called *serous* membrane. Between this and the mucous membrane is interposed another composed of three layers of elastic muscle which is called the *muscular* membrane.

No sooner is the food packed away in this snug little box than the middle membrane begins to expand and contract. One of its three layers of muscle runs the long way of the stomach, another the short way, and

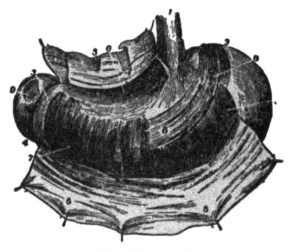

The Stomach.

Fig. XXIII. 1. The opening through which the food is passed into the stomach. 9. The opening through which the food is passed out of the stomach. 5. 5. The serous membrane turned back. 6. The muscular layer which runs oblique. 7. The muscular layer which runs shortways 8. The muscular layer which runs lengthways.

the other crossways. Each layer draws in and then spreads out, after the manner of India rubber, and this action is going on three ways at once, from the three layers, and with so much force as to jar and move the stomach. This imparts a steady, churning motion to its contents, which, with the pressure of food inside, crushes the ripe gland cells and makes them pour out their secretion.

The stomach is easily affected by the mind. Sudden disappointment, or bad news received during the progress of meals or soon afterward has been known to take away the appetite and even to cause vomiting ; force is diverted to the brain, and consequently action in the stomach is checked.

On the other hand, appetite is often lost upon the receipt of good news ; children can eat no breakfast on the morning of a picnic, or on the day of the ride to grandpa's.

A few glands remain to be described. The *pancreas* manufactures the pancreatic juice, an alkaline secretion. This gland is less easily affected by mental disturbances.

Fig. XXIV. 'A portion of the duodenum appears at the left of the cut. The pancreas lies between this and the spleen, which is seen at the right.

The *spleen*, a peculiar gland, varies from the others in having no duct to convey away the secretion, but appears to pour its product immediately into the blood. Its use in the body is as yet unexplained.

Glands Sympathize with Each Other.

One gland cannot be afflicted with serious trouble without affecting one or more of the others, and if the disturbance is of long standing all of them will fall under its influence. Thus the gastric and tear glands both enter into sympathy with grief-stricken emotions over the loss of friends, business or property. The stomach and liver often agree to complain together when only one of them is diseased. The spleen and liver are frequently united in suffering, and the stomach and other parts appear to be as much in pain as they, when in fact, the ailment is located in but one of them; they are then said to be *sympathetically* affected. If, however, the disease is not soon removed it is liable to actually spread to the part in sympathy with it, and from there gradually extend over the entire body, that which was at first mere sympathy afterward becoming reality.

CHAPTER XI.

The action of mastication; the vermiform motion of the walls of the stomach and intestines; the pressure of eyelids drooping in grief over the lachrymal glands; the pressure of the infant's lips upon the ducts of the mammary glands, are outside forces that cause them to yield their juices.

To distinguish these outside forces from creative force that builds and fills the cells, and also to distinguish from the inner forces of good and bad thoughts we will name them *physical* forces. Physical forces of every description go by the general name, *exercise.*

Physical Exercise Destroys Cells.

We have now learned some of the wonderful things that force can do; how it can build cells; how it has power to select some materials and reject others, and to form new substances out of its selections.

We see that force is greater than substance. We see that thought force is greater than body force; that it can made the body sick and can preserve the body in health. Exactly how it does this we cannot explain, but the facts are before us.

" As a Man Thinketh, So Is He."

The power of force over substance, of mind over

matter, of thought force over physical force, holds to a greater or less degree over all the organs.

The heart readily responds to the influence of thought. Fright affects the heart very quickly and powerfully. The pulse will stop and the heart seem to stand still for a moment and the next moment beat with a bound, keeping it in a flutter while the fright lasts. The blood retires from the face, leaving it "pale with fright," and passes inward to the brain, as if going to the assistance of the distressed parts.

Anxiety causes irregular palpitation of the heart. Grief causes it to move slowly and heavily, and has sometimes killed people by paralyzing the heart. They are said to have "died of a broken heart." Occasionally some great joy brought suddenly upon an invalid has had the same effect.

A sudden shock, either of joy or grief, will often produce an attack of diarrhea or dysentery. Others, in plump flesh and full health, on being thrown into adverse circumstances, have grown lean and weak, the tissues being gradually passed off through the intestines; while in still other cases the same change of condition takes place through the stomach by means of vomiting and indigestion.

With some, mental disturbance causes constipation. Violent weeping sometimes produces a flow of urine. Great loss of muscular strength accompanies prostrating mental emotions, as frights, shocks, bad news, with some people, while it seems to rouse others to redoubled exertions.

A person in fear is often covered with a cold perspiration. Fear has changed the hair from black to white in a single night, and in other cases caused insanity.

Dr. B. W. Richardson relates a striking example of the effect of *rage* upon the heart. "A gentleman told me that an original irritability of temper was permitted by want of due control, to pass into a disposition of almost persistent or chronic anger. Sometimes his anger was so vehement that all near him were alarmed for him even more than for themselves, and when the attack was over there were hours of sorrow and regret in private, which were as exhausting as the previous rage. In the midst of one of these outbursts of short, severe madness, he suddenly felt, to use his own expression, as if his heart were lost!

" He reeled under the impression, was nanseated and faint; then recovering, he put his hand to his wrist, and discovered an intermittent action of his heart as the cause of his faintness. He never completely rallied from the shock, and to the day of his death, ten years later, he was never free from the intermittency. 'I am broken hearted,' he would say, 'physically broken hearted.' And so he was; but the knowledge of the broken heart tempered marvelously his passion, and saved him many years of a really useful life." A hasty temper may early be placed under self-control, and young people who understand both the physical and moral dangers of self-indulgence will need few counsels from parents and teachers in regard to the matter."

" Let the farmer feel that his severe labor is sure to bring him in good crops, and how happily does he persevere in his severe toil month after month. And if the merchant can only know that his gains are great, how incessantly will he work day and night, and yet consider his no hard life. But if there be no encouragement, no prospect of reward to the working man in his employment, what drudgery does it become! Nay, how positively injurious to health and vigor of body and mind."—*Hitchcock.*

The willing student whose mind is free and spirits light, stores facts and principles in his memory with greater readiness, and his reasoning powers are more easily developed, than one who is depressed, or forced to study against his wish.

The worst effects of fright, grief, anxiety, etc., may be warded off by a "cheerful acquiescence in the divine will, which has often done more to restore the invalid and maintain good health against disease, than all medical remedies; and religious hopes have been more efficacious to prolong life on earth than all other hygienic prescriptions."

The following by Dr. K——, may induce some readers to avoid the risks indicated: "In games of chance (betting and gambling), where money is at stake, we see the play of the worst passions in all its mischievous intensity. Fear and anger, hate and grief, hope and exultation stand forth, one after the other, keeping the trepitant heart in constant excitement and under tremulous strain, until its natural steadiness of motion is transformed into unnatural irregularity, which if it does not remain permanent, is called up by the slightest irritation.

"The act of playing whist for high stakes is a frequent source of disease from this cause. I know that professed card players declare that however much may be played for, the losses and winnings are equalized by turn, and that after a year's play the player has, practically, neither won nor lost. I may accept this as true; but the fact, if it be one, does not alter the physical evil that results, one iota. The man who, after being engaged in business all day, sits down regularly at night to play his rubbers on rubbers; to stake heavily on his games, to bet on his odd tricks, never, I believe, escapes the effects of nervous organic shock."

The "Cornhill Magazine" publishes the incident below, which shows that people have scarcely begun to realize the great benefits (as well as dangers) arising from the influence of the mind over the body, and the extent to which it may be made of practical value:

"Mr. Crosse had been bitten severely by a cat, which the same day died from hydrophobia. He seems resolutely to have dismissed from his mind the fears which must naturally have been suggested by these circumstances. Had he yielded to them, as most men would, he might not improbably have succumbed within a few days or weeks to an attack of mind-created hydrophobia—so to describe the fatal ailment which ere now has been known to kill persons who had been bitten by animals perfectly free from *rabies.*

"At the end of three months, however, he felt one morning a severe pain in his arm, accompanied by severe thirst. He called for water; but 'at the instant,' he says, 'that I was about to raise the tumbler to my lips, a strong spasm shot across my throat. Immediately the terrible conviction came to my mind that I was about to fall a victim to hydrophobia, the

7

consequence of the bite I had received from the cat. The agony of mind I endured for one hour is indescribable; the contemplation of such a horrible death was almost insupportable. The pain, which had first commenced in my hand, passed up to the elbow, and from thence to the shoulder, threatening to extend. I felt all human aid was useless, and I believed that I must die.

"'At length I began to reflect upon my condition. I said to myself, either I shall die or I shall not; if I do, it will only be a similar fate which many have suffered, and many more must suffer, and I must bear it like a man. If, on the other hand, there is any hope of my life, my only chance is in summoning my utmost resolution, defying the attack, and exerting every effort of my mind; accordingly, feeling that physical as well as mental exertion was necessary, I took my gun, and went out for the purpose of shooting, my arm aching the while intolerably. I met with no sport, but walked the whole afternoon, exerting at every step I went a strong mental effort against the disease.

"'When I returned to the house I was decidedly better; I was able to eat some dinner, and drank water as usual. The next morning the pain had gone down to my elbow, the following day it went down to my wrist, and the third day it left me altogether. I mentioned the circumstance to Dr. Kinglake, and he said he certainly considered I had had an attack of hydrophobia, which would possibly have proved fatal had I not struggled against it by a strong effort of mind.'"

Good Thoughts and Bad Thoughts.

Good thoughts tend to health, happiness and longevity. A happy and harmonious home life gives healthful conditions. In the present state of society, however, many evil influences from without tend to mar the results of the best home training.

Thought Force Influences the Body.

Good Thought Force	Bad Thought Force
Preserves organs.	May destroy organs.
Invigorates organs.	May injure organs.
Preserves secretions.	May poison secretions.
Preserves life.	May destroy life.

Happy, peaceful and contented thoughts work in harmony with creative force in the glands, and tend to produce a regular heart-beat. Bad thoughts put everything out of place, and upset all of nature's calculations. A law of nature, hence a law of God, is to

Think Good Thoughts.

Obedience to this law is Life.
Disobedience to this law is Death.

Good Thoughts	Bad Thoughts
and their results:	and their results:
Love.	Hatred.
Kindness.	Malice.
Gentleness.	Rudeness.
Harmony.	Discord.
Sweet temper.	Hectoring.
Patience.	Fretfulness.
Amiability.	Sulkiness.
Forgiveness.	Revenge.

Trust.	Fear.
Cheerfulness.	Whining.
Justice.	Injustice.
Truth.	Falsehood.
Honesty.	Cheating.
Industry.	Idleness.
Economy.	Extravagance.
Reverence.	Blasphemy.
Dutifulness.	Disobedience.
Humility.	Pride.
Self-denial.	Selfishness.
Benevolence.	Penuriousness.
Temperance.	Gluttony.
Teetotalism.	Tippling.
Purity.	Vulgarity.
Chastity.	Prostitution.
Virtue.	Vice.
Self-control.	Indulgence.
Continence.	Incontinence.

The laws of God written in our nature agree with the laws of God written in the Word of Revelation.

In Ephesians IV. and Galatians V., and in numerous other places, we find the very words which we have used in our list of bad thoughts. These are called

"Lusts of the Flesh," " Works of the Flesh."

A student of physiology sees in these phrases an appropriate description of the result of wrong thinking. It proves disturbing and destructive.

On the contrary, good thoughts are called

" Fruits of the Spirit," " Being Led by the Spirit,"

and Paul speaks of finding in himself two laws, the

"law of God," or the "law in his mind," and the
"law of sin," or the "law in his members;" that to
live after the law of the spirit is to go

The Way of Life;

while to live after the law of the flesh is to go

The Way of Death.

.All through the Bible "sin" is the name given to
evil thoughts.   In fact, the chief burden of the Bible
from beginning to end is in regard to these laws of
the thoughts.

"See, I have set before thee life and death, blessing
and cursing, good and evil; therefore choose life that
thou and thy seed may live."

"The wages of sin is death."   "The gift of God is
eternal life."

The teachings of the Bible on thoughts are true;
they agree with science; agree with reason; agree
with facts.   As physiologists, therefore, submit yourselves to God (good thoughts).   Finally,

" Whatsoever things are true,
Whatsoever things are honest,
Whatsoever things are just,
Whatsoever things are pure,
Whatsoever things are lovely,
Whatsoever things are of good report,
If there be any virtue, and
If there be any praise,
Think on these things."

CHAPTER XII.

ORGANIC LIFE.

The word organized comes from *organ*, meaning a tool or instrument by means of which something is done or made. The bodies or objects containing the most tools or organs would be considered the most highly organized.

The dust of the ground has no tools, parts or organs, hence is not organized at all. Plant organs or tools are root, stem and leaves, hence plants are organized.

Things having organs are said to be *organic*. The rest of the world, soil, air, water, etc., is called *inorganic* (without organs).

Human beings are the most highly organized of all created things. Our bodies are only dust made over. The Bible states a great truth, with which the testimony of science agrees, when it says, " God formed man of the dust of the ground."

" *Dust Thou Art !* "

is true of all of us. What has done this wonderful work of making over or organizing dust into living bodies? Force. Force is found everywhere. Plant force soaks up or draws up by means of the roots certain substances that are in the ground. There are lime, iron, sulphur, phosphorus, silica, in minute particles

ticles. There are decaying wood, bones of animals and ashes. Many of these would prove injurious to us if we should eat them. They do not kill plants, but on the contrary, are good for them. Plant force can use them. The plant is full of cells similar to human cells, and in that same mysterious, secret process changes them over into entirely new substances not at all like the dust from which they were made. We find that soil, and minerals, and bones, and salts have changed into stem, branches, leaves, buds, blooms, fruit. Plants are of purer quality, of firmer texture, more elaborate and of more agreeable taste and odor; they are finer, cleaner, richer substances than the elements from which they are made. They are in every way altogether better, choicer material. In short, they are more

Highly Organized.

Looking again at a plant, for example an apple tree, we find that some of its parts are more highly organized than other parts; thus, the branches are of a finer texture and are more elaborate than the trunk; the leaves are richer and more dainty than the branches; the flowers are sweeter and handsomer than the leaves; the fruit choicer and richer than the flowers; while the seed is the *bon bon*, the best of all

Each part is a little more highly organized than the part below it until we reach the seed, which is the most entirely perfect, or *highly organized* portion of the whole plant, so much so that it is capable of starting a new plant from the very beginning. Neither roots, stem, leaves or flowers—only the seed—is highly organized enough for that. Plants may grow from slips, but that is not starting them from the beginning; it is only continuing the growth already begun, and does not require so complete a condition as commencing from the seed.

Man belongs to the organic division or kingdom of nature. He possesses the most complete set of tools or organs, and a more highly elaborated organization than any other order of existence.

He may not eat inorganic substances, but he may eat vegetables. They have begun the work of organization, changing crude, poisonous matters into a pabulum of which he may partake in safety. The creative force that resides in him may, by means of his bodily organs or tools, organize these into yet higher conditions.

Frequent mention has been made of the fact that secretions or juices are produced from what we eat, and that muscle, bone, blood, brain, organs and glands, once grew in the ground, and floated in the atmosphere.

Bone and cartilage are firmer than trunks of trees; muscle is better than leaves; eyes, lips, faces, are more beautiful than blossoms; secretions are richer than plant sap; the brain and nervous system is altogether beyond comparison with anything the plant possesses.

Bones, flesh, nerves and brain are not highly enough organized to produce an image of man—a little child—only the seed or egg is sufficient for this creative work. Hence we find in this the most highly organized product of the body.

So step by step the dust of the earth has been made into the very choicest part of the human system.

Glands are Tools or Organs.

By means of their juices substance is made over into the solid and fluid constituents of the body.

Does force come from dust? Is instinct, hunger, thirst, desire to breathe, creative cell force and thought force mere highly organized dust?

"And God breathed into his nostrils the breath of life, and man became a living soul." Thus Revelation answers our query, and nothing in nature declares the statement false.

God is Life, Spirit, Force.

To man's living soul are given the gifts of sense, by which he becomes conscious of the manifestations of God's forces in nature. His *eye* sees the *color* produced by God's *light;* his *ear* receives the *sound;* his *nose* the *fragrance;* his *tongue* the *flavor;* his *frame* enjoys the *warmth* manifested by the forces which emanate from the Almighty.

Thus man works together with God, although it may be many times all unconsciously.

Sound force reaches the brain through the ear, by means of the nerves of hearing. There it produces a thought impression, as to its nature, as soft or loud, musical or harsh.

Sights are conveyed from the eye to the brain by the optic nerves, and in the mind is formulated the ideas of light and darkness, motion and velocity. Thus our primitive ideas develop.

That we cannot discover all these various manifestations of force in every object in nature, is no proof that it is not there existent, but rather is evidence of defect in our senses. We cannot detect bears and other animals by their odor, but we know they possess an odor which dogs can scent with their more highly perfected organ of smell. Some people having keener hearing, can discover sound in objects that others would declare possessed none. So of heat, and electricity.

Again, it is noticeable that each sense is affected by the force it was fitted to receive, and by no other kind. Savor is that manifestation of force which strikes the nose but falls powerless on the ear. Sound fills the ear, but makes no sensation on the eye. The tongue never sees, the ear never tastes, and only the brain is capable of receiving impressions of these various sensations, and of forming ideas and emotions of pleasure or pain. In other words, it is the only organ of conscious thought.

CHAPTER XIII.

FOOD ASSIMILATION.

Man a Microcosm.

Man is a little world, or microcosm, formed from the great world, for his body is earth-born, while his soul or vital part is God-born.

"God created man in his own image, male and female created He them—and formed man out of the dust of the ground, and breathed into his nostrils the breath of life."

These two elements, *dust* and *breath*, *earth* and *spirit*, united into this miniature existence—man—constitute him at once the *image* and the *temple* of his Creator.

Chemistry has reduced earth, water and air into their simplest elements. Of these there are sixty-four. Some fifteen of them enter into the composition of the human body. Among these are the gases oxygen, hydrogen, carbon and nitrogen; iron, phosphorus, sulphur, silicon and magnesium, are among the minerals.

While life force primarily controls our existence and without it life is not, our subject demands that we consider briefly the interesting changes by which inorganic substances are changed to organic.

Iron dust and sand are not only incapable of assimilation, but would prove positively injurious to the digestive organs; yet the system must have iron and silicon in some form.

No one would dare take undiluted oxygen or pure hydrogen to quench thirst. But united as *water*, it constitutes a large and most useful factor in the human organism. Again, nitrogen cannot be breathed with impunity, but united with oxygen as air, what substance more vital to humanity!

The mineral elements, likewise, must first be transformed into roots, fruits and grains before they can become constituents of the body. In these they have already made combinations which can be assimilated.

In a grain of wheat a layer of cells of food substance lies upon the inner side of the envelope.

Here are gluten and phosphate. This is the most nourishing part of the wheat, much of which is wanting in white flour.

The Use of Secretions.

Saliva, evidently, is not made to be wasted upon vain and useless longings. Bile fails of its true purpose when it gives a bilious hue to the skin, or nausea to the stomach. Tears were not created mainly for weeping, because that is weakening and destructive; but rather as a useful emollient for the organs of vision. God did not construct any of the wonderfully delicate and elaborate glands to be abused.

Special Use of Saliva.

Saliva is the first secretion that exerts a converting action upon food. It mixes with and softens the food, thus preparing it for mastication and swallowing.

By its peculiar alkaline power it acts upon the starchy elements, turning them into something like sugar.

A very large proportion of our food consists of starch. Potatoes, rice, peas, beans, corn, and wheat, contain it in great abundance. But before the body can make use of it, it must be changed into sugar. Should starch be swallowed without being acted upon by the saliva it could not be digested, but would be to the body a useless waste substance.

Many business men in a hurry to get back to the office or store, many boys in desperate haste to resume a game of ball, cannot take time to chew their food and properly mix it with saliva. By aid of coffee, milk or water the half-chewed aliment is washed down into the stomach, and the heavy, useless load of starch is handed on from one organ to another—a mere burden to be got rid of.

It is constantly getting in the way, hindering and irritating the organs. Not being thoroughly incorporated with sufficient moisture to make it move easily, it gets impacted among the folds and glands of the Alimentary Canal; it may clog up the Colon and Rectum, and cause constipation.

Creative force puts up with this unnatural, lawless condition as long as possible, but sooner or later it will get discouraged, refuse to work any longer, and the process of digestion comes to a standstill. What happens next? One would die were it not that there is provision made by which the system can right itself.

This is by what we call sickness. One has headache, backache, pains in the bones; loses his appetite, experiences thirst, fever, perhaps vomiting, accompanied by severe pain.

" I am sick," groans the boy. How is he to be restored to health ? He is being restored even now by
this very sickness. All the forces of the body have
been apprised by the nerves that digestive creative
force is unable to get on without help. The Alimentary Canal must be cleared, so they all unite in a
mighty effort to dislodge the hurtful mass. Of course,
while the neighboring forces are engaged in this res-
torative operation their own work is being undone,
consequently the whole body is in one sense sick.
And this is what happens when physical laws are
broken.

This manifestation of force is called *recuperative
force*. All that the healing art can do is to find out
what nature is seeking to accomplish, and then
assist it.

What caused this boy's sickness? Did Providence?
Back of unchewed, undigested food and unused saliva
was wrong thought force. The boy *thought* that his
play or study was of more consequence than God's
arrangement for eating.

Providence has made these laws, and they must be
honored. Obedience is the best honor. God wants
good thoughts, that lead to honoring and obeying His
laws. Therefore, whether we eat or drink, or whatsoever we do let us do it in accordance with law, or,
what is the same thing, "to the glory of God."

Sickness is a merciful teacher. Some people are
slow to learn. Many honestly believe that there is no
way to prevent sickness. Those who continue to
violate health laws after they have become acquainted
with them, ought to be ashamed to be caught suffering from indigestion.

Is not such disease a disgrace? Animals in a natural state always obey God's laws for them, hence are not sick.

"I don't mean to, but I forget," is the excuse of the busy man, or of the greedy boy. Make a rule to

Never Drink with Food in the Mouth.

This will prevent the difficulty. If thirsty, clear the mouth of food before drinking. The dry food will refuse to be swallowed until thoroughly saturated with saliva. What is better, take no liquids during meals.

Food Converted into Chyme.

Food in being swallowed passes down the esophagus which lies in the back part of the throat, and enters the stomach. The vermiform (worm-like) motion imparted to this organ by the alternate contraction and expansion of its three layers of muscular membrane, gently moves the contents to and fro, mixing it thoroughly with the pepsin and hydrochloric acid. This *gastric digestion* reduces the food to a greyish, pulpy mass called *chyme*. In this process pepsin can have no action upon the saccharine group of foods, as sugars and starches, nor upon the oleaginous group, as oils, fats and cream.

The *nitrogenous* group is affected by the action of the strong acid secretion. Lean meat, white of eggs, curd of milk, gluten of grains, and some parts of fruits and vegetables, belong to this class. The most frequent abuse of the stomach is by failing to furnish a suitable proportion of nitrogenous foods.

Chyme Changed into Chyle.

For every one pound of solids in the human body

there are seven pounds of water. Thus a man weighing one hundred and sixty pounds has only twenty pounds of solid matter in him. The remaining one hundred and forty pounds are water.

It is necessary that in some way oleaginous food may be able to unite with this water, not merely to float in it but to be so combined as to form a part of it as it goes along. Bile and the pancreatic secretion subserve this purpose. The duct of the gall bladder and of the pancreas both empty by a common opening into the duodenum (Fig. XXI.).

Country boys who have watched grandma make soap, will readily comprehend how oil can be made to mix with water.

She fills the leach or barrel full of ashes and pours in water. The leach is raised from the ground to allow a bucket to be placed underneath one edge, where an opening is made to let out the—not exactly secretion, for no change has been made in the ashes— but to allow their juice to run into the bucket. It is a dark liquid called lye.

Lye is a powerful alkaline poison; eats the skin from the hands, burns holes in clothing, and if swallowed burns the mucous membrane from mouth, tongue and stomach.

Grandma next fills a large iron kettle with scraps of grease, lard, pork rinds, old bones and any fatty material she has at hand; hangs it over a fire and pours in the lye. The lye attacks the grease, eats it off the bones and rinds, and as it boils combines with it, making soap, which is a harmless and useful article.

The grease will now mix with water; the lye will not burn the hands. The antidote for alkali poisons is fat, cream or vinegar applied externally or internally, as the case may be. In either case the action of the alkali is diverted from the oil of the body and unites with the antidote.

The liver is a leach, the gall bladder is a vessel set to catch the alkali bile, which runs from it. The duodenum is the iron kettle; the chyme contains oleaginous matters; the fire is the natural heat of the body; the result is a thin, soft soap which mixes with water, or, scientifically speaking, saponification takes place.

The work also of changing starch into sugar which was suspended in the stomach, is here continued by the pancreatic secretion. Chyme passes from the duodenum into the small intestines, and is there brought under the action of the intestinal juice. This is produced in an immense number of microscopic glands just within the lining membrane. Here now, we find the result of the action of the salivary, gastric, gall, pancreatic, duodenal and intestinal secretions upon potatoes, bread, fruit and other foods which have been taken into the stomach. It is now made over into a soapy mixture, but is not yet complete.

The threefold coats of the intestines, like those of the stomach, also contract and expand upon their contents, moving them forward throughout their length of twenty-five feet. It is now losing its grey color and pulpy consistence, becoming thin like gruel, with a white, rich, creamy, milk-like appearance, and is called no longer *chyme* but *chyle*. This process is called intestinal digestion.

8

CHAPTER, XIV.

ABSORBENTS AND BLOOD MAKING.

The engraving below represents a part of the intestines turned inside out. It is seen to be thickly studded with points. Under the microscope these

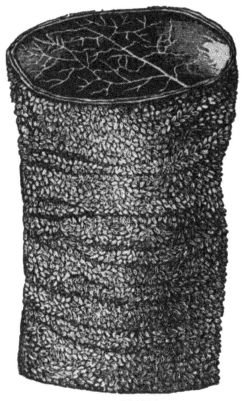

Fig. XXV.

points resemble minute hairs like the tuft side of velvet, and they give to the mucous lining a soft, velvety appearance. They are called *villi* (shaggy hair), and are absorbents.

These are directly the opposite of glands. As

their name indicates, they absorb, take in substance, while glands throw out, discharge substance. Each villus contains the beginning of one or more absorbent

Fig. XXVI. Villus containing three lacteals.

vessel, called a *lacteal.* They are here seen embedded in cells.

A network surrounds each villus. The dark lines in the cut are the artery ends, and the light ones the vein ends of the capillaries. Outside the whole is the mucous membrane of the intestinal canal. It is the office of the villi to take up as much chyle as is in fit condition for absorption, upon its entrance into the duodenum.

The capillaries also have the capacity of absorbing portions of the chyle; the thinner and more watery ingredients go into them while the oily, creamy portion goes to the lacteals. In this way the canal is gradually emptied; especially the fluid portion is drawn away. The remainder

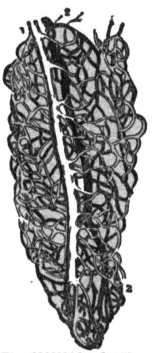

Fig. XXVII. Capillary tubing, showing 1, 1, veins ends; 2, 2, artery ends.

thus becomes thicker and passes on to the colon, or large intestine (Fig. XXI.).

Here other glands pour in secretions, and other lacteals carry on the work of absorption, leaving the waste matter to pass on to the *rectum* whence it is expelled by the *anus* (Fig. XXI.).

Mesenteric Glands. ·

Lacteals soon after leaving the intestines are joined to glands about the size of peas, called *mesenteric* glands, into which they discharge their contents.

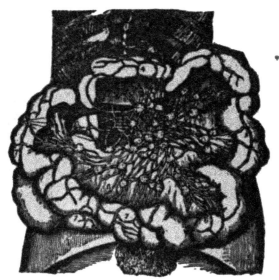

Fig. XXVIII. Mesenteric Glands.

All absorbents, including lacteals, have three coats which form their walls. The inner one contains folds falling loosely at intervals to form a sort of *valve* which prevents the contents from flowing backward. Chyle is worked over again in the mesenteric glands.

For the first time in its course, cells appear.

Glands have now, by the vito-chemical action of their secretions upon food and drink, produced other cells or corpuscles. In this chyle are multitudes of granule dots ; others arrived at the size and condition of nuclei ; and a few fully formed cells are distinctly visible ; all floating along together in the limpid current.

Coagulation takes place more readily now than when the contents were in the alimentary canal. When this liquid is allowed to stand a

Fig. XXIX. Chyle Corpuscles.

short time it will coagulate, and then the clot seen through a microscope shows cells entangled in numerous thread - like filaments. It is called *fibrine*. The clot is surrounded with a thin, watery fluid called *serum*. Fibrine is not seen in running chyle. Like jelly or glue, while warm it is liquid, but thickens upon cooling.

The color of chyle has also turned from a milky white to a pale, reddish, yellow hue.

Perfected chyle moves on to the *thoracic duct*, a tube about the size of a goose quill, passing in front of the spine to the neck, where it curves just in front of the

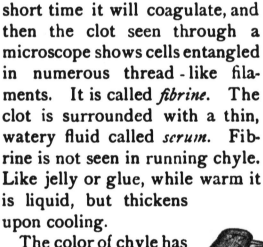
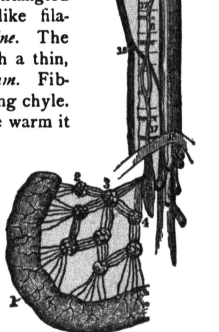

Fig. XXX.

shoulder blade and enters a large vein, the sub-clavian, and goes to the heart; 17, 6, 7, show the Thoracic Duct, in Figure XXX.

Venous Blood.

Venous capillaries in the alimentary canal also act the part of absorbents and draw into themselves that portion of the chyle which does not enter the lacteals.

These minute veins unite and reunite until they all join in one large tube called the portal vein, meaning venous gateway or door.

This vein enters the liver, where it again divides and redivides into capillaries.

The rich, creamy part of the chyle finds its way to the mesenteric glands; the thin, watery part comes to the liver gland.

Figure XX, p. 91, shows these veins and how they dip down into the lobules. The stomach is bounti-fully supplied with veins which likewise speedily take up liquids, as soups, gruels, alcohol and milk, with-out their being subjected to the process of digestion. These veins grow larger by union, and empty into the portal vein. The stomach, spleen and intestinal veins all converge and empty their contents through this very important tube, which distributes it throughout the liver. It leaves this gland by the hepatic veins, as seen in the center of each lobule in Figure XX.

While in the liver it becomes blood—it here gains liver sugar, additional fat, and a larger number of cells. There is also a greater perfection of fibrine, and consequently it clots more readily. There is less water, and of course more consistence.

Venous blood is of a dark purple color, as it occu

pies the veins. It constitutes three-fourths of all the blood in the system and is on its way to the heart, which it reaches by the vena cava.

That which comes from the veins of the head and arms reaches the heart through the *vena cava de-*

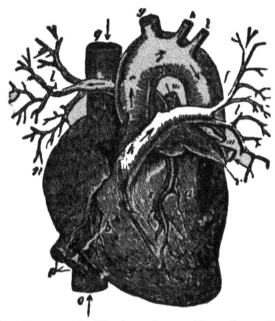

Fig. XXXI. Heart and Bloodvessels. o. Vena Cava Ascendens. k. Pulmonary Artery. l. l. Its right and left branches. q. Vena Cava Descendens. p. Portal Veins.

scendens (Fig. XXXI); that which comes from the lower extremities and the hepatic vein, arrives through the *vena cava ascendens* (same Figure).

CHAPTER XV.

ARTERIAL BLOOD.

The chyle from the mesentery, and all the venous blood brought to the heart by the *thoracic duct*, the *hepatic vein*, the *vena cava ascendens*, and *descendens*

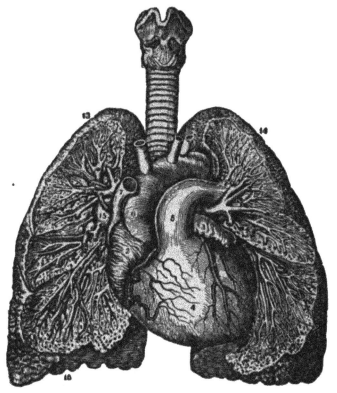

Fig. XXXII. Tubing view of lungs. 5, pulmonary artery; 7, ascending cava; 6, aorta; 4, heart; 14, left lung: 13, right lung.

enters its right side and passes out by the *pulmonary artery*. This divides and sub-divides like the branches of a tree, as seen in Fig. XXXII., and spreads over both sides of the lungs. Its minutest branches end in a delicate network of capillaries. These arteries are all filled with dark-colored venous blood sent here for the purpose of being still further perfected.

We find also in the lungs innumerable air cells or vesicles. All the cells hitherto studied are filled with

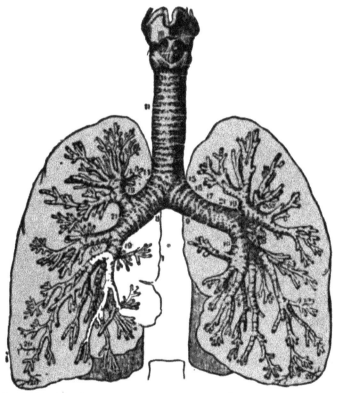

Fig. XXXIII. Cell view of the lungs. 11, trachea or windpipe; 8, 9, bronchial tubes; 19, 19, 19, sub-divisions of latter; 20, 20, cells.

liquid; these contain air or gas. The air is drawn in at the mouth and nostrils, and passes down the throat into the lungs by a tube named *trachea* or windpipe (Fig. XXXIII). The trachea divides at its lower termination into two branches, one for each lung:

they are called bronchial tubes.   These in their turn
divide and sub-divide until they become so small they
cannot be seen with the naked eye.

At their minutest ends are placed the six hundred
million-air vesicles.   These lie among the pulmonary
capillaries as in a plexus.   Air rushes down the
trachea and filling the bronchial tubes even to their
minutest branches, meets the venous blood through
the cell membranes.

Fig. XXXIV.   Bronchial tubes and air cells in lungs.

We here see these little air cells, through which
this wonderful process of osmosis takes place.   The
first cut gives them entire.   The second shows them
laid open.

Venous blood is impregnated with a poisonous gas
called *carbonic acid gas*.   This is upon one side of the
membrane, and oxygen is upon the other side.· They
exchange places by osmosis.   The former passes up
the bronchial tubes and windpipe and goes out of the
mouth and nose with the *outgoing* breath, called *expiration*.   It was the presence of the carbonic acid gas
which gave the purple hue to the blood; oxygen
now exchanges that color for a bright scarlet red.   A
multitude of ·cells mostly of a red hue, though a few
are white, fairly bound and dance with life, and all

float in a transparent, colorless liquid, called *plasma*.

With the unassisted eye, blood looks wholly red and we cannot see anything white in it, for the cells are very small and crowded together. It requires 3,500 of them to fill an inch of space.

Fig. XXXV. Arterial blood cells.

Blood cells are entirely mem-braneless, and have no nuclei. Crude material has here reached a very complete state. The blood coagulates promptly upon exposure, showing an improved condition of fibrine. It is consequently better adapted to human needs.

Respiration (in-breathing and out-breathing) has added a step in the series of changes organizing food into its highest capacity.

After venous blood has become saturated with oxygen, it receives a new name—*arterial blood*—and occupies another part of the tubing—the arteries—as soon as it leaves the lungs.

If we would have our blood of excellent quality we must select good food ; a constant supply of fresh air is equally essential, else muscles, nerves and glands cannot thrive; without it the forces of the system cannot do good work. Force came with the breath, and force must continue by breath, and work by breath, and fresh, pure, unpoisoned breath at that.

It will not do to shut ones self in a close room night or day, for that is to re-inhale carbonic acid gas over and over again, and this in excess poisons the arterial blood. Impure air cannot give to the blood the scarlet hue of health, but leaves it with the dark, purple color indicative of carbonic acid gas.

Circulation.

A strong partition membrane divides the heart into halves; the right half contains purple, unfinished blood on its way from the body to the lungs; the left half contains scarlet completed blood on its way from the lungs to the body.

It leaves the heart through the *aorta* at 6, Figure XXXII.; this is an artery, and measures an inch in diameter at its starting point. It becomes smaller as it proceeds and divides into branches until it terminates in the capillaries.

These lie so closely all along under the skin, side by side with nerves and absorbents, that a puncture with the finest needle will draw blood. They are also distributed, as we already know, through every gland and organ, supplying each cell with fresh, new blood from the heart.

Pause here and consider some wonderful things that force does! In the heart it operates so powerfully that if we place our hand over that organ we can plainly feel its action or, as we call it, the "beating" of the heart. The impulse of it—abbreviated "pulse"—is so strong that it is easily felt at the wrist, temples, neck, and several other places where the arterial branches pass near the surface.

The heart is largely composed of muscle, fibers and fibrous rings, similar to the middle membrane of the stomach and intestines, and it is in this that force resides. Also the walls of the arteries have a layer of the same kind of tissue, which slightly contracts as the blood comes rushing along, and this is one cause of the pulse being felt at a distance from the heart, even so far away as the feet.

Besides being divided lengthwise into halves each half of the heart is again partitioned by valves.

The impure venous blood enters the upper chamber of the right half of the heart by the two vena cava. When the walls contract the blood is forced through the valves, and as it enters the lower chamber they close behind it to prevent its return. Next the lower chamber contracts and a still greater force is required here, for the blood is now driven out of the heart through the pulmonary artery into the lungs.

At the same time this is taking place the upper portion expands so that it may be filled again from the cava. This alternate contraction and expansion is the pulsation or beating of the heart.

Meanwhile, on the left side of the partition the purified arterial blood is received *from* the lungs into the upper chamber. This again contracts, as described before, and the blood passes down through the valves which close behind it. Thence it is discharged by a forcible contraction into the aorta. A part of it goes on upward to the arms and brain, and the remainder passes down to the feet.

One-eighth of the body is blood. This all passes through the heart in two minutes.

CHAPTER XVI.

MATERIAL AND MECHANISM.

When men build houses, bridges, fences, wagons and machinery, or when boys make playhouses and kites, their first care is to furnish the *material*. Their next step is to find the tools to do the work with, as knives, hammers, saws, anvils, and engines. Equipped with these they proceed to construct the object they desire.

So, for the construction and repair of our bodies an abundance of *material* has been furnished in the inorganic substances. Wonderful tools are also provided with which to organize crude matter into the most suitable and perfect building material, and to erect these temples of God. Branches, leaves, and roots of plants do the primary work; grains, fruits, vegetables and other eatables are the materials thus prepared by them out of dust, air and water. The human organs, as the glands, teeth, alimentary canal, complete the work by doing the actual building.

The teeth are the axes that fell the trees and chop off the limbs; the stomach and intestines, with their vermiform motions, perform the work of the sawmills which split trees into *rough boards;* the secretions are the carpenter's planes which smooth them into *dressed lumber;* the lungs are the drying rooms where this green stuff becomes *seasoned lumber*. Thence it is *rafted* on the river of life, that stream called Blood, and portioned out to the shops—the cells—where the carpenters, Messrs. Creative Force, work, organizing it into still higher forms—the various departments and furnishings of the "house we live in," the body.

In order that man should be strong, a strong kind of dust should enter into his composition; and what is stronger than iron and manganese?

These human tools that manufacture fine lumber are indeed marvelous, for, when occasion requires they may be turned into smelters, crushing, smelting, and refining the raw mineral dust or ore, into a choice fluid iron, as found in the arterial circulation. In the lungs it becomes highly magnetized with the breath of life. Thence it is *shipped* on the river Blood to the foundries — other cells — where it is *cast* and *wrought* by Creative Force into required forms for use.

The framework of our bodies must, like the foundations of an enduring monument, be firm, compact, imperishable. In the ground are calcium (lime) and silicon (a flint sand). The same tools that anon were sawmill and smelter are now in turn stone quarry and mortar yard, and their products are *boated* on the same stream, Blood, to the glue factories (other cells, producing *gelatine*) where the finest kind of foundation material is produced.

For a good conductor from the great electric batteries of the brain, phosphorus is supplied, which of itself has neither strength nor endurance, but united with oxygen from the lungs it gives lightness, activity and *vim* to the whole man. The alimentary canal is a chemical laboratory on occasion; and the highway of traffic, Blood, *transports* all these materials to the nerve cells, where it is stored subject to the use of Creative Force.

The body must have heat. What makes a hotter fire than oil? Nothing. Starchy foods are converted into oleaginous matter, and in the cells this is stored for use. When fresh air from the lungs comes sweeping down the valley along with the waves of the Blood, combustion takes place in the innumerable furnaces (capillaries).

And now, having examined the elaboration and destination of *material*, let us go down to the dock— Heart—and take passage ourselves on a palace steamer "Pulse," that Captain Force propels on these proud waters of life and sail to the end of the world, the little microcosm. Let us step ashore and go a touring among these shops, foundries, glue factories and storerooms, and see for ourselves how the mechanics—Creative Force—work up the material brought to them with so much care and expense.

Bone.

Let us first visit the glue factories and stone works where bone, the foundation of the body, is made. These are cells built along the banks of minute branches of the stream of Blood. They do not lie in masses like gland cells, but are separated from each other by a plastic fluid called *blastema*, and are in various stages of growth, young, half grown, and mature.

The materials used by the workmen are lime (calcium) and sand (silicon), which mixed together, will, with the help of glue, form a hard plaster or cement. Glue or *gelatine* is made in the newly divided cells as it is wanted. The workmen heat, melt, stir and thicken their material, moving their kettles forward as they work, adding lime and sand as they go. How do they empty their kettles, for we do not see any ducts to convey away the product? When it has been cooked sufficiently it transudes by osmosis to the outside and covers them all over, taking the place of the blastema. It now cools and gradually stiffens until it becomes the finest white stone, with a polish almost like marble. Of course the cells cannot move any further; they have come to a standstill among their own blocks and chips. They have taken care, however, not to cut off all communication with

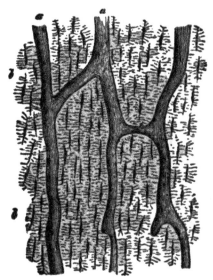

Fig. XXXVI. Vertical section through the human femur, (a) medul- lary canals into which the plexus opens, (b) bone corpuscles and their plexus. The intervening portions are the formed bone.

the river, having left little sluiceways or canaliculi (little canals) for the passage of air and blood, thus forming a network through the solid material.

Thousands of these cells lie side by side, forming a

9

thin stratum or layer, which now receives the name *bone*. On the top of this stratum will soon be formed a second, and then a third, and so on until the bone is of the required size.

The connecting canals are the canaliculi. The first layer cells die and are pushed into the plexus by other forces, and the bone they formed softens, liquefies and is absorbed likewise by the plexus, and carried out of the bone into the general circulation.

If we cut off the end of a long bone we will find it solid toward the outer part where the newest bone is, and spongy near the center where the oldest bone is gradually liquefying.

The formative blastema lies on the outside of the bone and over that is a tough, whitish skin or membrane called *periosteum*, supplied throughout with multitudes of bloodvessels.

The periosteum may be compared to the bark of a tree; the plastic blastema beneath, to the sap, which is most plentiful in the spring, running freely between the bark and wood, making it easy to strip off the latter. Boys choose this time of the year to make willow whistles. The new sap which forms the next layer of wood, in the autumn, is nearly dry, and the bark adheres so firmly that it must be whittled or chopped away. So in youth—human springtime—the periosteum and its sappy blastema is thick and abundant, making it very easily detached from the bone; but in the adult it is less thick and more closely connected with the bone, while in age—life's winter—it is thin, with few vessels, and no blastema. Bones, unlike trees, throw off their inner layers; hence do not increase in size after reaching maturity.

The Framework

is made in many pieces, of all shapes and sizes. Some are united with joints like hinges; others are made after the "ball and socket" pattern, which allows them to move in several directions; still others are fitted together like cogs. The movable joints are supplied with a fluid called *synovia*, which lessens friction. Most of the bones of an infant are soft like gristle, being all in the gelatine or glue stage. They are called *cartilage* and contain almost no silicon and calcium. For this reason a baby cannot walk. He has as yet no teeth, but in their sockets are small, soft patterns of teeth.

Creative force begins its work, lengthening and widening cells already in the blastema, building new glue factories by division, and filling up with lime and sand obtained from the mother's milk. The baby grows stronger; he is soon able to hold up his head, to bear his weight on his feet, to lift playthings with his hands. "How fast the baby grows," we exclaim; he creeps, he walks, he runs, as his bones increase in size and exchange the cartilage (removed from the centers) for *real* bone newly made on the outside.

Ossification.

Bones are said to *ossify* when cartilage gives place to bone. It requires about twelve or fourteen years for this change to take place, sometimes longer; the slower the better; for, with boys as with apples, slow development is most enduring. Bones are not completely ossified until a man is from twenty to twenty-five years of age.

Perfected bone has remarkable strength. Used as

a lever it is twenty-two times as strong as sandstone, and twice as strong as box or oak.

Bone is the last part of the body "to return to dust," and skeletons almost never decay, remaining

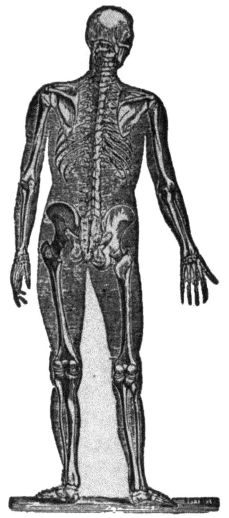

Fig. XXXVII. The Framework.

intact for many, many years. If burned, only the cartilage will be destroyed. The mineral part remains, and may be crushed to fine dust. The lime in bone can, however, be eaten out by certain acids. The enamel of teeth is the hardest substance in the body; in every hundred parts of them ninety-six are lime leaving only four parts of other matter.

Although so strong and enduring, bones are subject to disease, and are liable to be stunted in growth during boyhood.

Impure air is a source of bone disease. Oxygen must come freely to the bones down the valley of the stream of the blood, or they will soon deteriorate. Tobacco smoke and carbonic acid gas will not allow bones to flourish and develop.

Improper Diet

is a fruitful source of bone disease. Diet that is good for the stomach and the liver, is also good for bone building. White flour leads the van of the enemy— *bad diet.* Whole wheat is captain of the friendly army. White flour is chiefly starch. This is organized into sugar in the digestive organs, and sugar never makes bone.

The old Roman soldiers in the early days of their republic lived and fought on whole wheat. They won their most renowned victories without flesh, tobacco or alcohol. When they became more civilized (?) and had acquired a love for wine, flesh and rich cooking, this strength of bone and courage of heart diminished. They gave up grain and were in turn conquered by a hardy wheat eating nation.

Enduring national greatness must have for its foundation *strong men with strong bones and teeth.*

To grow into able bodied men, let boys use for bread that which is made from whole grains; oats, rye, wheat, etc., unspoiled by the miller's art.

CHAPTER XVII.

MUSCLE.

Let us next step into the shops and foundries, where the walls and coverings of the framework are turned out. These are cells called *fibrils* and are built in rows. Each row is inclosed in a delicate, transparent membrane, supplied with capillaries, and named *fiber*. It takes ten thousand fibrils to make an inch of fiber. Many rows of these, with their plexus, are bound together by another membrane in bundles and named *muscle*.

Muscles then are composed of cells, membranes and tubing.. With the naked eye the fibers look like strings, and the cells are not distinguishable at all.

Fig. XXXVIII. Muscle under the microscope. 1. Bundle of fibers inclosed in membrane. 2. A row of fibrils. 3. Bundle with membrane removed to show fibrils. 4, 5. Muscular fiber showing nuclei.

Under the glass the plexus appears like the finest and most exquisite lacework. Their membranes that seem as smooth and clear as glass now look coarse, tough, and full of specks.

The furnaces are in full blast here. All through

the shops it is as hot as August—winter or summer alike. The thermometer stands at 98° in the shade. When the ventilator (lungs) is open to the fresh air, a healthful breeze always blows down the valley of the stream of blood. Those who wear corsets reduce the capacity of the air box about one-half; one who keeps a wreath of tobacco smoke about the mouth of the ventilator impedes the entrance of. fresh air; one who pours whisky into the reservoir of the stomach fills the lungs with fumes of alcohol instead of air; one who even sits in a crowded church, lecture room, or his own air tight parlor, constantly takes in carbonic acid gas. Should we visit the cells of such an one we would be half melted with heat and suffocated by poisoned air.

"You have good ventilation in *these* shops," we suggest to a mechanic, Creative Force, whom we are watching as he works.

"Very good just at present, but 'tis not always the case."

"How is that?" we inquire.

"At some seasons of the year, especially in the winter, we suffer for the want of oxygen. There is scarcely a set of workmen in the world, I suppose, but now and then make the same complaint. Some. times we are treated scandalously."

"In this enlightened age! Is it possible?" we ask incredulously.

"You may not believe it, but every mechanic present will confirm it."

"Yes indeed," chimes in a medley of voices. "It has not been long since the last strike for better air."

"I noticed a bad smell the other day, and wouldn't

wonder if another breakdown were at hand," grumbles one louder than the rest.

"About the most serious time we've had," volunteers another, "was a few years since. The architect of this temple had spent a good many weeks reading law in an office where the air was fairly blue with other men's tobacco smoke—smoked sometimes himself. Weather was cold and no ventilation. We put up with it the best we could for a long time; sent him a good many sharp telegrams on these wires," pointing to the nerves, " calling for better supplies, but he didn't seem to understand what we meant. He only groaned, 'I've got a headache,' or 'It's a touch of rheumatism,' or 'Threatened with malaria,' according as we tried different plans of making him know there was danger that his fine temple would be destroyed unless given better air.

"But he didn't take gentle hints, so, as we were really in a desperate fix, we tried a heroic plan. We just shut up the shops, vowing we would never work any more until we had a good breathing spell again. So we all went out and had a jolly grand sail on the river. Of course the architect noticed that his muscles were stiff, sore and lame ; he got frightened and sent for the doctor, who ordered liniment, poured bitters and pills into the reservoir, and with a lancet partially drained the river. But we didn't care for that, and while we were frolicking around, swearing we would resign and go home for good unless we were 'treated' to fresh air, we heard a great racket among the bones.

"We rowed over there as soon as we could to see what the matter was, and found that Bad Air was making trouble here too ; but the stone masons said if we would come in and help, perhaps we might drive him out. We chased him round and round, got him into corners, and pounded him. The bones rocked to their foundations, and shouted to the architeet for 'fresh air.' But he only thought a new dis·ease had set in—'bone rheumatiz,' and sent for the doctor again, who poured some wine into the canal, put some calomel into the leach and blistered the covering of the framework.

"There seemed to be no help for us—no hope that the head mason could ever be made to understand our simple call—so we decided that it was best to close up stone works for the season. Just then we heard some hard pumping and thumping in the region of the air box. The whole force of us went up there and found Bad Air trying to tear the entire department to pieces. We just pitched into him and made him cry out with pain. The architect heard him and asked what was the matter. 'Oh,' said the lungs, 'I believe I've got the consumption.' 'Give us some fresh air and we'll cure it,' said we. But the architect as usual did not understand us, and sent for the doctor. He put some croton oil on the outside of the box, poured some cod liver oil on the troubled waves within, stuffed the reservoir with pork and molasses, shut down the windows and put the whole institution to bed for many weeks.

"We began to think we should all have to die and go home together, when fortunately it turned the spring of the year. That was too much for the owner of the temple. He declared he would stay in that bed no longer, live or die, doctor or no doctor. He coaxed them to open the windows so he could see the budding trees. That was just what we wanted. He made them take him to the porch so he could smell the bursting pines. We started for the shops. He began to walk. We got as far as the shop doors. He worked some at gardening. We built the fires anew and very soon everything moved on as usual.

"Well, one day the doctor came round and presented his bill, which the architect cheerfully paid, and *thanked him* besides, for the repairs *he* had made. We just took that as a great insult to us. Our architect is a very good man, means well, and seems to be exceedingly wise when he gets with his own kind, but he acts the fool about his workmen. Why he doesn't know the difference between bad air and good air. The only way we can get his attention is by putting him in pain, and it's mighty hard to make him learn even then what is wanted."

These talkative carpenters have secrets of their own, some tricks of the trade, that they keep to themselves, and after we have been all through their shops we shall not be able to imitate their work, even to making one single fibril of a fiber of a muscle. Yet we may learn many interesting points. As elsewhere, the muscle cells are in all stages of formation, and in turn are superseded by others. Their product is not a secretion, and like bone cells they need no duct. In color they are of a beautiful red. They possess contractile power. By this curious property they contract and expand in obedience to the will. This is as strange and wonderful as anything in nature— and for practical use is unexcelled by any properties of organized matter.

The vermiform motion of the stomach and intestines is caused by the contractile muscle fibers of the middle layer of their walls and the action of the heart is sustained by the same force.

Fig. XXXIX. Muscles of the front figure.

Muscles are of various forms and sizes, in thin layers, in rings, in strips, in thick piles, fan shaped, feather shaped, etc. They are bound firmly to the bones by white, hard, tough bands and cords, called *tendons.*

Strength is essential to muscles, for by them are controlled the powerful movements of the framework. They must also be soft and yield readily to pressure. For these reasons the furnishing of the proper nutriment is essential. Iron, potassium, chlorine, magnesium and sodium feed the muscles well. Phosphorus and sulphur give swiftness and life for the contractile property.

Muscles use up the larger portion of the food we eat. From the *cells* of blood they extract oxygen, magnetized iron and phosphorus; the *plasma* yields them albumen.

The *deltoid* muscle of the shoulder has power enough in it to raise 1,000 pounds. The reason the arm cannot lift so much is not for lack of inherent strength. It is hindered by its position with regard to other muscles, and by the way it is attached to the bones.

A great many diseases get seated in the muscles, for various reasons. Sometimes the blood contains no proper food substances, because we do not eat rightly. Sometimes it is lack of sunlight, or exercise, or rest, or oxygen. Like bones they may be stunted in childhood and youth, and never reach full development.

CHAPTER XVIII.

BRAIN.

The brain is also one of the workshops in which the human temple is builded. There is situated the great electric battery of the body. The brain of a child is more soft and delicate, and shows more beautifully its convolutions and folds than that of an adult.

Michelet, the noted French author, calls it a "hieroglyphic flower, the flower of flowers," and says, "The brain of a child seen from its base has all the effect of a large and splended camellia with its ivory nerves, its delicate rosy veins, and its pale azure tint. It is of an immaculate purity, and yet of an exquisite and tender softness, of which nothing else can give an idea, and to my mind leaves every other earthly thing far behind." In order the better to understand the working of these batteries which present so beautiful an exterior, let us compare them with an ordinary magnetic battery. In a glass case is placed weak sulphuric acid. A strip of copper and another of zinc are immersed in this, with wires attached.

Acids and alkalies (as in soda water), alkalies and oleaginous matters (as lye and grease) have chemical affinity. When placed in contact they meet with such intensity as to liberate the force that is holding together their atoms. In the battery cell the metal and acid unite in this way, eating or destroying each

(149)

other, and in uniting evolve a mighty force called electricity. Like other forces it can neither be seen, weighed, counted or pictured, but may be felt.

Chemists have devised a method of chaining it. This is done by wires. Electricity prefers to follow straight lines or zigzag edges, and to enter and leave by points. This peculiarity is a great convenience to man, for if it radiated in every direction as do light, heat and sound, it could neither be so usefully employed nor so easily controlled.

Lightning and thunder is a familiar manifestation of the electricity of nature, illustrating the law of preference for points and narrow lines, and how light and sound accompany it. In the process of evolving artificial electricity, light, sound, motion, smell, taste and heat are liberated. By the telephone, sound is transmitted. The brilliant, dazzling light of electricity illuminates our cities. Medical science fiuds in this agency a valuable therapeutic remedy. By telegraphic wires man makes electricity his servant to carry messages and do errands. By them thought passes instantaneously from mind to mind beneath the sea, and· thus is space annihilated, and continent clasps hands with continent.

We may now with Michelet visit the azure petals of the flower. Behold, the "delicate rosy veins" are capillary tubing filled with blood; and in the "exquisite and tender softness" we find cells of the batteries. Nearly a billion battery cells are there. The "ivory tracings" are the wires that catch the electricity.

If our sense of smell were keen enough we should exclaim, "Whew! whew! what a stench! How are

we ever to get through this department?" For there
are the fumes of burning sulphur, phosphorus, fats
and oils, out of which the professional chemists and
electricians, Messrs. Creative Force, are making
electricity. Yet these may have become so highly
organized in the body, that by the time they reach
the brain their crude perfume is changed into the
sweet fragrance appropriate to so beautiful a flower.

These brain cells, although constructed upon the
same essential plan (given before) of envelope, protoplasm and germs, are somewhat different in shape
from any we have seen. They have projections,
points or tails, by which they are joined to other cells,
and which may be compared to connecting tubes or
halls of communication between them.

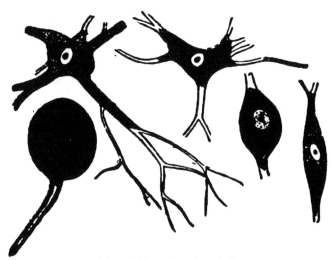

Fig. XL. Brain Cells.

This aggregation of cells. like a powerful many-
celled magnetic battery, is connected with every part
of the system by nerves. These are the ivory tracings whose beauty and delicacy are described by the
Frenchman, with a just enthusiasm.

The cells are of a gray color, and the nerves are white. To the eye brain substance looks like a soft gray jelly with white threads running through it. The gray matter lies in bunches or piles called *convolutions*, which give to the surface an undulating, wrinkled appearance. The white nerves issue from them, converging from every direction and meeting in the center of the brain.

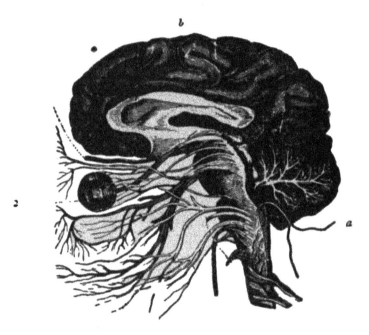

Fig. XLI. Vertical section of the brain. a, b, c, cerebrum; d, cerebellum; 2, the eyeball.

Over the whole are spread three membranes and a protecting wall of bones called the skull. Upon this is the integument covered with hair. The first membrane directly under the skull is white, tough, enduring, like the ligaments that bind muscles to bones. It is named *dura mater*. The next membrane is composed of thin, delicate fibers, and is compared to a

spider's web, hence called the *arachnoid membrane.*
The third one is a plexus, made up of capillaries, veins
and arteries, nerves and delicate fibers. It dips down
among the convolutions, carrying blood, loaded with
material for the manufacture of electricity. It is
named the *pia mater.*

The nerves are collected into bundles which are
distributed all over the body, resembling the branches
of a tree in their divisions. One branch goes to the
eye, another to the ear, another to the mouth. There
is a large bundle of them running down the center
of that part of the bony framework called the *spine.*
There are sixty-two openings in the spine giving exit
to thirty-one pairs of nerves, one on each side, to the
arms, limbs, stomach, liver, etc., supplying the nerve
tubing to every gland, muscle and bone plexus, inter-
mingling with capillaries, becoming there exceedingly
small and delicate.

Each white thread is a *tubule* (little tube) filled with
transparent fluid, and through it nerve force is communicated. The bundles of them are inclosed in a
membrane and the whole is called a nerve.

Distributed at intervals through the body are
minute clusters of cells and plexus called *ganglia.*
They too are little batteries and are united with one
another and with the spine and brain by nerves.

The brain with its system of nerves passing down
the spine and its branches therefrom, together with its
chain of ganglia, is called the

Cerebro-Spinal System of Nerves.

Cerebro means brain, and spinal, referring to the
backbone. The cells of the brain develop electric

force on the same principle as man makes artificial electricity.　Creative force draws into each cell atoms

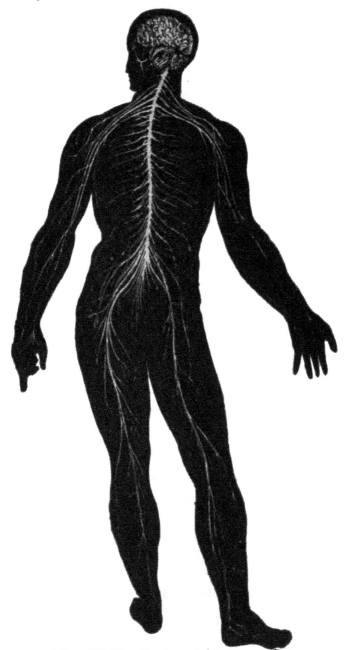

Fig. XLII. *Brain and Nervous System.*

having an opposite character—positive and negative—the acids and alkalies of the blood. Phosphorus
and oxygen couple together, or perhaps fats and sulphur. Uniting they form a new article, *salts*, and
liberate electric force in the process. The salts are
disposed of by absorption, and the electricity is gathered in the nerves, and as illustrated in Figs. XLI.
and XLII., distributed throughout the system.

Human electricity is called *nerve force.* It is much
finer, more highly organized than that made by man.
It is subject to the same laws of attraction and repul-
sion, and gives off light, sound, heat, in the same way,
e. g. sparks of light are often emitted with a crack-
ling sound, when woolen garments, worn for some
hours next to the skin, are removed in a dark, cold
room; and also by the hair when combed in clear,
crisp weather.

We find the same succession of young, old and destroyed cells in the brain as in all other organs. A
German histologist has computed that 3,500 cells are
destroyed every minute, and immediately replaced
with as many new ones, and that once in sixty days a
man has a totally new brain.

The Sympathetic System of Nerves.

This is another set of batteries, distinct from, yet
united to, and having free communication with the
cerebro-spinal system. Its nerve ducts are pinkish
threads instead of white. It contains innumerable
ganglia, the size of small peas. It is distributed mainly
to the glands and to the organs in the cavity of the
body, whose action is largely involuntary, as the
lungs, stomach, heart and intestines.

Pure blood in the arteries, made from good food and good air, insures health in them. But nerves are subjcet to disease when these two essentials to health are withdrawn. Then the nerves ache with pain and suffer with sickness.

The Use of Nerves

is to convey force, they bring outside forces, as light, heat, sound, the breath of life, etc., to the inside of the body. They transmit thought into actions. They make manifest hunger, thirst, desires, wishes and intentions.

If all the nerves could be severed from the spine without cutting an artery, or wounding a muscle or gland, or disturbing the bones, death would result as surely as it would if the bloodvessels were divided, or a vital organ removed, because the body cannot live without force, and the nerves are its channel.

If the nerves which supply a single limb, or organ, are severed, paralyzed or diseased, the muscles of that part may shrink away and die; the bones will no longer continue the process of replacing old cells with new, and the entire organ will become a lifeless, useless appendage. A familiar example of temporary paralysis is when the hand, arm or foot becomes numb, "gets asleep," from being in a cramped position. The stinging, tingling sensation felt when pressure ceases is in the nerve.

Warning of Danger

is given by nerves. Were it not for them we should soon destroy ourselves. We might be consumed in the fire, or frozen in the snowdrifts. But consciousness informs us that we are in pain and warns us of greater danger.

A loving, Heavenly Father has made pain a means of protection, a safeguard. This is his way of reminding us when we disobey any of the physical laws He made to keep us well and happy. So when we are in pain, we should remember that it is because we are astray from His presence, pause to reflect what laws we have broken, and hasten to return to the straight and narrow way of health.

The Divine Purpose.

We have learned that the glands, teeth, stomach, heart, lungs, etc., are instruments of organization, changing inorganic substances into a highly refined material—blood.

We have learned that in the process of blood making, substance became incorporated with force. This is organization—the union of life with matter, of *spirit* with *clay*.

We have learned that the life stream is still further organized into bone, muscle and brain. Blood deposits with bone its appropriate substance, other elements are assimilated by the nervous system, while muscle in its turn takes up and uses what is best adapted to aid its structure.

Why were bones, muscles and nervous system made? We cannot believe that all this trouble and care is for nothing ; that this infinite elaboration accomplished in myriads of mysterious cells teeming with life is made without special object. We ask again, of what use are the bones, muscles and brain ? What good is to be gained by head, hands and feet ?

Bones, muscles and nerves are turned out by the workmen for the exclusive use and benefit of the mind; the Ego, the real man, who is master workman, head mason, overseer and electrician-in-chief. It is his place to furnish generously the material for the workmen. When he does so, everything moves off prosperously and happily. But oftentimes he gets cross, bad-tempered, bitter, worried or discontented. Then he sends irritating telegrams by the nerves, quarrels with the workmen, breaks up their partly finished work, damages their tools and hinders operations.

Sometimes he allows himself to remain in ignorance of the needs of the workmen, as we have read in former pages, and does not supply the right kind of material. In consequence of all this the system becomes deranged, and what we call disease ensues.

Very often when a man suffers the results of his own badness or ignorance, he is so unreasonable as to blame it to the Creator, or call it a "mysterious and inscrutable Providence."

The mind governs the body. Yet there is a limit to the supremacy of thought over the involuntary functions of the body. The Creator has not empowered us to make the lungs stop breathing, the heart cease beating, nor to suspend digestion.

The glands and the involuntary organs are only partially under control of the mind, but the limbs are at its command, and move only at its bidding.

The Cerebro Spinal System

of nerves is the special instrument of the mind. It is called the voluntary system. There is a force in the

body called *life force*, whose authority is superior to
that of conscious mind. It links us to the Great
Source of life, and upholds us in existence. It maintains its authority in the

Sympathetic System

of nerves, or the involuntary system. Life force is
vital; is often called *vital* force. It binds body and
thought together. Conscious thought may be suspended in disease, as in insanity, and still the organic
processes move on by this life force acting through
the sympathetic system.

Human beings were placed in this world to honor
the Creator by using bones, muscles, and brain to
carry out good thoughts.

A ragged, dirty, rude, swearing boy gives evidence
of bad parentage. A neat, well trained, thoughtful
youth reveals unconsciously his origin and breeding.
Our Creator desires us to show forth all that is divine,
upright, and pure, and thus reflect the perfect character of our Parent.

Although thought force is for this life outranked
by vital force, it is not so forever. There comes a
time when blood, bone and muscle, glands, nerves,
brain and organs have accomplished their allotted
work. Then vital force surrenders authority over
this earth-born part. They return again to the dust
whence they came, and the spirit to God who gave it.

CHAPTER XIX.

TRANSMISSION OF THOUGHT.

Thought originates in the mind, filling the brain with its power and presence. It acts upon the brain cells, developing electric nerve force. This hastens with the swiftness of lightning, to the end of the nerve, carrying, as it were, the thought with it to gland, muscle, or bone, according to its purpose. Here it meets with other cells, of gland, muscle or bone, as the case may be, which it strikes with power, breaking them as the organ moves in obedience to the thought.

For example, a boy sees a young rabbit hopping in the grass before him. The sight rouses this thought in his mind, "I will catch the rabbit." It presses on the brain cells as the telegraph operator uses the keys of his machine, and more swiftly than the telegraph, the message rushes down the spinal column and through the openings in it leading to the legs and feet. "I want to catch the rabbit; run, bones, run; run, muscles, run," is the order that comes to the muscles. The fibrillæ are in a relaxed condition when the order reaches them. Being elastic they draw themselves together, which makes them shorter in length and broader and fuller in width.

This arrangement is for the purpose of drawing up the tendons which fasten muscles to bones. The bones can do no other way than follow. They change position. Muscles and tendons are to them what sails and yards are to a ship, while nerves are the ropes, and the power that moves the ropes moves all the other parts.

In running, the spine bends forward on the hip joint, the knee is drawn up, the ankle bent backward and the foot thrown forward. Nerve force then slackens its tension and the muscle cells relax for a moment, while the same operation is repeated in the other leg.

"Run faster," comes an order from the brain and "faster, faster," is the thought that strikes the brain cells, faster comes their discharged nerve force down the tubing, tighter becomes the tension of the muscle cells, quicker takes place the change of position of bones upon their sockets and hinges, faster goes the boy after the rabbit.

The motion and pressure of parts upon each other, and the thorough jarring and shaking which every portion of the boy's body undergoes as he runs, causes, it will be readily comprehended, hundreds of muscle and bone cells to be worn out by the time he reaches the animal.

"There he is close to you. Put out your hands," says thought. "Now catch him," and bones and muscles obey the will.

"Examine him and be sure it is really a rabbit," thinks the mind. "It looks like one," reports the eye to the brain, as the color, form, and other peculiarities are noted. "It feels like one, warm, hairy, soft," testifies the nerves in the finger tips. "It sounds like one," would decide the ear if the poor little frightened thing should dare to make a noise.

"It is truly a rabbit," confirms the mind, and sends a telegram to hands and feet to "take it home."

Arrived at home, the boy's thought moves his feet about the house, gives strength to his arms while they carry his prize to show to his mother and sisters; makes his lips, tongue and vocal organs rehearse the story of its capture, plans a little house for his pet, and uses hands and feet in its construction.

So it is from morning till night. Impressions are made through the medium of sunlight and atmosphere, upon one, or all of the senses. These are transmitted by their nerves to the brain. The impressions act upon the mind, arousing thought in their turn. Thought takes various forms, expressive of wishes, desires, necessities or will, and all day long the limbs and organs are used by it in many ways.

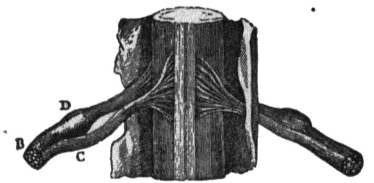

Fig. XLIII. Spinal cord, with nerves issuing from it. c. Motor nerves. d. Sensory nerves.

Nerves are used in two ways; one, in carrying sensation from without, inward, the other transmitting impulses from within outward. They are adapted to these two purposes. Each nerve bundle is made up of two kinds of nerves, placed side by side in the same sheath. Those occupying the back part of the tube, transmit sensations to the brain and are called nerves of sensation, or *sensory* nerves. Pressure on the finger tips, light falling on the eye, and sound entering the ear, use this half of the nerve to convey impressions to the brain.

The others occupying the front of the tube are used by the brain in sending orders to the body, and are called nerves of motion, or motor nerves.

If the motor half of the nerve is severed or diseased, the limb cannot obey orders to move, although the sensory nerve still carries sensations as before. If the latter is destroyed it cannot convey sensations, but its power to move remains unimpaired.

CHAPTER XX.

LYMPHATICS.

Use or exercise wears out everything. Boys understand this when holes come in the toes of their boots, and the elbows of their jackets. Constant treading over the carpet loosens its threads and wears off its outermost fibers, and the broom sweeps them away. At last the carpet is destroyed. Wagons, axes, spades, and all other tools have some of their particles jolted and pushed out of place every time they are used, and gradually dislodged and destroyed until they fall to pieces. Worn out material must be replaced with new. A large part of business consists in manufacturing new things and distributing them to take the place of worn out articles. It is the same way with the body. The stomach, intestines, glands, and lungs, are kept busy preparing crude matter to take the place of worn out tissue; worn out in the service of the owner of the temple.

Hunger, thirst and weariness are the sensations which convey to the brain by the sensory nerves the message that a new supply of cell making substance is needed. The boy who has chased the rabbit a mile, carried it home and made a house for it, has lost so many cells that he is tired, and is hungry for his dinner. Thought sending his body after the rabbit, caused it to be tired and hungry. Next it orders rest and a new supply of food. Worn out bits of leather fall to the ground ; atoms of carpet are swept into the fire ; shreds of Jack's sleeve are made into paper. Some worn out things go into the compost heap and are used to fertilize plants. What becomes of bits of bone and muscle that have been dislodged by physical exercise ?

Special Absorbents.

Frequent allusion has been made to the absorbent tubing forming part of the plexus which surrounds cells. While cell membranes, veins and capillaries have the power of absorbing matter, there is a set of vessels exclusively devoted to this work. Among these are the lacteals, whose business it is to take up the most nutritious portion of the chyle. Others are found, similar in many respects. They are called *lymphatics*, and contain *lymph*. These are found everywhere except in the nails, hair, and a few other parts of the body. Into them are introduced microscopical bits of bone, muscle, cartilage, tendon and brain cells, in fact, waste atoms from every tissue.

Nature is a great economist. She never throws away anything simply because it has once done service, but is like a good housekeeper who saves rags for paper making, ashes for soap, broken bread for puddings, and throws away only that which is absolutely useless. The frugal housewife burns again her sifted cinders.

Dr. Carpenter says: "The *death* of the tissues by no means involves their immediate and complete destruction ; there seems to be no more reason why the body should not derive support from its own dead parts, than from the dead body of another animal."

The lymphatics take all that may be again assimilated. Atoms absolutely unfit for further support of tissue are swept into the capillaries. It is so when the body is in a normal condition. When there are poisons introduced, or when the capillaries and veins are overloaded with waste particles, the lymphatics are obliged to take a share and help dispose of the burden.

When a mother would wean her child, she is aided by the lymphatics. At first the supply of milk is as great as before, and whether she weans the child gradually or at once, the surplus left in the breasts must be absorbed by the lymphatics. The secretion grows less and less, and finally ceases.

Unused saliva causes no trouble, but is carried away by these absorbents, and again enters the circulation.

Were the flesby part of the arm or leg to be tightly bandaged for a long time, it would waste away by impeded circulation, the plump muscle and other tissue being removed by the absorbents.

Again, when in sickness, little or no food is taken, life is maintained by the lymphatic vessels imbibing the stored up fat and conveying it into the blood. It is this which causes emaciation in fevers, and consumption. In extreme cases the muscles and other solid parts are thus removed.

These vessels begin in a plexus so fine and delicate that when injected with mercury it presents the appearance of a sheet of silver.

They soon unite into a few large trunks and take a direction toward the heart where their contents are emptied into it along with chyle and venous blood.

The minute lymphatics unite into larger trunks and pass through small glands, as lacteals pass into mesenteric glands. *Lymphatic glands* vary in size from a mustard seed to a pea.

In these glands lymph is subjected to cell action by which it becomes changed into a higher quality. White cells, resembling the white corpuscles of fully formed blood are found in it.

It is considered that something less than one-third of the volume of arterial blood was once lymph, which had already served a term of existence as bone, muscle, brain, etc., and is now on its way to feed some other organ, rather the better and stronger that it has passed through a second glandular action.

It is important to health that waste atoms be removed as soon as possible, for if they remain they clog up the passage ways, preventing the deposition of fresh, new material, become overheated by the natural warmth of the body, and cause disease.

A multitude of movements takes place every instant of our lives, by night in breathing, in digestion, in circulation and assimilation; by day in addition to these are the never ending mandates of the ever restless thought, occasioning the destruction of millions of cells which must be removed. Rather than that these dislodged atoms should be carried to a large gland centrally located, which would necessitate an extra set of tubes, the gland itself is divided into small parcels and distributed all over the body, where the allotted substance is received without delay.

Animal Heat.

The system maintains a uniform temperature of

ninety-eight degrees, winter and summer. The heat
of the fire or the warmth from the sun would in themselves be quite insufficient to create anything like this
degree of heat.

All animal life has within itself a power to originate
and maintain its own heat. By the food we eat and
the air we breathe, uniting under the influence of vital
force, this heat is produced.

The body may be compared to a furnace, the food
eaten to fuel, and the air breathed to the draught,
without which no fire will burn. This vital flame
was lighted in our first progenitor and descends to
all. The fuel is principally furnished by the oleaginous foods, with the addition of the surplus sugars
and starches which are stored for use in the inter-
stices between the muscles, whence it is taken by the
absorbents for use in the capillaries. When by privation or illness the supply of nourishment is insufficient,
this store is sometimes very much depleted, causing
emaciation.

Chemistry shows us that the primary elements,
uniting by chemical affinity, liberate heat. Wood and
coal contain carbon and hydrogen, and the air contains oxygen and nitrogen. In the body, again, the
food and stores of oleaginous matter contain carbon
and hydrogen, hence do for the fire in the body, what
wood or coal do for the fire in the stove when united
with air.

The oxygen of the air and the carbon of the body
form a chemical union liberating heat.

Ashes and smoke remain after the wood is consumed, as salts are left in the cup of the galvanic battery. The corresponding *debris* left in the body is

water and a gas called *carbonic acid gas*. This last is
a deadly poison. It is passed out by expiration.

Perspiration and other processes of excretion assist
in maintaining uniformity of temperature, and any
considerable diminution or acceleration in the activity
of these functions affects unfavorably the degree of
vital heat.

11

CHAPTER XXI.

EXCRETION.

Nothing in the science of physiology is of greater importance than the laws pertaining to the removal of effete matter. For in time each particle of food, drink and air becomes worn out and good for nothing. It is computed that the human body is newly rebuilt once in seven or at furthest, ten years. The processes by which waste matter is eliminated from the human system are called excretory functions. The matter removed is called residuum or excretions. One of these methods has been described in the account given of the expulsion of carbonic acid gas from the system through the lungs.

Seeds of fruits, the outer covering of wheat, and the woody parts of vegetables have little nutriment in them, but are in liberal quantities conducive to health, as they excite the vermiform motion of the intestines and cause a free discharge of the digestive juices. These substances and others which are not taken up by the absorbents are thus hastened on their way through the digestive tract, and pass away through the colon and rectum.

Constipation is often caused by lack of this kind of food material, and while fine flour produces it, graham or whole wheat flour is a preventive. A person of sedentary habits by neglecting to attend promptly to the calls of nature may bring on a torpidity of the bowels. In all cases the fecal matters instead of being properly and healthfully disposed of, are taken up by the absorbents. The blood is thereby poisoned, caus- ing headaches, eruptions, boils, fevers and other ailments.

Some of the residuum is removed by excretory glands, which are like secretory glands in action and construction, being composed of cells, tubes and ducts. But secretions are used in building up the system, while excretions are poisonous and remain in the sys- tem only long enough to be ejected.

The Kidney Glands.

The kidneys are excretory glands, two in number, situated just beneath the " small of the back," and are usually inclosed in a large amount of fat.

The average size is between four and five inches in length, two and a half in breadth, and one in thick- ness. The kidney is of a reddish yellow. In construction it varies somewhat from the other glands, its cells lying near the surface, while its ducts occupy the interior and converge toward the center.

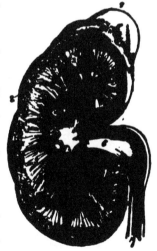

A plexus of vessels brings blood to the cells, which with unerring instinct extracts from them the ex- cretory fluid. Any elements that are available are taken up by the *Fig. XLIV. Section of Kidney.* lymphatics; the heat making atoms are taken into the capillaries, while the utterly useless urine is retained by the gland, and passed into the bladder through the ureters.

When a sufficient quantity has accumulated, the vital force gives notice of the presence of the poison by a pressure on the sensory nerves of the cerebro-spinal system. *Thought* sends orders down the motor nerves of muscles which attend to the duty of expelling the *urine*.

If *thought* fails to pay attention to the call of vital force, then the lymphatics come to the relief of the bladder and the poison is conveyed to the blood, to be entered again into the general circulation and cause disease.

Bad diet, beer, and other alcoholic drinks cause disease of this gland, by overloading it, as they contain no nourishment and cause too hard work and consequent injury.

The Sweat and Oil Glands.

There are some seven millions of minute pores upon the surface of the skin, visible only through a microscope. They are the orifices of as many *perspiratory* or *sweat* glands, tubular in form, placed just beneath or within the cuticle.

Another excretion takes place through these tubes in the form of perspiration. It can neither be seen nor felt as it passes out, so it is called *insensible* perspiration. By inserting the hand in a cold glass tumbler turned bottom upward, a moisture collects on the glass, caused by the condensing of the vapor.

It becomes *sensible* perspiration when the vapor passes away faster than it can be taken up by the air, as in running or working, or from excessive heat.

Oil Glands.

Clustered about each hair on the body are from four to twenty *sebaceous or oil* glands. These pour out a se-cretion which keeps the hair moist and lively, and also gives flexibility and smooth-ness to the skin. It is not of the nature of residuum, but it may unduly collect in greasy scales and stop up the sweat pores.

The cuticle itself is being constantly replaced by new particles and the old atoms are apt to remain and obstruct these passages. Then the vapors cannot escape, but are turned back into the lym-phatics and re-enter and poi-son the blood.

Hence the importance of frequent bathing, and also that clothing which is worn next to the body should be changed at least once a week, as it becomes saturated with poisonous and oily matter.

Fig. XLV. Sweat gland from the palm of the hand, mag-nified 40 diameters.

Another way of closing the pores is by taking cold. Cold contracts, warmth expands; chills cause the pores to close, and the vapors which can no longer pass out turn back, and settle upon some of the vital organs, causing disease. Sitting in a draft of air when the body is unusually warm, throwing off a coat when in a perspiration, are common ways of causing the pores to suddenly contract, and the individual takes cold.

When one does not bathe sufficiently and the skin becomes harsh and dry, vapors are not being evaporated freely and the effect is precisely the same as if a cold were just taken. In fact, it all goes by the name of a "cold." The symptoms are the same. The remedy is a hot water or hot air bath. Perspiration should be freely induced, after which the body should be bathed quickly in cool water. In this way taking more cold will be prevented.

PART II.

CHAPTER I.

SPECIAL PHYSIOLOGY OF MAN.

A consideration of the father part of the human tree of life, is the particular purpose of this volume. The foregoing chapters were designed to prepare the way for a clear understanding of the subject.

To win the prize of health and strength in a fully developed manhood, is an ambition worthy of every youth.

To aid him in attaining this end, there will be given special physiology and special hygienic laws to be followed in connection with general laws of health.

A lofty purpose to gain useful information from rightful sources, is most ennobling. To connect the thought of shame with such a pursuit of knowledge, is a false and degrading sentiment.

Each young man naturally desires to make the most of his every power, mental, moral and physical. He aspires to excel his comrades in strength and endurance, as well as in judgment, wit and understanding. To attain this praiseworthy ambition, it is essential that he know himself. The sexual system holds the balance of power, and by its elevation or degradation many a young man is made or undone.

(175)

For this reason he is asked to study the pages of
this book with an eye single to a noble manhood.

The Testes

are the most important of the male sexual organs.
The Greek alchemists melted in a crucible or *testa*
their precious metals, silver and gold, when they
would separate them from the baser metals and other
dross. .Thus they examined or *tested* coin or plate
when suspected of alloy. The foreign or baser parts
would separate from the pure metal, either floating
or sinking. The *testa* was the instrument of the purifying or refining process.

Hence the peculiar force and propriety of giving
to the organ which originates human male seed the
name of *testes*. The health and integrity of its internal
operations. is the measure of manhood, and may be
aptly compared to the trying, refining processes of the
old chemist's crucible. All the other sexual parts
may be present, but if this is lacking they are thereby
rendered useless. The *testes* then are the test or cri-
terion of sex. They are the testators or witnesses,
giving trustworthy testimony to the state of the
physical man. These and other words pertaining to
testimony, are derived from the same root.

Another method of ascertaining the quality of new
or unknown substances, was by the *touchstone*. This
name, "the touchstones of the man," is given by
some writers to these organs, and probably from this
source comes the name "stones" in common use.

The *testes* (or testicles) lie side by side with a division wall or *raphe* between them. Upon the back
part of each lies a narrow flattened body called the

epididymis. The two spermatic cords, one for each testis, pass upward into the pelvis upon either side of the bladder. The sac within which the testes and epididymis are suspended is called the scrotum.

Just within the surrounding outer cuticle or *integument* is a muscular tissue called the *dartos*, a muscle which, with the cord, sustains the scrotum in position.

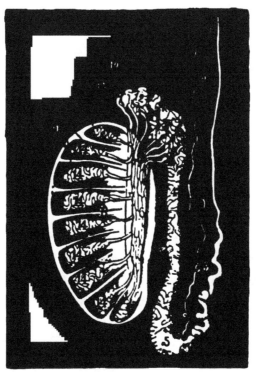

Fig. XLVI. Inside view of testis and epididymis. 1, vas deferens of spermatic cord; 2, spermatic artery; 3, vas aberrans; 4, 5, 12, epididymis; 6, rete testis; 8, vasa recta; 11, vasa efferentia; 14, 14, 14, seminal lobes.

The testicles are glands. Like the other glands of the body they are composed of a countless number of cells, a plexus of tubing, and a duct to convey away the secretion.

In structure this gland reminds us of the liver, in

that it is built on the lobular plan; its cells, vessels and ducts being gathered into separate bundles called lobules.

Each lobule is covered with a network of blood-vessels. Over this lies another coat or membrane, composed of fibers of white muscle interlacing in every direction, and called the white tunic. Still a third, a serous membrane or sheath coat, envelopes the entire gland. See 10, Fig. XLVI.

In a full grown man each testis is a little over an inch long, not quite an inch wide, and about half an inch thick, and contains some four hundred lobules. Inside of the lobules are the seminal tubes, laid in a coil. By holding them under water they may be un-raveled without being torn, and laid in a straight line, as a pile of rope may be uncoiled. Each then measures nearly a rod, thus making about four hun-dred rods of tubing in each testicle, or nearly two miles in all. It requires about one hundred and sev-enty of these minute hair-like tubes lying side by side to cover an inch of space.

The walls of the seminal tubes are lined with cells. How very, very small must be those cells which line a tube not so large as a hair—mere dots, smaller than the point of a fine cambric needle. Fine and delicate is this network of tubing, and consists, as in every other plexus, of capillaries, absorbents and nerves, and under the lens looks like the most exquisite, beautiful lace.

The cells are full of force and life as all cells are, able to take in and give out by osmosis, food sub-stance from this plexus, and out of it to manufacture a new secretion. different of course from the product of any other gland, containing ingredients not found in the blood, yet being derived from the blood.

The tubes are nothing more nor less than the ducts which convey away the secretion of the cells. In Fig. XLVI. it is seen that before leaving the lobules the seminal tubes become straight. From this circumstance they are called by a new name *vasa recta*, or straight vessels, 8. They all meet together at 6, and interweave with each other, so they are re-named to describe their appearance, *rete testis*, testicle net. At 11 the rete forms into from twelve to twenty ducts, which are called *vasa efferentia* (bearing away), or vessels that carry the secretion out of the lobules. The epididymis, 4, 5, 12, is simply a continuation of the seminal tubes, bunched up in a tortuous or convoluted mass; hence is but another change of name for the seminal tubes. The contents measure, when unraveled, about twenty feet. Following its course to 3, we find it becomes narrow, but still convoluted in a measure, and is called *vas aberrans* (deviating), to distinguish it from the straight line it next assumes at 1. Once more its name is changed to *vas deferens* (to bear away), or vessel by which the secretion is borne out of the scrotum.

Thus we have seven different names for the one duct:

> *Tubuli seminiferi*—seminal tubes,
> *vasa recta*—straight vessels,
> *rete testis*—net of testicle,
> *vasa efferentia*—bearing away vessels,
> *epididymis*—upon the testicle,
> *vas aberrans*—winding vessel,
> *vas deferens*—vessel to bear away.

The frequent change of name is a convenience to the anatomist, but is not essential to the purpose of this work.

The Spermatic Cord

is composed of the vas deferens, of a strong *cremaster muscle*, an artery, veins, lymphatics and nerves.

The cord, after it enters the pelvis, opens into the urethra or excretory canal of the bladder.

The spermatic arteries (as those connected with this cord are called) are given off from the aorta just below the kidneys, and enter the testes after leaving the cord by many subdivisions. The spermatic veins follow a direction quite near the arteries on their way upward to join the vena cava.

Sperm.

Two miles of minute seminal tubing lined with a multitude of infinitesimal cells!

Miles more of plexus tubing enveloping the cells!

Twenty feet yet more of seminal tubing (the epididymis) coiled in a few inches of space!

Arteries, bringing the richest and purest of blood directly from the heart!

Veins, taking charge of vitiated material!

Absorbents—general regulators—accommodatingly taking up superabundant nourishment or extra waste, as the case may be, holding the balance evenly adjusted!

Nerves, distributing a constant current of vital force, and holding all under the control of the brain!

The product resulting from a machinery so complicated, and constructed with such infinite painstaking, must be an exceedingly important one.

The testis is the seed-bearing organ—the male half of the seed—of the human tree of life.

The terms *sperm, seminal, semen,* etc., are all derived from similar words, meaning in the original language *seed.* Hence spermatic cord is a seed tube devoted to bringing seed material and taking away seed; tubuli seminiferi, seed tubes; semen, seed secretion, etc.

As in the vegetable kingdom the seed is the most highly organized and valuable production of the plant, so the seed of human kind will answer to the same description. Sperm is the most precious secretion of the male as the ovum is the most precious product of the female.

One physiologist calls it the *essence* of the blood. An essence is a refined extract of the predominant or essential elements of an article. The essences of lemon, vanilla and peppermint, are examples.

One author of note, *Tissot,* maintains that one ounce of sperm equals forty ounces of blood. The testimony of chemistry proves the principal solid constituents of this secretion are phosphate of lime, binoxide of protein, phosphorus, and a fatty substance. Thus it is the strongest, richest and finest secretion of the system, and represents the three most important organized formations of the body; bone, muscle and nerve.

These gland cells of the testicle, endowed with that marvelous and mysterious discriminating power common to all cells, *test, try* the blood flowing through their capillaries, retaining only those ingredients which will answer their purposes, allowing the re-

mainder to pass on. By this *refining, purifying* process they re-create the extract of the man, sperm.

The gland was well named *testes*, the crucible of
manhood.

Sperm in Childhood.

Most of the glands of the body are tools or instruments of organization used in building the human
temple out of raw material. The testicles, too, may
be classed among these instruments of organization.

Strictly speaking, the term secretion may be applied to substances of every kind which are separated
from the blood, but for convenience it is restricted
by physiologists to such as have a liquid form and
are destined to become a part of the new fabric.

For the first few years the sperm is scarcely entitled to the name secretion, but resembles in its removal rather the product of bone and muscle cells,
which are passed by osmosis into the lymphatics.

For the first dozen years of a boy's life, not a particle of juice made by these cells falls into the duct,
but is eagerly abstracted by the lymphatics.

Why is this?

He is not only growing rapidly, but in active exercise of brain and limb. He needs building material
for both increase in size and the replacing of lost cells.

In the testicle gland is the needed and appropriate
store. There is essence of phosphorus and lime for
the hungry, growing bones; quintessence of tissue-
formers for the restless, stretching muscles; and su-
perfine electricity for the eager, busy brain. The
incipient, developing manhood within appropriates
every particle of sperm as fast as it is made, so that
it cannot accumulate as a secretion. Without this

the blood of boyhood cannot be perfected any more than it would be perfect without bile, or gastric juice. The food eaten could not attain the highest organization. The saliva, bile, pancreatic and testicle fluids all combine to perfect the work. The entire volume of blood does not pass through the testicle, but it is all made stronger, richer and finer by the addition of sperm.

Once absorbed, sperm moves on to the lymphatic glands where, together with other lymph, it is subjected to their peculiar glandular action; thence through the heart to the lungs, whence it is returned to the heart and distributed to all parts of the body to be *assimilated* into the various tissues of the growing boy.

Eminent Testimony.

Dr. Acton, the eminent English surgeon, in his work on the Reproductive Organs, says: "I am disposed to agree with Haller that it is not certain elements remaining in the blood and not being eliminated from it, which produce manly vigor or virility; if so, castration would produce it, instead of preventing its development. That semen has an influence on the system is obvious, from the marked differences between castrated and non-castrated animals. These differences cannot depend upon anything retained in the blood and not excreted, but upon the fact that the greater part of the semen—that which is the most valuable and which has most force—is pumped back again into the blood, and there produces, as soon as it reaches the circulation, changes the most marvelous. It perfects the beard, the hair, the horn; it alters the voice and the manners. These effects on the system are only noticed in men and animals who enjoy virility. Age does not produce these changes; it is the seminal fluid alone which can effect this, as we never remark these changes in eunuchs."

His entire book is based on the spirit of this conviction. He gives further proofs and names other men of eminence in the profession who hold the same views.

Previous to puberty no spermatozoa exist in sperm, and consequently there is no reproductive power. Yet the testes are probably not wholly dormant. The nervous organization is acute, and consequently harm results even at a tender age if self abuse is practiced. The nerves will become unstrung, the whole system deranged, and the natural growth and development be interfered with; it may be through the nervous system, but it is a change, nevertheless.

Puberty.

It requires at least twelve years for the cartilaginous bones of babyhood to become the partially ossified bones of youth. Twenty-five years is the average time for perfecting this process. A long maturing time is indicative of the best formation, and other things being equal, gives the surest prophecy of vigorous old age.

Puberty arrives at the close of the period of most rapid growth, that is between the years of fourteen and eighteen. Climate, temperament, constitutional and hereditary tendencies among other influences, combine to hasten or retard this period.

It seems altogether probable that part of the surplus sperm now no longer needed for growth in height aids in further physical development. Some of it may go to the chest and shoulders. A little boy's breast is comparatively narrow and contracted and his shoulders are but little, if any, wider than his hips. They now gradually increase faster in proportion than the rest of his body ; his shoulders broaden, and his chest expands. A noticeable alteration now takes place in the boy's voice. By degrees it loses its childish melody, and is at first squeaking and some-what harsh ; apparently unmanageable, it slips and slides upon the gamut. After a longer or shorter time it settles into a deep chest tone, steady and agreeable. The larynx—his music box—has partaken of the general impetus of growth.

The mind acts with new vim and brightness. It is a pleasure to live, and life opens up with new meaning. He feels as if he could almost tread the air. Hope and courage are booming, and to whatever occupation he turns his attention he enters into it with vigor and energy. As a student he acquires knowledge with greater rapidity, and it becomes more thoroughly his mental possession. In athletic sports he has redoubled strength and elasticity. The world looks different to the youth because he sees it with clearer vision and keener intellect. He rests quickly and is up and at it again.

A distinguished French physician says: "Semen re-absorbed into the animal economy augments in an astonishing degree the corporeal and mental forces. This powerful vital stimulant animates, warms the whole economy, and places it in a state of exaltation ; renders it in some sort more capable of thinking and acting."

12

The Proof.

Country boys sometimes see men on the farm cas-
trate or alter the male calves, colts and pigs, and
know why it is done.

To perform the operation the scrotum is grasped
firmly in the hand and opened at a single stroke with
a very sharp knife, and the testes or "stones" severed
at the spermatic cord and removed. Blood from the
arteries soon clots, and the parts heal readily. This
is an operation that needs to be performed with
precision.

Bull calves, when castrated, are called steers.

Bulls' horns are thicker and heavier, their necks
larger, and they have more abundant hair on the fore-
head than steers. They are more fierce and vicious,
hence are less easily tamed, and when used can pull
a heavier load because stronger. The flesh on account of its toughness is not so desirable for food.
Their muscles are probably firmer and denser than
those of steers.

Among horses, those allowed to remain natural are
called stallions or entire horses ; the others are called
geldings. A writer of good authority testifies, "There
can be no doubt that entire horses are capable of un-
dergoing more work than geldings. It is a saying in
England that a stallion is equal in draught to one
gelding and a half. One such horse is often kept on
a farm and works a certain number of months in a
year. Any one who has traveled in France must be
aware of the fact that stallions are used by preference
as draught horses, and by means of hard work and
driving in teams together they are made very gentle,
though well fed and in excellent condition."

Sir Philip Egerton says: "Fawns when cut prior to the formation of any horn, will never hear horns, however long they may live. They will be more slender and more porous in their internal structure."

Eunuchs.

In ancient times castration was practised to a wide extent, and to this day in some Oriental countries it is still customary. Slave boys are treated in this way, and the operation is performed when they are from seven to twelve years of age. Those thus operated upon are called eunuchs.

The results following this operation form an interesting study for the physiologist.

The beard never grows and the voice does not change, the face remaining as smooth and the tones as soft as in childhood. These men are not nearly as strong as others. They make very good servants to do the drudgery of a family where not much strength is needed, but they make very poor soldiers or sailors, for they cannot bear hardships. Their minds only partially develop, and they are incapable of attaining a high education. A marked effect is seen in disposition and temper. Courage is lacking, and they are more easily kept in servitude. They are unmanned, robbed of strength in body and character, in the loss of this important gland.

At one time boys were served in this way on purpose to make singers of them, because of its effect upon the voice, as they can then sing parts that are ordinarily carried by ladies. This was done to supply Catholic choirs where women were not allowed to appear. But later, the Pope forbade the practice.

The following description of a eunuch is by a late writer in the *Herald of Industry :* " In Egypt they are spoken of as the third sex. They speak in crescendoes and that at the sound of a bass note. Col. Charley Long, formerly of the Egyptian army, and now American Consul, told me all about them, and introduced me to one, the head eunuch of Cheriff Pasha. He was a big, broad-shouldered, tall, well formèd chap, black as night. It was almost startling to hear this fellow speak. Every time he opened his mouth it was a new surprise. One expected a diapason flow, but heard instead high pipings, not unmusical it is true, but pitched even higher than a woman's voice. I am told that this is the only eunuch in Egypt (except the one owned by the Khedive) that speaks French, or indeed any tongue except the Arabic. *Weak of mind and body, they never learn much, and die early."*

Thus actual facts carry out Acton's theory. There is the same food substance, the same amount of blood in the altered as in the natural male, but the final organizing change is lacking.

Eunuchs are large, tall, broad shouldered, fleshy men, with loose joints, flabby muscles and porous bones. They lack solidity or density in structure, and are inferior in strength and endurance, both mental and physical. A natural man may be both large and compactly built, and is then of course correspondingly stronger than a small man. But for this perfection of frame the man must be complete.

In one case all is flabby and relaxed; in the other, fine, solid and taut. It is like the strings of two bows in which one is left loose, and the other drawn up with tension and snap. The testicles are the tension regulators of the whole man.

Colts are generally allowed to become two or three years old before the operation of castration is performed. They will then have thicker necks, more solid bones, and firmly knit muscles, and correspondingly greater strength and higher life than if it is done when they are a week or two old, the time usually chosen to alter cattle. But with cattle, beef, not strength, is wanted, while the reverse is desired in horses.

We now understand why steers make tenderer beef than bulls; their flesh is not so dense and firm. Pigs when altered, produce fat easier and in larger quantities on the same amount of food than others, and probably it is the same with all animals.. With horses, however, the object is to tame their dispositions and make them safer to harness and drive. Had they intelligence this would be unnecessary. Man is the only male who is capable of exercising self-control, and in this it is his privilege to live superior to the brute. Reason and conscience bearing sway over his animal passions, he, more perfectly than by any excision of the material, casts out from himself all that would lower and degrade the creative function, his most god-like attribute.

CHAPTER II.

MANHOOD ABUSED.

The custom of blotting out a boy's manhood by castration is now unknown in civilized lands; but many boys have sacrificed this precious inheritance by a yet more degrading and ruinous practice.

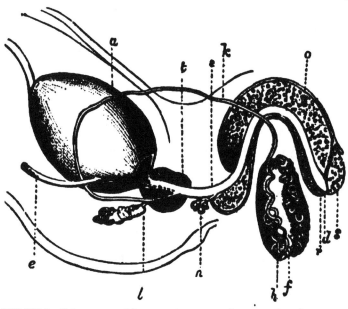

Fig. XLVII. *Diagram of inner view of male reproductive organs and appendages. a, bladder; c, urethra; l, vesiculæ seminalis; t, prostate gland; f, testicle; h. epididymis; k, vas deferens of spermatic cord; d, meatus urinarius; e, ureter leading from kidney to bladder; n, Cowper's gland; o, r, penis; s, glans penis.*

Through curiosity and for a temporary physical pleasure they have acquired a habit of handling and thereby exciting the sexual organs. This practice is known under the various names of masturbation, meaning to defile with the hand; secret vice; and self-abuse.

It is believed that every boy who has yielded to this prevalent temptation, will be deeply grateful for instruction as to the wrong he is doing and the right course to pursue. Before we can properly explain this important matter we must examine further the formation of the sexual apparatus.

At *o*, we have a lateral or side view of the body of the penis. The part marked *s*, is called the *glans*. Surrounding the outside of the glans are several folds of cuticle integument called *prepuce* or *foreskin*. In· childhood this completely covers the glans, sometimes extending beyond it.

The penis is not a gland. There are, however, some small glands placed about the glans penis which secrete and throw to the surface an oily matter called *smegma*, serving to keep the parts soft and healthy.

Erectile Tissue.

The body of the penis is composed of what is called *erectile tissue*. This consists of fibrous tissue arranged in bars and columns resembling the structure of a sponge. It is divided into three compartments, two of them lying side by side, as shown in cut, above the urethra, and the third below it.

The lower division is called *corpus spongiosum* or spongy body; the other two, *corpora cavernosa*, so called because full of little holes or caverns.

These apertures are lined with an intricate plexus of veins mingled with arteries, nerves and lymphatics.

The veins are in a greater proportionate number than is usual in the other networks of the body and capable of holding a large quantity of blood.

Precisely as a sponge may be swollen out by filling its holes with liquid to two or three times its ordinary dimensions when dry, so may the erectile tissue be increased in size, or diminished by the action of the plexus. The outer integument and the inner tissue are of the elastic sort, expanding to make room for the inflowing tide of blood ; and then in turn contracting or shutting down upon the veins, pressing the blood back again, or falling into its original condition after the retreating stream. The walls of the veins are of course contractile, and the entire structure is under the control of the nerves.

When the veins of the spongiosum and cavernosa become gorged with blood and the penis consequently enlarged to its utmost limit, it is said that an *erection* has taken place.

The urethra *b*, the remaining part of the penis, Fig. XLVII. is a hollow tube beginning at the bladder, *c, d,* and extending through the organ to the outlet, called the *meatus urinarius*, meaning mouth of urethra. It is lined with three coats ; the first a mucous membrane, like the lining of the alimentary canal ; the second, a thin muscular membrane ; the third a vascular or plexus membrane. The chief use of this canal is to convey away the urinary excretion of the kidneys.

Among the many changes which come at the age of puberty is increased growth and energy of the erectile tissue.

The product of the testicles also becomes greatly

improved in both quantity and quality, so much so as to assume the title—*secretion.*

On account of these two changes this period is one of the most critical in a man's life.

Probably the majority of boys learn in childhood to expect something of the kind. And now finding the anticipation being realized in their own case— unless taught how to conduct themselves with regard to it, they are extremely liable to make some disastrous blunders.

Or, if a boy had never heard of such a thing, and it should come upon him unawares, it could scarcely fail to arrest his attention, arouse his curiosity, and tempt him into error. It is better in all cases that the entire truth should be learned beforehand.

These changes are not sudden, but gradual, and require several years to perfect. They are not difficult to account for. The parts naturally augment in size with the rest of the growing body ; hence the testicle is able to turn out a more abundant secretion, and besides, the framework now nearing completion, no longer consumes the whole supply. It is improved in quality, because not being absorbed quite as rapidly as heretofore it has time to become more highly elaborated, riper and more mature.

The framework is not thoroughly consolidated until about the age of twenty-five, and up to that time will continue to use up a considerable portion. What is left over must be disposed of in either of two ways:

1. It may be all incorporated into the texture of the chest, vocal organs, beard and brain, in the manner already described ; or

13

2. It may be conveyed away from the body in the form of a secretion.

If it is poured out as a secretion it cannot be absorbed ; per contra, if it is absorbed it cannot be thrown out of the system. Every boy may, nay must, *does* choose, which shall be done. He cannot have both. It is just here that the danger lies. Should there or should there not be secretions *induced* during the age of puberty, becomes an all-important question.

Before this can be wisely determined he must understand the relation between the penis and testis, the method of procuring a secretion, the power and consequences of habit, and other vital points.

The penis and testis are closely united by means of the spermatic cord, as will be seen by examining Fig. XLVII., *k.* The *vas deferens* only, which runs through the center of the cord, is there shown, but we recollect that this is a continuation of the tubuli and that it is, at the cord, surrounded with muscles, bloodvessels and nerves. It is seen to join the urethra at *t.* In one sense the uretha is a continuation of this tube.

These organs have more arteries and nerves distributed to them in proportion to their size than any other part of the body. The nerves lie thickest upon the outer parts of the penis, nearest the surface. The reverse is true of the testicle, the nerves being most abundant in the deeper parts of the gland.

This causes the penis to be particularly sensitive to impressions ; to feel pleasure and pain very quickly. Especially is it the case with the glans where the nerves are finest and most plentiful. The thinness of the cuticle increases the sensibility of the parts. On the other hand the tubuli seminiferi of the testes are extremely susceptible and readily respond to nervous influences, because here the supply of nerves is greatest, while the surface of the scrotum is quite inert.

Filaments of the sympathetic system of nerves ramify from one to the other, and by means of them sensations felt on the outside of the penis are conveyed to the inside of the gland, and the state of the gland is communicated to the erectile tissue. When one is diseased, in pain or at ease, the other knows it and partakes of the same condition. Both are intimately related to the brain by means of the cerebro-spinal system of nerves. One of the thirty-two pairs branch off from the lower part of the spine and are distributed all through them. This brings them into direct connection with *thought force*, and on account of their generous possession of nerves they are, of all the organs of the body, the most emphatically the servants of the soul.

All parts of the system are more or less related to them by means of these two systems of nerves, and may be sympathetically affected by their various states. " If one member suffers, all the members suffer with it."

CHAPTER III.

The process of re-absorption by osmosis, by which the tubuli cells are made to yield their secretion to the lymphatics lying upon one side of them, has been fully explained.

It remains to show how they may be made to pour their product instead, into the duct lying upon the other side of them; in other words, the process of inducing a secretion.

As in the case of the salivary, lachrymal, gastric and other glands, it must be done in one of two ways. Some outside force greater than the hungry lymphatics which, undisturbed, soak up their rich juices, may break their envelopes and let out the contents, which will then of course fall into the duct.

Or else the *power of thought* may be sent from the brain, down the spine, along the tubing of the nerves, and reaching the cells through their plexus, give them, as it were, an electric shock that will break up the cells and liberate the secretion.

Either method may be operated separately, but usually both of them are united in the process. What are the outside or foreign forces used to destroy *these* gland cells?

Masturbation is one of them. But this is not practiced upon the scrotum where the cells grow, but

(196)

upon the penis where there are no secretory cells.
How then, can it have any effect upon the cells?

To illustrate, let us inquire into the physiology of
tickling. Webster defiues tickling: "To pat, to
touch lightly, so as to cause a peculiar thrilling sensation, which commonly causes laughter, and a kind of
spasm which may become dangerous if too long pro-
tracted." Some one else aptly calls it " an exquisite
. pain."

At first the sensation is rather pleasant than otherwise, exciting to laughter, unless repressed by a
strong effort of the will, but if long continued it becomes unbearable, and finally, if forced upon one
after that stage is reached, it may cause spasms.

A little school boy was once found by his playfel-
lows to be unusually ticklish. So they thought it
would be fine fun to tickle him every day at the re-
cesses on purpose to see him laugh. This was persisted in many days, the little fellow begging piteously
to be let alone, for though forced to laugh he was
suffering at the same time exquisite torture. But the
others could not understand how any one could be in
pain and still laugh, and the more he begged the
harder they continued the sport. He complained to
his parents and cried and plead to leave school, but
they did not understand, thinking it only the excuse
of an idle boy; so they flogged him and sent him on
to school. A very sad stop was put to it at last, but
too late. Convulsions came on; light at first and not
noticed until his nervous system was racked beyond
recovery; gradually he became a hopeless idiot.

The will can overcome the sensation if exerted in
the beginning, and some children find this out, and

take pride in challenging their mates, "You can't tickle me." All ought to know how it is done. Strongly determine not to laugh. After a few minutes of steady resistance a reaction will come to the part, and the thrill change to a senseless stroke of neither pain nor pleasure, when the experimenters will desist their efforts.

The little school boy had been shockingly abused, through ignorance, not malice.

Precisely in this way the masturbator abuses himself in sport, ignorantly, and without evil intention. The school boy was abused by others; the masturbator abuses himself. The penis is the most extremely sensitive to the "light touch" of all parts of the body, on account of the thinness of the skin, and particularly on account of its abundance of delicate nerves. Especially is this the case when it is in the state of erection. An erection is liable to form momentarily, at any time, without any apparent cause; as a boy may stretch, yawn, whistle, etc., scarcely knowing why. If let alone no harm occurs.

But here is the temptation; once begun, the most natural idea in the world is to keep up the excitement as long as possible, which for a while becomes more and more intense. It is followed by a nervous spasm of these organs.

And what is a spasm?

The pleasant thrill is first felt in the nerves, but the force of it soon spreads beyond them, filling the muscular bars and columns of erectile tissue; spreads into the deep seated nerves of the testes which lie in the tunica vasculosa (plexus) enveloping the lobules;

spreads from there into the tunica albuginia (fibrous membrane) beyond.

While the excitement is still in the outer nerves of the penis, before it has passed into the erectile fibers it is *voluntary*, and under the boy's control; but once extending to other parts he cannot control it; the actions which then follow are *involuntary.*

The muscle fibers vibrate under the excitement; they contract and expand alternately as only muscle cells can do. The vibrations take place very rapidly and with *force*, forming the spasm. It is involuntary, or beyond control when it has reached that stage.

The heaviest strokes occur in the tunica albuginia of the testicles. The boy does not realize pleasure there; it seems to him to be entirely located in the other member.

The muscle fibers interlacing in every direction, are by the rapid contractions pressed down upon the gland cells with such force as to break the ripest ones. This is done so rapidly that the lymphatics have no time to absorb the secretion, therefore it falls into the duct.

The spasm takes place through the whole length of the tubuli—rete, epididymis, vas deferens—for the secreting cells line them as well, and their contents pass into the urethra and out of the *meatus.* They are thrown away—wasted, *good* for nothing more.

The parts are now exhausted. The nerves relax, because their force has all been used up: this allows the erectile tissue to collapse, the sponges contracting upon the veins push the blood back into the great veins of the body from whence it came.

Nature now sets to work to repair, if possible,

The Mischief Done.

And what mischief was done? Supposing some semen was wasted, what of it? The consequences if this practice is continued are more serious than if the testicles had been removed by castration.

Bad as castration is to an undeveloped boy, masturbation is a hundred times worse. If it were known for a certainty that a given youth could not be induced to forsake the habit, it would be a merciful kindness to him to remove the glands entirely.

For, besides carrying about in his body similar marks of arrested development, the masturbator is liable to trials and sufferings in addition not known to the *castrato*.

In the latter case when the wound made by the surgeon's knife is well healed it is once for all. The parts are gone forever and will give him no more trouble; for, like an amputated arm or leg, they will never grow again.

How is it in the other case?

A fever or inflammation may set in, not very bad at first, and it will go away, and get well if allowed; but after a time if the abuse is continued it will increase and make much trouble. How would it be if the finger or cheek should be rubbed ever so lightly for a long time? It would first be red, then heated, and finally inflammation would follow. The finger would become of a dark red or purplish hue and grow very painful and tender, causing severe suffering.

There is always a little fever left behind after a *forced* ejection of semen. It takes time for that to subside, but if *entire* rest is not had before another one is brought about, there will be a still greater fever the next time to contend with. A little more fever is added each time to the last. In extreme cases *stricture of the urethra* occurs. This tube becomes so inflamed and swollen that the sides close up together; the urine and semen can no longer pass, or only with difficulty, giving great pain.

If the urine is not excreted, it accumulates in the bladder. Some of it will be re-absorbed by the lymphatics and go back into the blood to poison the whole system. Extreme pain and sickness must be endured. The doctor's art may give relief, but if the fever has progressed too far death will ensue.

All this could never happen to the eunuch. The masturbator is worse off than he.

Besides this, if the tubuli cells should in addition pour semen into the duct, it would complicate matters very badly. Not being able to escape through the closed urethra it must remain in the duct. The lymphatics could take care of it once or twice, but if allowed to occur often they could not possibly dispose of it all.

What remained would dry and become a hard, irritating substance; or else it would putrefy and decay, in either case causing fever, swelling and soreness. It would end either in a painful boil or tumor which would have to be opened by the surgeon, or in gangrene and mortification, in which event the gland must be removed to save the patient's life.

Sometimes these disorders are months and years in developing; in the meantime a partial or *semi-stricture*

13

with irritation and feverishness is constantly present; at times causing pain in passing water.

There is a disease of the urethra called *priapism*, resulting from self-abuse, in which erection is constant, with extreme pain in the penis, and extending beyond into the bladder, or the spine. This is a severe affliction; one that eunuchs never have.

Secret vice does not serve all alike. With some, all the evil effects settle upon the gland, and do not trouble the urethra.

The ripest cells are first destroyed, then the next ripest and so on, as we have already learned. Sometimes the act is so often repeated as to destroy the tiniest, youngest cells, and even to cause blood to ooze through the capillaries into the duct to be passed out of the urethra.

Impotence.

It is possible to continue this terrible practice until the power of the gland is destroyed forever. This is called impotence, and is seldom cured. The youth is as effectually *emasculated* as though an operation had been performed by the surgeon's knife. Besides the physical effect, the mental results are most debasing. It is quite possible for a eunuch to be a pure minded and noble hearted man. But the masturbator is subject to a flood of impure thoughts and evil imaginings. His soul is enslaved to his body, and all his nobler faculties are degraded.

The scrotum remains, a useless appendage. Instead of being drawn up close to the body, plump and round, as it is in health, indicating that the muscles are full of vigor and strength, it is elongated, relaxed and flaccid. This condition is called *prolapsus*,. or falling of the scrotum.

The prolapsus begins a while before entire impotence sets in. It indicates a depression and weakness extending through the entire system; all being dragged down together.

To avoid these sufferings and discomforts, never tamper with your sexual nature; or, having done so, *stop at once*. Nature will then set to work to repair all this mischief done and restore the whole system to normal working conditions.

It must not be expected that after months of such indulgence the body will afterward acquire the strength, hardihood and development that it would otherwise have attained; but life will be prolonged and a fair measure of health and enjoyment may be expected. Where the constitution is very good such recuperation may be surprisingly rapid and complete. One who has thus abused his nature arrives too soon at puberty. His physical nature is stunted. There should be full development otherwise, before this maturing begins.

Further Mischief.

Others experience directly the opposite effect. The sexual organs apparently take on new vigor and increase in size much faster than they would naturally have done. It does not seem to hurt them; no inflammation follows; new cells rapidly replace the old ones after each ejection of semen; there is an unlimited supply always on hand and that too, without impoverishing the gland. This may go on for some time and the organs mature at an early age, becoming at fourteen, sixteen and eighteen years as large as they will ever be ;‘ whereas they ought to have had from five to nine years longer to grow in, and would, but for this vice.

How is it with the rest of his body ? Is he increasing in general maturity, and becoming tall, strong and healthy all through?

The exercise of any organ draws an excess of blood to that part, and to a certain extent increases its growth and vigor. But when such exercise is excessive, it not only causes an unhealthy activity in the member thus used, but draws vitality from other parts of the system.

In the constitution of most individuals there is one part more vulnerable than any other. It may be the heart, lungs, kidneys or stomach. The constitutional injury which is effected by the masturbator is very marked, and is more generally disastrous than the injury to the sexual organs. The weakest spot will break down soonest, robbed as it is of blood and nerve power, to say nothing of the vital fluid which is wasted, and which ought to have been re-absorbed and gone to strengthen and replenish the system.

If a boy who falsely and foolishly prides himself upon his manlike development in this direction, should examine his physique carefully, he will find many humiliating defects. Instead of the ruddy, fresh hue he once had there may be a sallow or dead pale tint, with a greenish cast. Eyes that should be clear, bright and moist, are seen dull, dry and hazy ; sometimes weak and inflamed, and surrounded with greenish blue rings. Lips and ears bloodless, and of a lifeless white color, instead of vermilion ; hands cold ánd clammy. There may be rushing of blood to the head, with headache and flashes of heat in the face.

Again, he may find defective muscle; being soft and flabby rather than full and firm; face thin and emaciated; eyes sunken, giving the features a haggard, old expression. There is general wasting away, and this too, although the appetite is good, and he eats most ravenously. Sometimes he suffers with dyspepsia, loses his appetite and craves vinegar, pepper, cloves, mustard, pure salt, etc. Again he may have a variable appetite, eating heartily one day and almost nothing the next.

Palpitation of the heart and asthma are often found. The walk will proclaim the secret; instead of a light, springing step, the gait is inelastic, as of stiffness in the hips, resembling the walk of old men. A most marked deficiency common to all, is loss of strength and nerve. This becomes evident in trial matches of work or games. Given, two boys, same age and size; the one who has never abused himself can perform a certain piece of work in a stated time, or can run, row, jump, wrestle at a certain rate, and scarcely feel tired after it; while the one who has abused himself gives out before the goal is reached, or going through to the end, finds himself weak and exhausted. Endurance is lacking.

Nervousness and irritability follow close upon such a condition of weakness; perhaps taking the form of St. Vitus' Dance, or convulsions and epilepsy.

The worst robbery is perpetrated on the brain. His memory and power of attention fail; he forgets where he laid his books, playthings, hat; his mind wanders upon other subjects while the teacher is giving out the next day's lesson, or his father is giving directions for doing an errand; and he has to be told the second time. He cannot study; recites bad lessons; is reprimanded at school and at home for stupidity, until he loses all ambition to succeed as a student. He is fretful, cross, unstable.

He takes less and less interest in things going on about him; more and more frequently his thoughts engage in the favorite topic of his life, and he seeks solitude that he may indulge in his secret pleasure.

How does he think it will end if he persists in draining his brain of blood and nerve force?

After awhile, as a result, he will dream about it at night, just as he dreams of other things he does through the day. Even in his sleep his hands may engage in the same acts, causing loss of semen. These organs are kept in a turgid state day and night, gradually becoming so unnaturally sensitive that simply a thought may cause a loss of the secretion. Riding on horseback, running, the pressure of the clothing may affect him thus, and he finds a most distressing complaint fastened upon him.

How earnestly do those who know what the future will bring to such a one, repeat the words of Ellis: "Would that I could take its melancholy victims with me in my daily rounds at Hanwell Asylum and point out the awful consequences which they do but little suspect to be the result of its indulgence. I could show them those gifted by nature with high talents, and fitted to be an ornament to society, sunk into such a state of degradation as wrings the heart to witness, and still preserving, with the last remnant of mind gradually sinking into fatuity, the consciousness that their hopeless wretchedness is the just reward of their own misconduct."

He may imagine that others are ignorant of his practices, and very likely his friends attribute his ill health to every cause except the right one, but physicians and the informed are not deceived. The youth becomes uncomfortable in society, for he fears lest friends and acquaintances may read the visible signs of his wrong doing.

Instead of a frank and guiltless bearing, he feels and looks sheepish, blushes and stammers with conscious shame, and exhibits a telltale uneasiness of manner. Yet this lack of self-confidence must not be too certainly ascribed to a vicious life, for many pure-hearted boys during their growing years are distressingly bashful and self-conscious.

All these symptoms do not come to each person at once. As was mentioned before, it is the weakest organ that breaks down first. Weak livers show the sallow complexion; weak stomachs have the dyspepsia; weak lungs are liable to consumption.

Now and then one who has a strong, equally balanced constitution, will hold out for a long time; may even reach the age of manhood without any disease. But he will not be perfectly formed in every way. His voice will not be full and deep, or his beard will not have grown very much. Sometimes one only, sometimes both will be deficient.

How humiliating it must be for one in this situation, to have arrived at man's estate in age but not in manly physique.

"How different is the picture presented by the boy who has kept his sexual function unimpaired. His body is firm, vigorous and elastic; his countenance rosy and healthy; his complexion bright and clear; his manners frank and candid; his spirits buoyant; his memory quick and ready; every function of his body properly performed; he has that firmness of will and purpose which give him a happy self-control; he has no cause for shame, and as he feels his stature increase and intellect expand, his whole life is a joy, and his heart a fount of thanksgiving to the great Creator, that he is permitted to exist."

CHAPTER III.

VIRILITY.

Virility, from the Latin *vir*, a man, means adult manhood, manly character, also the power of procreation.

The beard has now grown, the voice become settled and modulated, the chest broadened, the bones hardened, and the general growth completed. Boyhood and youth have departed. Having kept himself from disastrous errors the young man is overflowing with strength and energy. He is in the family circle the exponent of cheer and vitality, the embodiment of ambition and energy. He looks back to no past experience of sowing wild oats, for his mother and sisters never drove him out to bad associates during the years when possibly his turbulence swept like a cyclone through the home, overturning all the quiet and order of nice housekeeping. Exalted and steadied by the dignity of manhood he is leaned upon proudly and fondly by those who have hitherto been his guardians and mentors.

Although the growth is generally considered to be attained at the age of twenty-five, there is further development during the next twenty years. A man who conserves all his forces and allows no prodigal waste of seminal secretions during the age of virility receives a sure reward. His frame becomes more closely knit, his step more sturdy and elastic, his voice rich, harmonious and magnetic, his mind clearer and his judgment more reliable. He can endure a greater strain of business or study, as he goes on in years, and in every way is the reliable man.

This progress in many desirable points may in large measure be attributed to the absorption and assimilation of the conserved sperm.

A large quantity of the secretion may be taken up by the brain and expended in thought. No uneasiness need be felt if, after strenuous mental exertion, there should be a temporary arrest of the secretion. Excessive manual labor also under some circumstances arrests the secretion, and both body and brain may be affected thereby. The better life is that which is equally apportioned between mental and physical labor. With these there should be rest, leisure, recreation and social enjoyment interspersed, to bring the best results.

The depressing effect upon the system, of tobacco, alcohol, opium and chloral, prevents the secretion and assimilation of sperm, robbing both mind and body.

Like barley, oats, corn, wheat, rye, nuts and other seeds, so the human seed seems to have for its chief object to renew and sustain man's life and perfect his development. In the language of a popular physician, "Nature knows well what to do with these precious atoms. She finds use for them all in building up a keener brain and more enduring nerves and muscles."

The Prime of Life

is ushered in as the crowning reward of a well-ordered virility. That man who has not "wasted his substance in riotous living" now enjoys to the full extent his accumulated store of physical and mental vigor.

There should be, there *is* such a season extending over a period of from fifteen to twenty years, in which the organism seemingly remains at a standstill, neither gaining nor losing; a sort of harvest season of life. These years are his best. He is able to do his hardest work either of mind or body; he has a power of endurance not known in his younger days. His knowledge of life and the world; his insight into human nature, gained by experience, serves to temper and guide him in the use of these ripe powers, and to make him the valued leader of younger men.

History records many illustrious examples of men whose ablest achievements were executed after the age of forty-five. Columbus was at least forty-six when he discovered America. Washington was forty-three when he was made Commander-in-Chief of the army, and fifty-seven when chosen for the first time to the presidency. The "Principia" of Sir Isaac Newton was published when he was about forty-five, and his great public services were performed later.

Many a man may assert that to judge from his own individual experience this is mere theory; that his best and most vigorous days were between the years of sixteen and twenty-five. Granted; but why was this? Is he sure that he conserved his best physical powers? Was not his life such that he exhausted his resources? Is not the impoverishment of his maturity due to the efforts of nature to pay the debts of youthful excesses?

With the prevalent habits of life, few examples of a

typical manly prime are known. On every hand we see men old at fifty, and often broken down still earlier.

Old Age.

Parise says of this season, "The activity of the generative organs diminishes, their functions abate, languish, and then cease entirely. Blood now flows in small quantities toward the testes. Their sensibility becomes blunted, and is reduced to what is sufficient for the nutrition of the parts. The scrotum becomes wrinkled and diminished in size, the testicles atrophy, and the complicated vascular tissues which form them become obliterated. The semen is not only less abundant, but has lost its consistency and its force. The zoosperms, far from being as numerous or as active as formerly, are, on the contrary, few and languid."

Dr. Napheys says: "It is evident that mere age does not destroy virility, but that it endures with the other bodily powers. There are some striking examples on record" (some of which he cites) "showing how a good constitution supported by proper care can escape the action of this law for many years. Thus it becomes a matter of no little interest, since we see such vigor is possible, to investigate the means by which it may be obtained."

"He who would secure a green old age must commence when young. Not many men can fritter away a decade or two of years in dissipation and excess, and ever hope to make up their losses by rigid surveillance in later years. 'The sins of youth are expiated in age' is a proverb which daily examples illustrate. In proportion as puberty is precocious, will decadence be premature; the excesses of middle life draw heavily on the fortune of later years."

How to make the best use of the privileges and powers of the virile age so that a grand prime may be enjoyed, and so that one may "grow old gracefully," will be the burden of succeeding pages.

CHAPTER IV.

PROCREATION.

Among the parts of the generative organs not already described are the Vesiculæ Seminales, the Prostate gland, Cowper's gland and the Urethra.

The *vesiculæ seminales, l,* meaning seed vessels or receptacles, are two membranous pouches lying just · under the bladder. They are attached to the *vas deferens* and also to the *urethra* by a canal called the *ejaculatory duct.*

The use of the vessels is to secrete a liquid that is discharged into the urethra during the sexual orgasm and meets and mixes with the product of the *tubuli seminiferi.* It is supposed that the reception of this fluid causes the zoosperms to take on their vibratory motions. Also that semen without this addition is not perfect and will not fertilize the ovum.

Dr. Davy says: "Admitting that they are like the gall-bladder and bladder of urine, receptacles, the fact may be viewed as a fortunate circumstance in our economy, and admirably adapted to the condition of man. Like the bile or urine, the spermatic fluid in the healthy adult appears to be in a constant process of secretion, and to pass as it is formed into its appropriate reservoir, from which, without disturbance to the system, in a state of continence, it is either passed out and voided during the act of alvine evacuation, or it is in part absorbed."

A writer in the *Edinburgh Medical and Surgical Journal* sums up an examination of this subject in the following forcible words: "They are essentially designed to enable man to control and to exercise that moral check on the passions by which he should be distinguished from the brute animals, and without which no considerable advance can be made in civilization or in elevation of individual condition and character."

These are very important organs. They become inflamed and diseased in sexual abuses, and their position with regard to the bladder, spreading as they do over its base, see 6, 8, figure below, explains why it is that the bladder is so easily implicated in sexual

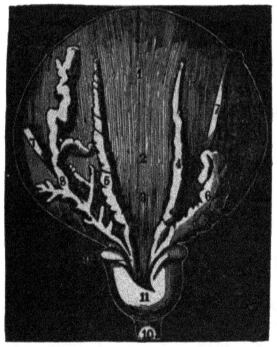

sufferings. It also on the other hand shows that urinary and bladder diseases arising from the kidneys may cause abnormal conditions, sympathetically, in the sexual organs.

The accompanying figure gives a good idea of the appearance of the under side of the bladder, and organs near it.

Fig. XLVIII. Base of Bladder. 1, 2, 3, bladder; 4, 5, vas deferens; 6, vesicula seminalis; 7, 7, ureters; 8, same as 6, unraveled; 9, ejaculatory duct; 10, urethra; 11, prostate gland.

The *prostate gland*, 11, Fig. XLVIII., also *t*, Fig. XLVII., surrounds the neck of the bladder. In the latter cut it is opened to show urethra passing through it. It resembles a horse chestnut in shape and size. It secretes a fluid which is poured into the seminal secretion after it reaches the urethra.

Two small glands, *n*, Fig. XLVII., called *Cowper's glands*, about the size of peas, are joined to the urethra by ducts about an inch in length, a short distance in front of the prostate gland. These also add a secretion to the others.

The male *urethra* extends from the neck of the bladder to the meatus urinarius. Its length in the adult is usually eight or nine inches; its course has a double curve, in its flaccid state, but in the erect condition it forms only a single curve, the concavity of which is directed upward. It is divided into three portions, the prostatic, membranous and spongy.

The *prostatic* portion is the widest and most dilatable part, and passes through the prostate gland. It is about an inch and one-quarter in length. Upon the floor of the canal is a narrow ridge, formed of mucous membrane and its subjacent tissue. When distended it serves as a valve to prevent the passage of the semen backward into the bladder.

The *membranous* portion of the urethra extends between the apex of the prostate and the bulb of the corpus spongiosum.

The *spongy* portion is the longest part of the urethra, and is contained in the corpus spongiosum. It is about six inches in length, and extends from the membranous portion to the meatus urinarius.

The *meatus urinarius* is a vertical slit about three

lines in length, and is the most contracted part of the urethra.

Manhood's Distinctive Sign.

Complete development of spermatozoa is the evidence of virility. This product is the very heart and core of the semen, the germ of the male half of human seed. It is really the nucleus of the germ cells.

The changes in the seed are known only by microscopic investigation. No perfect germs are formed in youth, and possibly few in the first years of virility. A single drop of semen contains many hundred cells. In each sperm cell is a single zoosperm, and when their envelopes are ruptured, liberating them, they enact rapid vibratory motions.

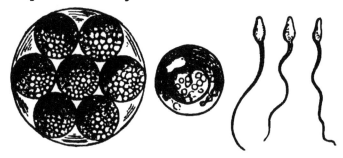

Fig XLIX. Cells and Spermatozoa.

The first cut shows a parent cell containing vesicles from the sperm of a dog; the second, vesicles containing spermatozoa in process of formation; and the third, complete spermatozoa of man.

Procreation is the crowning function of sperm in virility. Those wonderful germs that contribute toward perfecting and sustaining the life of man are thereby capable of perpetuating life.

In order to attain this result it is necessary that semen be conveyed to the ovum in the uterus of the

14

female. This is accomplished by contact of the parts and constitutes what is known as the sexual act, connection, intercourse, coition or copulation.

At the virile age the seminal product is placed in the keeping of the man. Whether he will waste it, and thus impoverish both mind and body, or use it up in mental and physical exertions, or preserve it for the nobler purpose of procreation, lies with him.

In manhood the judgment is, or ought to be matured, the will trained, the emotions subordinated to the highest objects, the motives consecrated to sacred uses, and the reason enlightened.

The continent man is he who holds this human seed as a sacred gift, too sacred to be either wasted or perverted, whose soul dominates this part as all parts of his physical nature, and who allows no waste of this secretion except for its appointed purpose.

CHAPTER V.

Thoughts and wishes with regard to eating, and longings after dainties of the palate locate themselves in the salivary gland, but have no effect upon the tear or other glands.

It is the eye, not the mouth, that waters upon the receipt of sorrowful news.

Bitter feelings expend themselves upon the liver, but do not affect the salivary glands.

Joyful expectations may take away the appetite by their effect upon the gastric glands, but act less directly upon other glands.

In blushing, the face also is sympathetically affected by thought. Intense and sudden emotion, shame or embarrassment will instantaneously suffuse the cheek with blood.

Emotions do not move muscles and bones; it is the *will* or conscious thought that causes them to act. Glands, as hitherto stated, are ruled by unconscious thought, rather than by the direct command of the will.

Each gland is subject to a special kind of thought or direction. Yet, if such thoughts are unduly prolonged or exciting, a constitutional disturbance is produced which is liable to affect through the sympathetic system, all the other glands of the body.

Thoughts of sex operate on the testicles. So powerful is the influence of the brain over this gland that mere thought without the intervention of any outside force is sufficient to produce or prevent secretions.

What is Sex?

Boys and girls are born in the same home, and of the same parents. Both are brought up exactly alike, partaking of the same food, breathing the same air, basking in the same sunlight.

Why is it that the boy should in youth have a deep, bass voice, and the girl a high, soprano tone? Why should he grow a beard and she retain a smooth face? Why should his shoulders become broad, his hips narrow, while the opposites are her characteristics?

Because the life element, the vital and creative forces that permeate every cell and tube in their bodies is different, the one from the other. The feminine force pervades one, the masculine force pervades the other.

A great many people suppose that sex is a term restricted to the reproductive organs; to the testes and erectile tissue in man, and to the ovaries and uterus in woman. This idea is most debasing in its effects upon the mind of the individual, and disastrous in its results upon his life and that of others.

Sex is quality, not substance. A principle, not material. An energy, not matter. It is indescribable but quite as real as any other force, and permeates the entire individual. The man is masculine all through and the woman is feminine all through. Sex is an attribute of the soul. Its manifestation in the physical is secondary.

God "created man in his own image, male and fe-male created he them." All animal life throughout the universe is sexed, being either masculine or feminine.

The soul is the man. If it is possessed of the masculine attribute, he appropriates to this end the substance he eats and the air he breathes. He transforms them, by this principle, into a male body. A soul having the feminine' principle transforms these substances into a female body. The ovaries of the female, as well as the testes of the male, are organizers, but they produce unlike results from the same material.

The physical manifestations of sex in face, form and voice, are the outward signs of an inward power. Sex then, really and truly is in the soul.

Masculine and feminine qualities are often compared to the positive and negative forces of electricity. As these mighty energies of nature irresistibly attract each other so are men and women, young men and maidens, drawn to each other. By suitable association life's happiness and usefulness are greatly augmented.

One sex or principle is not superior to the other. Both are equal in power and worth.

A Girl is as Good as a Boy.

Men and women are equal halves of the human tree of life. They are different, but the differences are equalized. A man can lift a heavier weight than a woman, but she can endure more privation and pain than he. He makes the better soldier, but she the better nurse for the sick and wounded.

Boys and girls have the same faculties of soul; can learn the same books; can write, draw, paint and sing equally well. One displays feminine grace and tenderness, the other masculine strength and force. Both may read the same poem and sing the same song, conveying thereby the very same idea; yet a subtle something pervades each rendition and leaves its own peculiar impress on the spirit of the listener.

Thoughts of Sex

are either good or bad. All good thoughts agree with the functions of the body, while evil thoughts are productive of derangement of bodily powers. If a boy would develop into that "noblest work of. God," a true *man*, he must exercise his mind in noble thoughts only.

Good thoughts of sex tend strongly to prevent excess of secretions, and assist the lymphatics to take up every drop as fast as formed for the use of the growing man.

All study of sex throughout creation, when entered into with the spirit of the true student, is elevating and ennobling. The evidences of design in the adaptation of means to end; the infinite variety of plans displayed; the beautiful adornments of nature—all inspire admiration and adoration of nature's God.

All enjoyment of the artistic in the tints, rounded outlines, musical tones, graceful gestures, laughing eyes, speaking features, etc., of the other sex, when regarded with reverent admiration as the handiwork of creative skill, as one gazes at a rare flower or painting—is a true and pure exercise of the soul.

All enjoyment and admiration of sex in soul is to

be sought after and cultivated. This secures inter-change and equalizing of magnetisms on the higher planes of being, and calms and tranquilizes the phys-ical forces.

Boys and girls should play, study and recite to-gether, enjoy holiday excursions, explorations after specimens, picnics and the like, in company, as brothers and sisters of one large family. The same socia-bility continued through life, with added dignity and a delicate reserve is conducive to a fully developed and pure manhood and womanhood.

It is a pity that pure and innocent children should hear of sexual matters first from coarse and evil-minded men, should hear these truly serious and sacred subjects treated as a vulgar jest. It some-times requires years to undo the effects of such teach-ing, and is the cause more than all else of sufferings presently to be discussed.

If the reader has formed no such acquaintances, having received instruction from the pure lips of his parents only, he may be truly thankful. Yet he may have imbibed the false yet prevalent opinion that everything pertaining to the sexual relation is impure, and all thoughts of it shameful. To change this thought is to revolutionize the morals of the world.

The boy enters puberty with increased size, and altered appearance of the organs ; greater erectile and secreting power ; voice changing ; hair growing upon the pubes, under the armpits and upon the face ; with a new start in mental power and general bodily growth. Instead of understanding the magnificent possibilities foreshadowed to him in this mysterious change, regarding it with pride and waiting for its completion with patience and calmness, he very naturally recalls all the debasing things he has ever heard, and allows his imagination to augment the sensual pleasure which he has been led to believe constitutes the whole of sexual life.

Perilous time for the boy! if no word from his mother, no hint from his father, no good friend or pure book comes to counteract the impure thoughts that now spring up as the result of evil associations and false ideas!

A properly instructed and right-minded young man will avoid the reading of books that stimulate such thoughts; will drop the acquaintance of those who retail coarse stories; will absent himself from attendance upon low theaters and impure plays. He will admire in statuary the skill of the sculptor in presenting an image of the Creator's handiwork; he will find in the society of lovely girls no temptation, but a stimulus to higher living.

An eminent physician says: "A heavier curse can hardly hang upon a young man than that of possessing a polluted imagination." Another, giving directions for the cure of the disease thus induced, says: "He *must shun evil companions*, keep watch and ward over his emotions, avoid, as he would the pest, all prurient literature, and live a chaste life. Nine-tenths of all the misery arises from mental sources. The thought as well as act must be put away." Still another in warning against disease urges, "*The only true safety lies in keeping the thoughts pure.*"

Another, writing more at length, says: "All overt sins and crimes begin as we know, in evil thoughts or imaginations. These become habitual and haunt him, until at last the sexual passion absorbs not only his waking thoughts but his very dreams. All the other forms of licentiousness put together are as nothing to this. A host of husbands deplete their strength by legalized excess; myriads wander in shameless promiscuity. Numerous though such offenders are, they seem but few beside those who keep shut up in their souls libidinous fancies which burrow and fester there.

"So far as the record is preserved, unchastity has contributed above all other causes to the exhaustion and demoralization of the race. And we shall not be likely to vanquish the enemy unless we make the *thoughts* the point of attack."

Further Testimony.

Dr. Dio Lewis, in his valuable work entitled "Chastity," gives some marked illustrations of the physical effect of an unchastened imagination. He speaks as a man to young men strong words of warning and counsel. His warnings have not fallen unheeded. The following cases given by him will be read with interest :

"A young man of fine culture and morals, who for four years had filled a prominent pulpit, came to me with a derangement in his nervous system. I immediately suspected that his peculiar symptoms had their origin in some abuse of the generative function; but knowing that a person of his character was not likely to be thus guilty, I inquired somewhat reluctantly, if he had not suffered from nocturnal emissions. He answered, ' No, thank God, I have been preserved from all those wicked follies.' I still sought for the clue, and said to him at length, 'You will pardon me, but I cannot help suspecting that your difficulties are due to some sexual exhaustion.'

" He replied, 'You are mistaken; I never practiced masturbation; I never had intercourse with a woman, and never but once had a nocturnal emission.'

" I asked, 'Are you engaged?'

" 'Yes.'

" 'How often do you see the object of your passion?'

" 'I spend every Thursday evening with her.'

" 'You caress her?'

" 'Perhaps so.'

" 'Is your mind occupied with sexual fancies?'

" 'It is, very much.'

" 'Do you not feel worse on Friday than on any other day?'

'I do, and I have wondered at it. I have wondered that my visit to my friend, which is the happiest event of the week, should be followed by such a wretched day.'

" He had allowed his thoughts of his friend to be based upon a physical plane, rather than soul union, and had thus dishonored her and lowered his own vigor of mind and body."

A Case in Point.

" A gentleman of some intelligence had lived a chaste life up to the age of thirty-nine. A successful manufacturer, he had acquired wealth and kept up a hospitable home, but had never married. In point of personal purity he was regarded as a very Joseph by his friends, among whom I had the honor to enjoy a place. What was my surprise when he consulted me with reference to seminal weakness! I made careful inquiries about his habits. Had he practiced masturbation? 'Never!' Had he indulged in familiarities with some woman? 'Never.' And yet here was a case of frequent nocturnal emissions, with all the usual symptoms of exhaustion.

" I said, 'There is but one explanation, and that is, that you have morbid imaginations.'

" He owned it. 'If that is important, I am free to confess that I am rarely alone a moment without being occupied with erotic fancies. And my dreams, too, are full of them.'

" I explained the mischief and warned him that unless he could break up the habit altogether, he was a ruined man.

" 'But,' said he, 'I can't prevent my thoughts. I can't decide what shall come into my mind.'

" 'Yes, you can,' I answered; 'you can decide precisely what shall occupy your mind. It is just herein that a man is superior to a horse.'

" 'Oh,' he replied, 'I am sure that is impossible; the thoughts will come unbidden.' "

The doctor gave advice and instruction which resulted in a complete cure at the end of two months.

Another Case.

".A young man who had visited the East Indies twice as supercargo of a vessel sailing out of Boston, consulted me two years ago in regard to 'sexual nervousness,' as he called it. He told me that while he had kept a native mistress in the East Indies, he had never indulged himself excessively, and yet he felt that he was losing his virility.

" The symptoms, as I thought, indicated a masturbator's exhaustion, and I told him it was best to speak freely, concealing nothing.

" He said, ' I never practiced masturbation more than five times in my life, when my mother began to suspect something, and talked to me in such a way that I never was guilty again.'

" I then proposed to examine his urine, and to that end brought in five long test tubes, directing him to fill them in my presence.   I saw nothing unusual with my naked eye, and after a time proceeded to scrutinize the sediment with a microscope.   Discovering nothing of interest, I finally asked him if there was anything in his sexual life which he had concealed from me.

" ' Nothing that I know of,' said he, ' except that I indulge in thoughts about women.   During my long voyages I have given myself a good deal to such things.   I have taken with me a score of French novels, in which sex has been treated in a very fascinating way.   Certain passages in these' books I have read over and over, and then I have indulged for hours and days in thoughts to which such reading naturally gives rise.'

" ' Have you observed after several hours' abandonment to such fancies that your nervous system was greatly exhausted ? '

" ' I have constantly observed it.   I have noticed that intercourse with my Indian woman did not exhaust me half so much.   But sir, it is impossible to control my thoughts.   Such fancies will haunt me and it is impossible to get rid of them.'

" I then said, ' Come to see me again in two days,

and I will prepare in writing the course you are to pursue.'"

The instruction given, urged, above all else, the importance of keeping the mind free from impure thoughts. This like the preceding case, was brought to a successful issue.

"Upon his return from another voyage, a few months ago, he called to see me. His face told of improved health, and as soon as we were alone, he began about ' My great victory.' ' Cleaned out, sir! I wouldn't go back again to wallow in the mire for my life. And now I am going to marry, and I shall marry the woman's soul. If I had married two years ago it would have been her body.'

"I have the impression that the service I rendered that gentleman was really more precious to him than to have saved his body from the jaws of death."

CHAPTER VI.

Thought, an apparently much weaker element than the body, is in reality the more powerful. What we call the physical organism is the most unreal part of human nature.

Air seems an unsubstantial, harmless element, so nearly impalpable that we call its sole presence vacancy or emptiness. Yet in motion it is far more potent than many objects of apparent density and substance. It overturns houses, uproots trees and devastates villages.

Like air operating on material objects, so thought controls and moves the solid atoms of the material body. In the creation of mankind, body is made the administrator of thought.

One must understand that there is a conscious and also an unconscious action of the mind. All the processes of the body under the control of the sympathetic nerves, such as digestion, are involuntary or unconscious phenomena.

Evans says: " They take place in accordance with the highest intelligence, and consequently, must be the resultant of some form of mental action. But it is an interesting fact and one that has its practical importance, that all these so-called automatic movements may be modified, and even controlled by the voluntary action of the mind. Take as a familiar illustration of this, the act of respiration. Breathing is usually automatic, and accomplished without any conscious, volitional effort. All the muscles concerned in the respiratory movement act when we sleep and when we wake, and without any expenditure of will-force on our part, yet we can, by our will, take those muscles under our control, and the breathing passes from an involuntary automatic movement to a conscious and voluntary act.

"The action of the heart is almost always an involuntary movement, and effected by an unconscious action of the mind. Yet the distinguished physiologist Weber of Leipzig found that he could completely check the beating of his heart.

"The contraction of the iris, the colored circle that surrounds the pupil of the eye, under the influence of light is a purely reflex or involuntary action, and to close the iris would seem to be an impossibility. Yet there are men who have learned how to do this.

"These facts go to prove that all the muscles of the body are made to obey the sovereign will, and that there is no real and essential distinction between what we call voluntary and involuntary organs. The motor influence in both is the mind, in the one case acting unconsciously, in the other consciously, and by a volitional effort.

"There is no part of the body that is not under the dominion of the mind, and that cannot be influenced by an intelligent voluntary action. It is an error to believe that these movements and functions of an organ *cannot* be affected, and that they are altogether beyond the interference of mind with their action."

If the automatic actions of the heart, the lungs, the iris can be thus placed under the guardianship of conscious thought, who shall say that the same control may not be obtained over those organs which are destined for the sacred purposes of procreation?

Although the testicles, like other glands, are apparently controlled by involuntary thoughts or unconscious mind, yet they can be put under the control of conscious thought. Indeed, the unconscious or involuntary powers can be brought into subjection, by steadily holding the mind to desired conditions. The law of action, as regards the effect of conscious thought on the sexual life, is just as certain as any other law of the system.

It is Accomplished

by persistently affirming the nobleness of the procreative attribute, and holding firmly to this thought; at the same time ignoring and denying, over and over again, the debasement usually allotted to these organs. In other words, train the spiritual to control the physical man.

You will then live above the organic and sensual, forgetting the physical part of sex. In your associations with women let your communion with them be on the plane of the higher life. Let their sprightliness, their vivacity, their womanly gentleness and tenderness win your manly regard. Cultivate the habit of noting and enjoying in them their sweet sisterly impulses. Be to all what Louisa Alcott in " Work," called Mr. Power, " a brother of girls." He realized in his intercourse with every young woman the beauty of the fraternal relation, and thus was a pillar of strength to those whom more sensual men would have looked upon as a temptation.

It is not claimed that this higher mastery can be accomplished at once. The thought must be trained to control feelings. There is a contest between these two, which one shall govern the other. We can change the *direction* of our thoughts, but the feelings cannot be changed or suppressed by any *direct* act of the will, but only indirectly through the thoughts.

The Thought Can be Trained

to a lofty ideal of purity and manly honor. Entertain noble thoughts and there will be no room for ignoble and erotic fancies. As a consequence, impure and sensual feelings will be subdued. In no other regard does the physical respond more fully to the mental than in this.

No discouragement need be felt if an undisciplined mind is some time in obtaining this mastery over the physical. Perseverance in so noble an effort will win the richest victory of which a human being is capable. " He that ruleth his own spirit is better than he that taketh a city."

Effects of Wrong Thoughts.

The most frequent result of self-abuse and debasing thoughts is spermatorrhœa or seminal weakness.

Dr. Jackson describes this affection as follows: " The patient has as often as from once a night to once in three or four weeks, when asleep, involuntary erection of the penis and general genital excitement, creating orgasm of the parts, and resulting in a flow of the seminal fluid. He is liable to be visited in his

15

sleep by images, more frequently than otherwise, lewd, and which cause lascivious dreams. As respects the activity of his imagination, its *unpleasant* and *unhealthy* action is the source of more mischief to him than any other faculty which he possesses. The disease divides its victims into two classes. The first is marked by involvement of the nervous system, showing great depreciation of power. The other type may be seen in persons who are of a bilious temperament, and who, whenever they are sick, are likely to put on signs of bilious derangements. This class do not show seriously impaired nutrition, nor great mental excitement, but exhibit symptoms of dyspepsia, torpid liver, constipation of the bowels, with diseased state of the skin."

We may find emaciation, headache, cold extremities, ringing in the ears, tenderness of the spine, lung difficulty, sleeplessness, weak digestion, loss of strength and memory, with gloomy, jealous, irascible temper. In short, the symptoms and effects are similar to those of masturbation, for both proceed from the same causes, loss of semen and nervous derangement. In its advanced form the emissions pass in the night without effort or dreams, on account of increased weakness of the organism. And even when about his business, the patient finds that the friction of clothing, or the exercise of horseback riding or merely talking with women will often cause a discharge of semen.

Some eminent authors have given the opinion that

The Only Sure Test

of spermatorrhœa is the presence of the vibratory

bodies, or spermatozoa, in the semen discharged.
But Dr. Wm. Acton, an eminent English physician, in
his work on *The Reproductive Organs*, says:

"Spermatorrhœa may really exist though it may
be impossible to discover spermatozoa in the urine.
I would urge my professional brethren to depend
less upon the discovery of spermatozoa than on the
consideration of the symptoms. If the patient has
that peculiar worn or haggard expression, complains
of lassitude, indisposition to work and loss of memory, etc., what does it matter to the surgeon whether
he can or cannot detect semen in the urine?"

Donné gives some interesting particulars of cases
of suspected discharge of semen, watched for days
together without finding any traces of spermatozoa.
All at once they were found to contain large quantities. In one case during eighteen days the urine was
most carefully examined several times a day, and yet
on three occasions only could spermatozoa be detected.

In other instances all the urine passed during the
night may contain them, while that passed in the day-
time be perfectly free from them. It may be that
fully formed spermatozoa can only be found in the
most mature cells. Constant excitement in the gland
prevents rapid ripening of the cells. Hence, may
not absence of these bodies be as likely a sign of an
advanced stage of the disease, as freedom from it?

A lad of sixteen had been complaining for some
months of loss of appetite, weakness and headache.
He grew thin and pale. Finally he took cold, not
very severely, and had he been well and strong it
would soon have passed away. But his system could

not react and the cold took firm hold on his lungs. He had for two or three years wasted his strength by self-abuse, and as the consumptive cough progressed he grew paler, thinner, weaker, was soon confined to his room, and at length to his bed. He wasted away to a mere skeleton; lost his mind so that he did not know his nearest friends, nor take any notice of what was going on around him; in short, became idiotic.

His friends thought he had quick consumption, until the doctor called their attention to the incessant oozing of semen, as a symptom of spermatorrhœa, and a certain sign that their boy had been guilty of sexual abuse, either physically or mentally.

If this lad had been guarded in regard to purity of life and thought, and taught the necessity and possibility of controlling his physical nature through a lofty determination to hold his thoughts on a noble plane, this sad and untimely death might have been averted.

CHAPTER VII.

SPECIAL AIDS TO SELF-CONTROL.

Each man or boy must be his own physician. No man can do his thinking for him, and in this lies the chief secret of reform and recovery.

We reiterate, because pre-eminently important, certain points which may be helpful in this line.

Never repeat vulgar stories. If unavoidably within hearing of coarse talk, do not listen with complacency, but repel it with scorn. Be exceedingly guarded in the selection of reading. Let your chosen literature be of the best; if fiction, choose pure and bright books, stimulating the imagination toward the mental rather than the physical. The natural sciences, travels, the accounts of great explorations, are fascinating reading to the young, while nothing is more stirring to manly ardor than history and biography.

"The Card Plan,"

prescribed by Dr. Lewis, and here quoted, has been found by many to be effectual.

"Write on a card a number of words, each suggesting a subject of interest, or a familiar train of thought. Fix in the mind that a sensual idea is dangerous and harmful; then the instant one comes it will startle you. When an impure notion obtrudes itself, the idea of danger which has been associated with it will arrest the attention, the card is taken out, and a glance at it will help to shift the switch at once."

The following is one selected from many testimonials to the efficacy of this prescription: "Whenever an impure thought entered my mind, I remembered my card at once, and taking it out, never failed to change the subject. It was not a complete victory at first, but now I have no need of the card at all. I have cleaned my soul of impure thoughts, and can talk with any of my lady friends for an hour without a single sexual impulse. I cannot tell you how clean and manly I feel. I would not go back again for a mine of gold. All that is essential to its success is a

Good, Strong Will."

An absorbing interest in the benevolent and social affairs of one's neighborhood is a stimulus in the right direction. Active participation in Sunday school work, or a Chautauqua Circle, or Young Men's Christian Association, or Farmer's Club, or any organization tending to the betterment of society, in which a young man mingles with ladies either young or old, elevates his habit of thought, and consequently his life.

The bent and occupancy of the mind is the thing of paramount importance. He should enter society with the noble and manly intent to seek the happiness of others rather than for selfish gratification. This will turn the current into wider channels; and grander thoughts, sweeter joys and purer delights will flow through his soul.

Simultaneously with efforts at pure day thinking must be begun a special course of training for pure

Night Thinking.

It is here the hardest part of the battle will take place. It has been fought by many and successfully won, and from their experiences others may learn how to vanquish the enemy. The point to be gained is to set such an alarm in the mind—a picket guard— that the moment a lascivious dream begins it will waken the slumbering I, in time to prevent an emission.

The ability to waken when desired is not peculiar to this phase of need, but is frequently brought into requisition for other purposes. A well-known example is furnished in some night watchers by sick beds, who by previously charging the mind, arouse from profound sleep at the slightest movement of the patient, or at the exact moment set to give medicine, no matter how frequently required.

One who was subject to taking cold every time the mercury dropped in the night, trained himself to awaken with the first sensations of chilliness, sufficiently to draw on an extra quilt and so prevent taking cold.

A certain frontiersman among hostile Indians was so overpowered by a sense of danger, that no matter how stealthily and noiselessly the savages approached, they could never get within gun shot, without waking him ; while other and louder noises made no impression. The instinct was unerring and became so well known that he was much sought after by camping expeditions, the men feeling perfectly safe if he were in the company.

A girl twelve years old was speedily broken of somnambulism by a new guardian. She had walked in her sleep around the walls of a house, just before the roof was put on, leaping from window sills, etc., to the imminent danger of life and limb. For this her guardian whipped her soundly, after talking with her as to the necessity for serious measures. He assured her that every offense would be followed by a repetition of the punishment. But there was no necessity for a second resort to the whip. This operated according to the same principle, instinctively causing her to set a night guard over her actions before dropping to sleep.

Dr. Acton reports instances in which the adoption of the plan suggested was attended with perfect success: "An Italian gentleman of very high station and character, consulted me for quite a different affection; but in order to put me in possession of all the facts in reference to his state of health, he related his history. He had been inconvenienced five years before with frequent emissions, which totally unnerved him. He determined resolutely that the very instant any libidinous idea presented itself to his imagination, *he would waken;* and to insure his doing so, dwelt in his thoughts on his resolution for a long time before going to sleep. The remedy, applied by a vigorous will, had the most happy results. The idea, the remembrance of its being a *danger*, and the determination to waken, closely united the evening before, were never dissociated even in sleep, and he awoke in time; and this reiterated precaution repeated during succeeding nights, absolutely cured the complaint.

"A letter I received on this subject from a very distinguished provincial physician, corroborates the

statement as to the possibility of schooling the will
so as to awaken in time to prevent emission. I had no
success in overcoming the tendency until I adopted
the plan of being lightly clad in bed (on a mattress).
Even with this the trouble used to come on about
once a month. Indulgence in wine or ale always
made it more troublesome ; but brandy was invariably
followed by emission, during sleep, without a dream.
Yet I have learned so to school my mind during
sleep, that I awake in time to prevent a catastrophe."

This interesting case of self-cure is taken from
"Chastity," already referred to. "A young man of
particularly bright faculties and good family asked
my advice about spermatorrhœa. His seminal losses
had been so frequent that he would probably have
become insane but for his exceptionally rich endow-
ments. I urged him to attempt what may be called
moral self-treatment. He had long thought that if.
by some means he could awaken before the emission
occurred, he should soon recover his health. He
had slept with a towel tied about his loins with a big
knot upon his spine, so that he could not turn on his
back, and had tried several other expedients, but
without avail. I charged him to fix in his mind the
idea that a lascivious image was dangerous—to think
of it some minutes before going to sleep—and resolve
firmly that if such a fancy entered his brain he would
start up instantly. He has had but two emissions within the past year ; and what is quite as
important, has learned the art of controlling his
thoughts, so that the libidinous imagination which
was the source of all his troubles is completely subordinated to his will."

Every salacious thought put to rout through the day strengthens the night watch. Each effort will become easier, both by day and night, and soon the contest will be ended with a victory for the right. Thus is shown by these various examples the wonderful watchguard which the conscious mind is able to exercise over unconscious thought.

The old monks and friars made the mistake of secluding themselves from the·

Companionship of Women,

as a safeguard from impurity. They failed to understand that temptations are from within. They had not taken home to their minds the truth that soul is sexed, otherwise they might have done God and man better service outside monastery walls, and gained much to themselves in pure social intercourse.

Nothing can be more stimulating to all a young man's best powers than the society of bright, earnest and lovely women. Mutual benefits flow from such associations. To be appreciated the one by the other; to sympathize in aims and efforts; to mutually criticise with a view to eradicating faults; to be educated together; to meet on a basis of political and business equality; all these redound to the best good of both.

A physician testifies: " When an intelligent young man comes to me for advice about sexual weakness, if his health and age be proper, I am in the habit of advising him to cultivate the intimate acquaintance of a pure woman, with reference to marriage. Nothing ennobles manhood more surely than such associations. And if for any good reason matrimony is out of the question, I still advise him to form a friendship with some true lady. It is best that she should be older than himself, a wife and a mother. The wife of a manufacturer of my acquaintance has taken into pleasant intimacy a dozen or more of the young men employed by her husband. One of them told me that a half hour spent with her has driven out of his mind for days impure thoughts which were wont to harbor there. One of the most potent safeguards against lust is an intimate association with pure women."

Few heads of families realize the opportunities for grand missionary work that lie within their own doors. In every city, in every town of any considerable size, there are many youths and young men practically homeless and motherless. To keep "open house" for such at all times is a mission having far reaching results. We have seen some noble exhibitions of this broad, open-hearted Christian parenthood which have been richly blessed. To feel that there is a true *home* open to him when a spare evening or a Sunday afternoon offers no other alternatives but a dismal boarding house, or outside temptations, has been the moral and physical salvation of many a struggling and homesick young man.

The same physician also relates the following:

"A gentleman of position gave me an interesting account of his own experiences. He was haunted by impure longings, awake and asleep, and in his calmer moments loathed himself. He noticed that the company of young and pretty girls inflamed his passion, and that exclusive association with men did not help him; but he did not fail to observe that the society of his mother, sister, and other dignified, intelligent, middle-aged women did help him. He found the companionship of a certain lady of his own age to be particularly helpful. She was full of zeal and interest in reform movements, and talked much of woman's duties, dignity, mission and opportunities. He was glad to find that an evening spent with her discussing such subjects left him free from prurient imaginings. He gladly read such books and papers as she gave him, and at length found that thoughts of this lady did not excite his sexual passions. In other words, this man was for the first time introduced to a woman's soul, and found so much there to interest him that he forgot her person. He experienced such a sense of manliness when in her company, that he was with her almost constantly, and after two months' intimacy asked her to become his wife. He instinctively sought in her companionship the completion of the cure she had so unconsciously but happily begun."

In one case woman is a temptation, and in the other a safeguard. The same sexuality exists, but on the one hand it manifests itself in the physical, on the other hand in the mental.

" There are periods in the life of every one," writes a man, " however well regulated, when sexual desire is powerfully stirred, and when continence may seem well nigh impossible. Many imagine them to be seasons of special temptation, while others regard them as nature's demand for sexual intercourse. But there is a wiser view."

Vigorous Exercise

is a special safeguard in such an hour of temptation,

To rise at once and attack a task requiring attention and care, with vigorous bodily movements, will effectually drive away all unclean thoughts. Dumb bells, bean bags, brisk walking, sawing wood, gardening or any other exercise requiring attention and strong will, answers the purpose. Such efforts seldom fail to cure seminal weakness.

A distinguished man related his experience in this line to his physician, as follows: "During my University career my passions were very strong, sometimes almost uncontrollable, but I have the satisfaction of thinking that I mastered them; it was, however, by great efforts. I obliged myself to take violent physical exertion; I was the best oar of my year and when I felt particularly strong sexual desire, I sallied out to take more exercise. I was victorious always; I never committed fornication. You see in what robust health I am; it was exercise that saved me." This gentleman took an excellent degree and has since reached the highest point in his profession. It was his boast that until his marriage he lived a continent life.

Food and Drink.

A proper habit of diet is one of the chief aids in counteracting sensuality. Few parents realize their responsibility in this regard, and load their tables with food which tends to make more difficult their children's struggles after a pure and temperate life.

Stimulating food is not strengthening food. That which is adapted to add permanent strength to the system nourishes and builds up with little excitation of the nervous or cerebral organism. Vegetables, fruits, and especially properly prepared cereals furnish such sustenance. The process of milling has been so greatly improved of late years as to place cracked wheat, rolled avena and the best grades of whole wheat flour within the reach of the multitudes. These cereal foods build up the strength without supplying the nervous excitement so dangerous to purity. Tea and coffee on the contrary, should be used in moderation, as should pepper and other condiments which tend to inflame the mucous membrane.

Animal food partakes of both characteristics. It is both nourishing and stimulating. On this account young men will find it to their advantage to be guarded in regard to excessive meat eating.

A. E. Newton says: "They who have ever carefully noted the effect on themselves of most kinds of alcoholic stimulants, of coffee, oysters, eggs, spices and an excess of animal food of almost any kind, and especially they who prefer these things *because* of their stimulating effects in this direction, cannot surely with any justice charge upon 'nature' the exuberance of their amatory desires."

If this advice is necessary in regard to meat eating, where can we find words strong enough to warn our youth from the alcohol habit? Even an occasional glass of ale, wine or beer has often sufficed to arouse latent sensuality, or to produce involuntary emissions. All the excretory processes are overtasked to get rid of this foreign element, which nature cannot transmute into living organism. Alcoholism contains the seeds of death, both spiritual and physical, and overturns perhaps more quickly than aught beside, the self-mastery which is all important.

Maintain Normal Action

of the excretories. This is one great secret of sexual health. Thus no waste will accumulate. By vigorous bathing and friction the pores of the skin should be kept open. Through deep breathing of pure air the lungs are enabled to do their share of purifying the system. The kidneys and digestive organs must be kept from derangement, and will thus co-operate to prevent any undue excretory function being forced upon the testicles.

"It is a gross and dangerous error to suppose that ardent desires are a sign of vigorous health. This is a delusion which should be destroyed. Those men who have the finest physiques, the most athletic frames, and are in thorough condition, experience least acutely the spur of desire. It is nearly a constant symptom of certain dangerous diseases (as consumption, obstinate skin diseases, leprosy and slow poisoning by diseased rye flour) that the passions are easily excited."

Put to yourself frequently the question, "Which shall be master, body over mind, or mind over body? And remember that no matter how great the transgression and how deadened the conscience, the promise holds true: "Let the wicked forsake his way, and the unrighteous man his thoughts, and let him return unto the Lord and he will have mercy upon him, and to our God, for he will abundantly pardon."

Newton affirms: "It is no easy matter to acquire the mastery over a tendency strong by inherited force and increased, perhaps, by long and ignorant indulgence. Especially is the mastery difficult to those who have not learned the full meaning and the better uses of the sexual impulse, and know not the aids that are available for its wise control. To all who are struggling in such conditions, heartfelt sympathy is due. But experience has proved that the mastery can be attained. A determined will—an earnest, constant aspiration for power from above to overcome—with a careful abstinence from exciting foods, drinks, acts and *thoughts*, and the use of appropriate means to allay excitement—these, persisted in, will bring the victory in due time."

CHAPTER IX.

CONTINENCE.

Many scientists and philanthropists now maintain that the law of continence is the true rule of life. By continence is meant the voluntary, entire abstinence from sexual indulgence in any form, except intercourse for the purpose of procreation; and the complete control over the passions by one who knows their power, and who, but for his pure life and steady will, not only could, but would indulge them. All men of intelligence are willing to admit that reason not impulse should govern action in other matters. This belief carried out in sexual life would mark a new epoch in the history of man. Heart and thought culture, we reiterate, must, however, precede this great reform of life. "Keep thy heart with all diligence, for out of it are the issues of life." This is solid

Scientific Truth.

For the purposes of self-development, a youth must live a continent life up to the period of virility. He must not waste, but *contain, hold*, within himself the vital fluid. This is continence. This is science, reason, nature; "*Vox naturæ vox Dei.*"

It must be a cheerful, willing, and even a joyful continence, or else it is not continence; it is, in that case, only repression, and in secret reacts upon the

16 (249)

glands causing emissions and waste of seed. "Let every man be persuaded in his own mind." An outward continence results in no personal benefit without inward acquiescence.

"Don't nature know what she is about?" "Nature is our best guide," etc., are objections brought against the Law of Continence. What is nature? And under what conditions does nature produce most perfect fruitage? From the *Rural New Yorker* is taken a case in point on

Strawberry Culture.

"The first effort a plant makes is to propagate itself, and it will throw out runners when it is too young and immature to produce fruit, as may be seen in the woods where the vines are left to follow nature. Poverty of soil hastens a redundant but inferior fruitage."

Applying this to human plants the parallel reads: The first effort or instinct of a youth when he awakens to the idea of sex is to exercise his reproductive powers, although too young and immature for proper parenthood. Poverty of mental soil tends, later, to increase of progeny, but decrease in quality thereof.

The *Rural New Yorker* continues: "A strawberry plant, with a rich, moist soil back of it, does tend to run to vine; that is the first law of its being on all soils. But suppose you restrict it—cut the runners off—what must follow? It can't stop growing; indeed this restriction seems to double its vigor. That it can expend its vigor in useless leaves is impossible, for the foliage is the plant's digesting organ, and the more it digests, the more vigor and power it acquires.

Since it can't run, it must do something with all of
its accumulating force, and what can it do but *develop
fruit buds* in the large, bushy stool which is rapidly
formed under this system of restriction which curtails
the growth of an indefinite number of small plants."

Thus when a youth restricts by continence the
seminal waste, this conservation of force tends to
preparation for future fruitage.

" In other words, all the energy and vitality which
would go to produce runners are thrown into fruit.
Fruit is the only outlet, and the rich, moist, yellow
soil demands a large outlet, therefore you secure
large, elegant berries, one crate of which is often
more profitable than a dozen of inferior specimens."

It is quality, not quantity of population the world
needs to-day. One good man like George Washington, Peter Cooper or Dean Stanley, is worth to the
world many hundred ordinary people.

Excesses operate upon a man as tapping does on
young sugar trees in the early spring. The tree becomes useless for timber and dies prematurely. Let
a youth rather restrict and cultivate nature, and regard sexual impulses and temptations as nature's
friendly notices that fresh supplies of mental and
physical vigor have come to him in life's springtime.

" The procreative element is not necessarily limited
to increase of human beings. It may be taken up by
the brain and may be coined into new thoughts—
perhaps new inventions—grand conceptions of the
true, the beautiful, the useful, or into fresh emotions
of joy, and impulses of kindness and blessing to all
around. This, in fact, is but another kind or department of procreation; is just as really a part of the

generative function as is the begetting of physical offspring. Indeed, it is by far the larger part. The continent youth will soon find his intellect blossoming with new ideas—perhaps fresh flowers of poesy ; and the maturer man will realize the birth of grander conceptions, nobler resolves, higher life purposes."— *A. E. Newton.*

A Contrast.

" In the same New England home were born two sons, the only two. Good early influences surrounded both. One is now honored by the entire civilized world, a scientific gentleman of such attainments as give his name pre-eminence even among eminent names. He speaks upon abstruse subjects in many tongues before audiences of many nationalities, and the learned of earth do him honor. Scientific quarterlies reprint his opinions and defer to his decisions.

" The other son of the family, equally gifted by nature, has for years been an outcast from society, sent from one corporation to another, from one poorhouse to another, from one State to another. His is that peculiar form of half insanity, that strange mixture of mental and moral with physical disease, which baffles every physician. The man may entertain you with stories of foreign lands in which he has traveled, but you shudder as you look upon his distorted form, and a face sometimes idiotic, sometimes devilish. With wonderful tenacity of life he lives through spasm after spasm that tortures his poor racked body and mind. The poor wretch is the victim of excesses. Behold the wreck of what might be a noble manhood ! For the honored brother, too, is a life-long bachelor, whose continence has left all his life forces to enrich his brain, and his thought children have made the whole world wiser."—*Mary J. Telford.*

To quote again from Newton: "To the mature man this continence is essential to the maintenance of a high tone of vitality and of manly vigor. On it depends the degree of positive or impregnative force which characterizes the individual in his mental activities. A speaker or writer who is addicted to waste in this department, though he may talk and write with great profuseness, may expect that his words will be comparatively powerless in their effect upon others. They will lack *germinating power.* But he who retains this element, other forces being in proper balance, charges not only his words but his very atmosphere with a power which penetrates and begets new thoughts and emotions in those with whom he comes in contact. Reserve is everywhere the

Grand Secret of Power.

"And when the fit time comes to exercise the crowning function of manhood, to impart the germ of a new immortal—who shall repeat oneself in a nobler type, to expand and rejoice through the eternities—he who has reserved his forces has at full command the elements requisite for the God-like purpose."

CHAPTER X.

THE RIGHTS OF OTHERS.

While it is conceded by all thoughtful minds that mature man is the arbiter of the procreative element, yet the rights of others must in this, as in all things, be regarded. True freedom does not exist where the liberty of one interferes with the privileges of others.

To understand the wrong which may be done to others through sexual influences, and to set forth clearly the true and underlying principle which should govern them, requires serious consideration. We have hitherto looked upon these matters in the light of the man's own development. They affect momentously both children and women as well as society at large.

Children's rights have been sadly overlooked by parents, and by those seeking parenthood. A noble and essential truth is expressed in the aphorism,

To Be Well Born is the Right of Every Child.

"Like produces like" is an old saying. Christ emphasized the same law in, "A good tree cannot bring forth evil fruit, neither can a corrupt tree bring forth good fruit; and Paul echoed it in, "What a man soweth, that shall he also reap."

Wrong thinking and wrong habits of living on the part of parents must leave their impress on the incipient being.

The foundations of character and physical organism come to every individual as a special inheritance. These may be likened to the metals. The miner delves in the earth and brings to us gold, silver, iron and copper. These are by mechanism transformed into articles of use and adornment. Yet no elaboration or variation can ever change the individuality of the metal. The gold always remains gold. The iron, iron, and the copper, copper. So with human life. Although pre-natal and post-natal conditions may transform the original product into more comely development, yet the original heritage is strangely like the primitive ore.

"I know a lady of rarely noble character, temperate in all things, whose husband had left off drinking for one year in order to secure her hand, and continued temperate till after the birth of the first child—a boy—when he relapsed and went on regular sprees. The second child, also a boy, was born under these unfortunate auspices. The first has been a model man, high toned, talented, a devoted son to his widowed mother and a father to his brother, who could not restrain his desire for liquor."

"A married man addicted to smoking, resolved to abandon the habit. He suffered horribly. His longings for the accustomed sedative were indescribably tormenting. Tobacco became the desire of his life. All other blessings were as nothing to this coveted indulgence. He became morose and vicious. In this fearful state of mind he begot a son. He did not succeed in conquering his appetite, and his poor boy inherited propensities, the indulgence of which has become the scourge of his father's life, and the sorrow and humiliation of his mother and all his friends, who are highly respectable and keenly alive to the disgrace of having a relative an inmate of a house of correction, to keep him in any kind of safety. The boy's appetite for tobacco is insatiable and has been from babyhood. When it is forbidden, his cunning evades all rules and he is seldom without it. This father was capable of transmitting better conditions, as his later children show."—*Dr. C. B. Winslow.*

"In no instance is the sin of the father more distinctly visited on the children than in tobacco using. It produces in the offspring an enervated and unsound constitution, deformities, and often early death."—*Dr. Ruddock, of London.*

The fearful contagious disease which is frequently contracted through sexual excesses, involves not only the transgressor in suffering and mortification, but is transmitted in all its baneful effects to offspring, more certainly than any other affection.

Pre-natal Impressions

have often produced some marked instances of youthful depravity. "A woman, educated and well connected, who had brought her husband a large fortune, found him so penurious as to begrudge her the necessaries of life, although he spent her money without stint in the gratification of his own tastes and vices. 'When I was about to become a mother,' said she, 'my husband refused me money, and had I not risen from my bed after he was asleep at night and taken it by stealth from his pocketbook, my boy would not have had a single garment at his birth.' This communication was made by a broken-hearted mother, whose young son, detected in stealing by his employer, we were endeavoring to save from the legitimate consequences of his crime.

" This boy, in spite of light, intellect and high cul-ture, has been an inveterate thief from infancy, and could not withhold his hands from taking that which pleased him."

" A very lovely and high bred lady, whose son was hanged for murder, said: ' The crime of my boy was the legitimate outgrowth of my own criminal weakness in living with his father, whose violent pas-sions made my life a torture. I hated him as bitterly as I feared him. For many years previous to his death I never saw him leave the house without an involuntary mental prayer that he might not live to return.' For years this poor lady was a murderer at heart, and transmitted to her child the character that led to his death upon the gallows."

While it is true that the previous life of the parents —the whole of it—has a great effect upon the phys-ical, mental and moral constitution of offspring, there is no doubt that their transient impulses and moods, as well as brief deviations from established principles, often leave undesirable permanent results upon the character of the child.

" A well-known philanthropist whose companion was bright, loving and amiable, found great disappoint-ment in his only son, who should have inherited the virtues and talents of both parents and become a blessing, not only to his family but his country. He was wild and intemperate, and had more interest in a horse race than in his parents' humanitarian schemes. With broken health and incapacity for any good work

he passed out of existence in early manhood, his
whole life a miserable failure.   This boy was begotten
directly after a successful lawsuit, in which the father
was his own lawyer.   The effort called out all the
antagonism of his nature.   Greatly fatigued, he returned home and related to his wife the circumstances
of the bitter contention, with all the exciting and
irritating incidents.   The wife listened sympathetically, entering into the spirit of the contest and rejoic-
ing in the triumph of her husband.   These conditions
were transmitted to their son.   Not all the influences
of a beautiful home, with the tender love and example
and precepts of both parents could eradicate the
virus of irregularity and discord from this *seed* so
thoughtlessly sown."

Many stock raisers have found that infrequent procreation is one great secret of raising fine stock.
Some physiologists claim, and with a good show of
reason, that children are deprived, under the same
law, of their right to be well born.

Sexual excesses are exceedingly liable to defraud
children of their best and strongest physical organization, to produce discord in the nervous system and
to lay the foundations for sensuality and intemperance.

Children's rights are also invaded by precocious
parentage.   A young orchard, forced to premature
fruitage, soon degenerates.   Yet the same trees restrained from fruit bearing for a few years give ulti-
mately, the finest, fairest and most enduring results.

Pinch off the first buds on a rose tree, and added
strength and vigor give future blooms of greater
loveliness.   So it is with human blossoms and fruitage.

A Greek philosopher says: " In the entire animal

kingdom the fruits of the first signal of reproductive instinct are constantly imperfect, and have not any well established form. It is also the same with the human species, and the proof is evident, for precocious marriages procure small and contemptible men."

Breeders of valuable stock do not allow the animals to follow out their earliest instincts to procreate their kind; first, because it stunts them in size; second, because their progeny lack vitality and do not command a good price in the market.

"Montesquieu affirmed that the fear of military service induced a great number of young men—mere boys—to enter into matrimonial connections, and that the misery and diseases produced thereby greatly diminished the population of France."

Dr. Ryan records: "The ancient Germans did not marry until the twenty-fourth or twenty-fifth year, previous to which they observed the most rigid chastity, and in consequence they acquired a size and strength that excited the astonishment of Europe. This accumulated vitality has been handed down from generation to generation."

The tall, vigorous and splendidly developed citizens of Sparta, became the pride of all Greece. Grote, enumerating the causes which brought about their superiority over the other states, says: "The age of marriage was deferred by the Spartan law (both in women and in men) until the period deemed most consistent with the perfection of offspring."

Dr. Alice B. Stockham, in her invaluable work *Tokology*, gives in plain language the sad results to both the nursling and the unborn babe when too frequent child-bearing depletes the maternal vigor:

" The Unwelcome Child

is deprived of physical vigor, and may be endowed
with lustful passions and morbid appetites, if he does
not indeed curse his own existence.

"At the close of one of my health *conversations*
after speaking upon this subject, a lady tremblingly
but touchingly, gave her experience. She said:
'Ladies, when I was married two years I was the
mother of a puny, sickly baby; it had required incessant care and watching to keep it alive. When it
was only seven months old, to my surprise, astonishment and horror I felt *quickening*, and for the first
time, I knew I was pregnant again. I was abased,
humiliated. The sense of degradation that filled my
soul, cannot be described. What had been done?
The babe that was born and the babe that was unborn
were robbed of their just inheritance. Remorsefully
and tearfully I told my mother. She says: ' Why,
child, you should not grieve; don't you know your
children are legitimate?' My whole being arose in
protest; I stamped my foot and almost screamed;
'Although my husband is the father of my children,
they are not legitimate. No man-made laws nor
priestly rites can ever make an act legitimate that
deprives innocent children of their right to life and
health.' With sobs and moans reaction came, and I
fainted in her arms. What was the sequel? Two
years later both of these children after a brief existence lay in the " city of the dead," and until my husband and I learned *the law* we could not have children
to live.'

A wife will more surely retain her health and
youthful charms in bearing welcome children. Wo-

man will rejoice in a glad maternity, and a higher, nobler and more God-like posterity will people the earth."

Rights of Wives.

Throughout the animal creation in parentage, the mother instinct is the governing power. The female rules in the reproductive domain. Mother love has been sung by poets and depicted in art and story as the strongest, purest, and most enduring of human passions. The burden of parenthood, both pre-natal and post-natal, falls more heavily upon the wife, while at the same time she is by nature more fully alive to the spiritual and less largely dominated by the physical influences of the conjugal relation.

For these reasons does it not seem that with her rightfully and properly belongs the authority which shall decide as to the frequency of the sexual relation, and of the inception of a new life?

Dr. Acton says: "In a state of nature wild female animals will not allow the approach of the male, except at long intervals, and only at certain seasons of the year. The human female, probably, would not differ much in this respect from the wild animals if she were living under natural conditions. She would not for her own gratification allow sexual congress except at certain periods."

The male is adapted, without injury to himself, to remain continent for her sake and the good of their young, and our leading medical men declare openly the same thing of the human species.

Animals are not harmed by long periods of sexual restraint, neither is man when his heart is continent.

" If a wife conceives every second year, we usually

notice that during the nine months following concep-
tion, she experiences no excitement. I have known
instances where she has evinced positive loathing for
any marital familiarity whatever. In some cases, the
wife has endured, with all the self-martyrdom of womanhood, what was almost worse than death.

" Again, while a woman is nursing her babe, there
is usually such a demand made on the vital force by
the organs secreting milk, that sexual desire is almost
deadened." Where the mother's force is diverted
from her milk to sexual enjoyments, the milk must
inevitably be robbed in a corresponding degree, and
the infant deprived of its right to full vital energy.
Thus not only does the woman but also the child
sustain injury.

Acton continues: " I have been consulted by persons who feared, or professed to fear, that if the
sexual organs were not regularly exercised, they
would become atrophied, or that in some way impotence might be the result of chastity. This is the
assigned reason for committing fornication. There
exists no *greater error* than this, or one more opposed
to physiological truth. I may state that I have, after
many years' experience, never seen a single instance
of atrophy of the generative organs from this cause.
I have, it is true, met with the complaint, but in what
class of cases does it occur? In all instances from
the exactly opposite cause—early excesses."

It is reported on good authority that Sir Isaac
Newton, who lived to an advanced age and performed
intellectual achievements that have been of untold
benefit to the world, left in writing a statement
ascribing his remarkable achievements in science and

philosophy to the fact that not a particle of semen was ever allowed to pass from his body. His vitality was abundantly taxed to sustain the frequent, prolonged activity of his brain.

Dr. Napheys attests: "We emphatically condemn as a most pernicious doctrine, one calculated to work untold evil, and to foster the worst forms of vice, the theory that any injury whatever rises from a *chaste* celibacy. The organs are not weakened, nor their power lost, nor is there a tendency to spermatorrhœa, nor to congestions, nor to any one of those ills which certain superficial and careless physicians have attributed to this state. No condition of life is more thoroughly consistent with perfect mental and physical vigor than absolute chastity. Those only suffer who are impure in thought and act."

Such objectors to chastity as are mentioned above, fail, either ignorantly or wittingly, to express any fear as to atrophy of the lymphatics. This is without doubt liable to occur from non-use of the absorbents, accompanying sexual excesses.

Clear and unmistakable are the earnest words of Dr. R. T. Trall, when he says:

"God and Nature have given to the female the supreme control of her own person, so far as sexual congress and reproduction are concerned—indeed for any and for all purposes. I am not here advocating the doctrine that sexual intercourse, with human beings, as with animals, should be limited to reproduction. This question is not now in order. But what I mean is that for any purpose, under all circumstances, it is for the female to accept or refuse, and not for the male to dictate or enforce.

" Recognize in woman this God-given right, which man has deprived her of, solely because the function of maternity and a less selfish organization rendered her practically in this respect 'the weaker vessel,' and all questions of 'equality' would soon settle themselves; and man would find in the higher elevation and superior healthfulness of woman, his own nature correspondingly elevated.

" It may be objected, that to leave this great and important question of having children entirely with woman would endanger the extinction of the race. But such an objection implies little knowledge of woman and less of nature. The desire for offspring with all women who are in normal conditions, is the strongest of their nature. It is all-absorbing, all-controlling. It is only in diseased conditions that the pains and perils of child-birth and the cares of maternity are dreaded. It is well understood by physicians that the health of a majority of civilized women is seriously impaired and their lives greatly abbreviated by too frequent pregnancies. Thousands are brought to their graves in five, ten or fifteen years after marriage, and rendered miserable while they do live, for this reason."

Dr. Alice B. Stockham, in *Tokology*, thus confirms this view: "It is due to posterity that procreation be brought under the control of reason and conscience.

" It has been feared that a knowledge of means to such control would, if generally diffused, be abused by women; that they would to so great an extent escape motherhood, as to bring about social disaster.

" This fear is not well founded. The maternal instinct is inherent and sovereign in woman. With this natural desire for children, few women would abuse the privilege of controlling procreation. Although women shrink from forced maternity and from the bearing of children nnder the great burden of suffering, as well as other adverse conditions, it is rare to find a woman who is not greatly disappointed if she does not, some time in her life, wear the crown of motherhood.

"An eminent lady teacher in talking to her pupils, once said: 'The greatest calamity that can befall a woman is never to have a child. The next greatest calamity is to have one only.' From my professional experience I am happy to testify that more women seek to overcome causes of sterility than to obtain knowledge of limiting the size of the family."

"It is for woman," again says Dr. Trall, "to nourish and sustain the new being; it is her health and life that are directly imperiled by being compelled to bear children when she is unfitted and unwilling for the sacred office. For these reasons it is her absolute and indefeasible right to determine when she will, and when she will not, be exposed to pregnancy.

"Would it not excite the just indignation of a *man* to be told by any person, even though that person were his lawful wedded wife, that he must beget children when he did not desire them? Certainly he never would submit to such dictation, such tyranny, nor should he. And why should woman? Woman's equality in all the relations of life implies her absolute supremacy in the sexual relation."

Let neither man dictate to woman, nor woman to man, but with unselfish hearts and truest mutual re-

17

gard for the rights of both, let them seek sincerely the

Best Good of the Child.

Let those touching words of our Saviour, which have brought sweet comfort to many hearts, be their inspiration: "Suffer little children to come unto me, and forbid them not; for of such is the kingdom of God."

CHAPTER XI.

MARRIAGE AND PARENTHOOD.

" Marriage—the choice of the companion who shall make life beautiful and complete, and who shall become the true father or mother of good and pure children—this is the most important question which can meet any man or any woman.

" Ideal marriage is not one-sided. Both man and woman must be striving toward perfection. As the first important factor is the possession of high ideals, the second is the possession of knowledge—knowledge of the laws of life, of what married life is in all its phases, of its possibilities, its dangers, and its sorrows, as well as of its joys. How few men understand women! How few women understand men! And yet no man or woman ought to marry without each first knowing the whole life of the other, and having some understanding of the nature of the opposite sex. There is nothing more beautiful in life than a harmoniously wedded pair, yet nothing more terrible than a mis-mated couple.

" That factor which is most indispensable to the realization of true life in all its phases, is the possession of a high ideal—a standard by which all life's affairs may be modeled and thereby rendered more beautiful and complete.

" The first duty of every young man in this direc-

tion is to have a high ideal of a wife. I once heard a
lady say that her ideal husband was a man who should
be worthy of becoming the father of her children;
and perhaps no ideal could be higher, for every true
woman must desire (if she is to be a mother at all) to
be the mother of good and pure children, and of
these she cannot be certain unless she gives them a
good and pure father."

This is correspondingly true in a man's lofty ideal
of a wife. He will desire such a woman as will make
a noble mother for his children, a woman high-
minded, sweet-natured, well-balanced and true. And
he must himself be pure and good if he would be the
husband of such a wife. He will indeed hesitate
long before asking such a woman to unite her life
with his own, unless he is willing to make that life
worthy. Else she may respond in the earnest words
of Adelaide Proctor:

> " Do you know you have asked for the costliest thing
>   Ever made by the hand above—
> A woman's heart and a woman's life,
>   And a woman's wonderful love?
>
> *   *   *   *   *
>   I look for a man and a king.
>
> " A king for a beautiful realm, called home,
>   And a man that the maker, God,
> Shall look upon as he did the first,
>   And say , ' It is very good.'
>
> " Is your heart an ocean so strong and deep
>   I may launch my all on its tide?
> A loving woman finds heaven or hell
>   On the day she is made a bride."

A Help Meet.

"It is not good that the man should be alone; I will make him an help meet for him . . . and the Lord God . . . made a woman, and brought her unto the man."

Help for what?

To carry out a man's will? To help him as a servant, a subordinate, helps him? To obey *his* wishes and notions? To wait on *him* and forward *his* plans? To have no ideas, wishes, and individuality of her own? To drown her own nature and hold herself in a receptive attitude for studying his every whim and find it her highest pleasure to seek and to serve his desires? Is that what is indicated by the word help? By no means; although it has been and is to-day largely so interpreted.

Rather is it that she was intended as meet assistance in interpreting God's will; to help him live up to, and carry out the design of their Maker in their united creation.

He should study to know what revelation of God's will can be discerned through her. And let her seek reverently to learn of the divine intent through his relations to her. Both will thus begin to subjugate their own selfish interests and desires to the higher light. They will hear and obey the message: "Take this child and train it for me, and I will pay thee wages." This is the millennial marriage. Anything short of this is not love, but exquisite self-love. True love is thoroughly unselfish. Its test is the willingness to yield one's preferences to promote the happiness, honor or welfare of the beloved. Our heavenly

Father demands this token of our allegiance to Him,
and we expect such of each other.

A great reward for all self-restraint, self-culture,
mutual forbearance and mutual help to higher living
is realized by the young wedded pair when they are
called to the holy estate of

Parenthood.

A clearer understanding of the many-sidedness of
life, and of their own responsibilities prompts a grateful backward look over the upward steps already
taken, and stimulates to more heroic efforts at self-
conquest.

Dr. C. B. Winslow in the following words makes
practical suggestions of great value: "Unite your
interests in some useful enterprise—a pursuit that
will absorb your attention, gratify a laudable ambition and satisfy your conscience. Thus, living in
the fear of God, and meriting the respect of each
other, you will cement your souls with a stronger
bond and more lasting happiness than unrestrained
passion can ever give. This course will warrant an
increase of health and vigor to feeble ones, and a
buoyant happiness to the already strong, a blessing
in the consciousness of living that no sensualist can
ever experience ; and when the desire for offspring,
under proper circumstances and conditions, makes it
best for that lawful desire to be gratified, both husband and wife will have a wealth of reserved vitality,
clear minds and consciences, clean, healthy bodies, a
fitting preparation for that wellspring of pleasure,
that messenger of peace and joy, a lovingly desired
and intentionally created child, for which quality of
children the world to-day travails in ignorance."

It is *desired* children that bless the world, honor God most surely, and are the proof of true love. Disinterested love alone enables parents to lead the pure, continent life requisite to the highest good of children. In such a life there is no harmful *repression*, but under wise direction a higher *expression* conducive to the best interests of all.

Pre-Natal Culture

has already accomplished much for the improvement of mankind, and is destined to do still more. There is at the present a growing interest in the subject, and a desire to learn not only theories but facts in regard to this parental duty.

All genuine efforts conscientiously continued will secure an impetus in the right direction toward the good of the child. Dr. Winslow again says:

" It is not the surroundings and circumstances that make up life, but the spirit and temper in which we meet the inevitable—the trials that seem to be laid on us by human ignorance, malice and selfishness, as well as those called providential. Mothers need self-control and poise while moulding character for time and for eternity. Said a mother to me, ' There are some theories that I cannot reconcile with facts— such as the statement that expectant mothers should have the best conditions provided for them. While I was carrying my Charlie our affairs were in a disastrous condition. My husband's business was established by his grandfather, and had been successfully run by its founder and by my husband's father, and its apprehended failure in our hands was a great responsibility, felt by both of us. We had shortly

before purchased a new home and fully expected to
see that swept from us in the general ruin. Yet
Charlie is the bravest and most cheerful and frolic-
some of all my five children. He absolutely knows
no fear. How can you account for that?'

"' Did you sink under these trials, worry and weep
in despair?' I asked.

"' Why no,' she replied, ' I was obliged to keep up
to sustain my husband. I exercised all the hope,
energy and sympathy I could command, and felt
equal to any emergency if the worst should come.'

"' There is your reward for the exercise of mental
and moral force. You transmitted that part of you
to your son, to live forever, and thus taught a lesson
for all time.' "

All interested in the better development of humanity will read with pleasure the extracts here given
from A. E. Newton's treatise on *Pre-Natal Culture.*

" Unlike the animal, we have the capacity to become
spiritual beings. The germ of a spiritual nature is
doubtless present in us from the first; but it needs
to be quickened and developed into conscious activity, as has been the germ of the animal. When this
takes place, earlier or later, under impregnative *spiritual* influences, then we experience a *second birth*—a
new life is born within us, we enter upon a higher
grade of conscious existence. One characteristic of
this new spiritual consciousness is *regard and care for
others*, instead of for *self*, or, in other words, *universal
love.* When once the spiritual selfhood has been born
into consciousness, it tends to become the ruling
power in us, and in proportion as its divine prompt-

ings are heeded, it will overcome and remove all the evils and impurities of the animal or selfish nature.

"This being so, the importance, on the part of both parents, of attaining both physical health and mental and moral soundness—or of what in religious phraseology has been termed 'regeneration and sanctification'—before reproduction is attempted, will be apparent to every one. It is not impossible that such a state of self-abnegation and sweet surrender to the will of the Highest may be reached, as that this higher and wiser Will may come in and work to grander and completer results than the most intelligent mother would of herself be capable of effecting."

Interesting Incident.

"Not long since I met a venerable lady of marked intelligence and spirituality, who had formerly been for many years a preacher in the Society of Friends. From her I obtained a narration of some interesting facts in her pre-natal history, as she had derived them from her mother. They were to the following effect:

"Some months previous to her birth, and while anticipating that event, her mother, who was a Quakeress, had become exceedingly despondent and oppressed with gloomy forebodings, in consequence of severe domestic trials. Poverty, privation and disgrace seemed to stare her in the face, in connection with this expec----' 'e of family. While in a state of mi..d l ..; on despair, a prominent Friend called upon her one day, bringing with him two or three copies of a new book just published. This was the journal of a distinguished Quaker preacher. then recently deceased, who had passed

through great vicissitudes and dangers in the performance of the mission to which he had felt himself
called, but had been wonderfully supported through
all by an unfaltering *trust in God.*

The mother at once seized upon one of these books,
with a strong interior feeling that in it was help and
hope for her. She obtained a copy, and almost lit-
erally devoured its contents. It brought to her the
needed help. In its perusal she seemed to be lifted
up into intimate sympathy with its author, and to
partake of the same calm trust and unfaltering faith
which had sustained him in life. Her fears and forebodings all disappeared, never again to return, and
she received in some way a premonition that her
forthcoming child would be a daughter, and would
prove a great help and comfort to her through life.

This premonition proved true. The daughter at
an early age showed a remarkable predisposition to
spiritual concerns, and in due time became an accept-
able preacher in the society, notably resembling in
many respects the one whose biography had so deeply
impressed the mother during the period of gestation;
and she was able to provide a pleasant home for her
mother for more than fifty years of her later life.

"Surely, thus to become a willing and plastic instrument through which the Highest may work
unobstructedly 'both to will and to do,' and to co-
operate energetically with the Infinite Will, is doubtless the most desirable state to which a mortal can
aspire.

"It seems not improbable that in the way thus
suggested, that is, through the instrumentality of
matrons specially receptive to these hallowing influ-

ences, no matter how lowly their estate in other regards, nor even how ignorant of the law or process involved, have been gestated and brought forth the grandest and noblest souls that have illuminated the pathway of humanity in all time. She whom all generations with one consent have called ' blessed '—the mother of the Nazarene—appears to have been a prominent example."

Mary was in a very happy state of mind during Christ's nativity. She was "in the hill country" quaffing copiously the invigorating breezes, free from sexual intrusions, and was full of heavenly joy and spiritual exaltation.

A Striking Fact

is given by the author of the valuable book entitled " Husband and Wife." It is to this effect :

A teacher in a Western State had under her instruction five children belonging to one family. The two eldest were dull, inert and slow to learn ; while the third, a girl about twelve years of age, was remarkably bright, sensitive and talented. Not only apt and quick at her lessons, she possessed a fine poetic temperament, accompanied by a keen appreciation of the beauties of nature ; she could also write a theme in prose or verse with ease and facility. The children younger than this one were both physically and mentally superior to the two eldest, but far inferior to her in talent and refinement of manners. These differences were so marked that the teacher's curiosity was excited to learn the cause. Becoming intimately acquainted with the mother (who at first could assign no reason for the diversity), the teacher at length ascertained the following facts: Some months prior to the birth of the favored child, the mother (who, though reared in an Eastern State, in the enjoyment of fair advantages, had become the wife of a farmer in a new country, deprived of literary and social privileges, and overworked in the struggle to acquire a competence) had her attention attracted to a volume of Walter Scott's poems, brought to the house by a traveling peddler. She was so seized with a desire to possess and read the book, that, not having at hand the money to purchase it, she had walked four miles at night to borrow of a friend a sufficient sum for the purpose. " And a glorious time I had in reading it," she said ; "for often in the perusal of its pages I forgot my fatigues and cares." Having read the book so often, that she came to know much of it by rote, she used to sing the songs to the child when an infant, and afterward to repeat the stories to her when a little girl. Here, no doubt, was the source of the superior intelligence, refinement and poetic tendencies of the child.

" The Father,"

again quoting from Newton, "also seeking to obey the monitions of the spirit rather than the desires of the flesh, may experience a corresponding internal preparation for paternity. This is doubtless true—though men for the most part are less conscious of these delicate spiritual leadings than are women. Hence men, as a general rule, should defer to women in these matters, especially to those of keen spiritual intuitions. But the preparation on man's part, if earnestly sought, may be no less real though it be less fully sensed. And on no consideration should one ever enter the sacred relation whence parentage may result without due preparation in himself.

" In 'this pre-natal' culture the father should take equal interest with the mother; for he is equally concerned in the object in view, namely, the production of noble and worthy offspring. Having given due attention to his own antecedent preparations, he may perform essential service in the proper development of the embryo before birth. He can assist the mother, to some extent at least, in the various exercises appropriate to its unfolding, providing the proper facilities therefor (such as means for physical exercise and travel, books, pictures, etc.). He can lend his sympathy and encouragement at every step, guarding her against all untoward conditions or influences, and thus helping to secure such a result as will be a source of mutual joy forever.

If, on the contrary, he manifests indifference, neglect, or untoward conduct of any kind, he may thwart and defeat the best efforts the mother can put forth, and may excite in her such feelings of depression, disappointment, grief, perhaps of repining, aversion, or disgust, as shall enstamp upon the child she is hearing characteristics which will prove a

Life-long Burden

or a curse. Many a child has been impressed before its birth with repugnance and dread toward its father, caused by his selfish or harsh treatment of the mother during this critical period, which can never be fully overcome in after life. Such a child is robbed of its birthright in paternal affection, and such a father robs himself of the bliss of filial love and confidence. The mother of one of the most quarrelsome, ungovernable and unhappy families of children the writer ever knew, stated to him that she never had the sympathy of the father during pregnancy in a single instance, but only his anger and dissatisfaction at her condition. A terrible penalty was that which this unhappy man drew upon himself, and a terrible curse did he inflict upon his offspring.

"To what grander achievement can either woman or man aspire than to be an artist in that

Noblest of Arts,

the moulding and rearing of immortal beings? Fadeless renown has crowned the efforts of gifted sculptors and limners in the past to portray the perfect ideal of the "human form divine." That field of High Art is open to comparatively few competitors —those fortunately endowed with rare genius. But there is a field of Higher Art, worthy of still greater honor—as much greater as the living perfect man is better than a senseless image. And this field is open to almost every one, even the humblest. Yes! the godlike privilege is brought within the reach of the great mass of those now entering the prime of manhood and womanhood, as well as of those who have not yet passed its noon-time, of *endowing with the noble gifts of genius their own sons and daughters*, however lowly born.

"Young men of America—fathers of the future race—will you not accept this high privilege, and prove yourselves worthy of it?"

CHAPTER XII.

THE WHITE CROSS.

Within a very few years an organized movement in favor of social purity originating in England, has made a widespread impression through the world. The work has been taken up in America, and many organizations have been effected. The first leader in this country was Rev. Dr. B. F. De Costa of New York City, who has been most zealous and efficient. A department of preventive◆work has also been created in the Woman's Christian Temperance Union, entitled the Department of Social Purity, which works in harmony with the White Cross Army. It has published much helpful literature and pledges for the young and the mature of both sexes.

The work which the White Cross has in view is one of prevention rather than reform; the cultivation of that purity of heart without which no man can see God. It aims to elevate opinion respecting the nature and claims of morality, yet as far as possible all needless handling of undesirable themes is avoided. Evil is overcome less by depicting the blackness of sin than by making glorious and altogether lovely and desirable the light and joy of purity.

In this work of moral elevation and instruction, literature of a character especially adapted to form a high type of manly character is disseminated, and all movements looking to better laws for protection of women and children are heartily seconded.

The White Cross movement is a work by men for young men, and the societies are composed exclusively of men. It urges the necessity of a common standard of purity for both sexes, and presents for signature and observance the following

WHITE CROSS PLEDGE:

I, ——— ———, promise by the help of God:

1. To treat all women with respect, and endeavor to protect them from wrong and degradation.

II. To endeavor to put down all indecent language and coarse jests.

III. To maintain the law of purity as equally binding upon men and women.

IV. To endeavor to spread these principles among my companions, and to try and help my younger brothers.

V. To use every possible means to fulfil the command,

"Keep Thyself Pure."

Teachers often give this pledge to young men in Sabbath school, high school or college. Business men in positions of influence have many opportunities for quiet work in this direction. Thousands of these pledges have been circulated and signed within the past six months.

" The Silver Cross " was organized in 1886, and the following pledge prepared by Dr. De Costa has been adopted as the pledge of the new society for boys, who are known as " Knights of the Silver Cross."

I, ——— ————, promise by the help of God:

I. To treat all women with courtesy and respect, and to be especially kind to all persons who are poorer or weaker or younger than myself.

II. To be modest in word and deed, and to discourage profane and impure language, never doing or saying anything I should be unwilling to have known by my father or mother.

III. To avoid all conversation, reading, pictures and amusements which may put impure thoughts into my mind.

IV. To guard the purity of others, especially of companions and friends, and avoid speaking or thinking evil.

V. To keep my body in temperance, soberness and chastity.

King Arthur and his Knights of the Round Table may find in these Knights of the Silver Cross and members of the White Cross Army true successors to an inheritance of noble living and chivalric hearts. It is, indeed, a revival of the age of chivalry, wisely adapted to the perils and duties of the day.

These pledges may be grafted upon existing societies tending to the uplifting of humanity or the conservation of society, as temperance and literary societies, Look up clubs, Sabbath schools or college clubs. It is not in any way necessary that an independent organization should be effected. One young man united in heart with God and his purposes may form an efficient White Cross Army. In many cases youths have been encouraged to form circles of five for mutual help and encouragement in this direction; and after a period sufficient to confirm their strength and acquire an intelligent understanding of the work, these have each formed a nucleus for another circle of five, thus spreading through a community, quietly and beneficently the influence of pure hearts and lives.

A Worthy Example.

A young and attractive working girl in a Western city, making her home in a boarding house, was subjected to strong temptation through the assiduous attentions of a man-about-town, of whose lack of principle she was ignorant. His preference for her society, lavish expenditure of money for her pleasure and protestations of love had won her entire confidence and affection. No other calamity appealed to her thoughts as so unbearable as the loss of his companionship and endearments. In this state of mind she had been persuaded by him to leave her boarding place and occupy a suite of rooms provided by him. Just as she had reached this fatal decision the matter was brought to the knowledge of Mr. B., a young man boarding in the same house. It came to him as a great shock. He could not be indifferent to the self-destruction of this infatuated young woman. He could not say, "It is no affair of mine. She is nothing to me." No; for his thoughts went swiftly back to his country home, and his sweet, innocent sister Mary. And over and over again the thought came, "What if Mary were being beguiled from the right, and some other should coolly stand by and see her destruction? Should refuse to lend a hand to help her? I must do what I can."

He went to the young woman and with all the tact and wisdom at his command, endeavored to counteract the wrong that had been done. But she failed to respond to his brotherly overtures, and could see no evil in her lover's attentions. She left the house. Mr. B., nothing daunted, ascertained her whereabouts and again he sought her.

With all the earnestness of his nature and with the thought of " Mary " on his heart, this pure-hearted young man plead again with the misguided girl the cause of her own honor. He recalled her mother's love, her innocent childhood. He did not forbear to lift the veil of the future and paint before her the blackness of great darkness into which she was hastening. He was rewarded. She stepped back from the pitfall and yielded to his urgent pleadings. By his advice she fled to her country home and her mother's protection. " There was joy in the presence of the angels of God " over one sinner, nay, rather one sinned against.

This experience shook Mr. B. to the very depths. He felt that he and he only, under God, had stood between a young life and its destruction. He resolved that he would ever be thus ready to help those who were "somebody's sisters." Many a girl trembling on the brink of ruin, many a fallen one lost to all but God, has this " brother of girls " led with a strong, pure hand, by the way of the cross, back to a better life and a mother's home.

Although this incident occurred long before the organization of the White Cross Army, Mr. B. was actuated by its principles and was really carrying out the first clause of its pledge. While few are adapted to do the work that he has done, all can, as the opportunity offers, throw their influence, whether great or small, in the same direction.

The second clause of the pledge is peculiarly practical and practicable. Few boys or men who mingle freely with others of their sex fail to have frequent opportunities of protesting by at least a silent gravity against the sin of indecent language. This is especially so in intercourse with those who are younger. A gentle remonstrance, a serious " I wouldn't say that," or, "Mother would not like to hear such words," will do a vast amount of preventive work and serve to carry out the fourth clause of the pledge, " to help my younger brothers."

Perhaps the greatest reform looked forward to in this work is that proposed in the pledge to " maintain the law of purity as equally binding upon men and women." This is really the true foundation stone of this movement, and upon the development and spread of this principle depends all effectual progress in the direction of social purity.

" Is it not the very strength and intensity of a

Woman's Affections

that sometimes gives a man his fatal power over her, even though morally she is the stronger? A woman, if she falls, falls often by what is highest in her—the pity of it, oh! the pity of it—her longing to give herself to the man she loves, to fling herself at his feet, even if those feet in return trample her into the dust. The man falls, if he falls, by what is lowest in him— the longing for his own selfish gratification, the base willingness to accept at another's bitter cost, to run up a bill with the devil, knowing that he can sneak out when pay-time comes, and the woman can't.

" Yet the world has agreed to lay all the blame and disgrace on the woman. The man wipes his mouth and says, 'I have done no harm,' and is received into society. The woman is cast out as a defiled and ruined thing. The woman is pushed and jostled down those dread winding stairs that lead to ever lower depths, till the last steps are bathed in the blood and tears of a lost soul, a lot so dreadful that the common pity of mankind has agreed to call the one on whom it falls 'an unfortunate.' The man ascends the drawing-room stairs, and if he be rich or titled, finds anxious mammas who are only too proud and happy to give him their unspotted girl to be his devoted wife.

" But the Christian idea is that the strong are made for the use of the weak. The Bible tells us that the man is the head of the woman. So far Jew and Christian believe alike. But our Lord tells us what is the true meaning of being head or chief. He says, 'He that would be chief, or head, let him be the servant.' In olden days, to be chief was to make other men serve you, and use them for your own purposes, and to sit idle on a throne, while they slaved. But now men have worked out a truer idea—the Christian idea that he who would be chief must be chief in service.

" 'I'd sooner,' says Adam Bede, and every true man with him, 'do a wickedness as I could suffer for by myself, than ha' brought *her* to do wickedness, and all for a bit of pleasure, as, if he'd had a man's heart in him, he'd ha' cut his hand off sooner than ha' taken it. What if he did not foresee what's happened, he foresaw enough; he'd no right to expect anything but harm and shame to her. No, there's plenty o' things folks are hanged for not half so hateful as that. Let a man do what he wills if he knows he's to bear the punishment himself; it isn't half so bad as a mean, selfish coward as makes things easy to himself, and knows all the while the punishment 'ill fall on somebody else.'

" This is not our idea of the self-sacrificing woman, but God's idea of the self-sacrificing man; the man who gives himself, sacrifices himself, without stint or limit, for the good of the woman, as Christ gave Himself without stint or limit for the good of all, holding all that He has for their good.

" The man, if he be the head of the woman, is the servant of the woman, and she is made the weaker that he may have the exquisite joy of protecting her, and caring for her, and placing his strength at her service.

" Do you ask how?

" First of all by working it out in your own life. Remember your strength belongs to the woman you will love and make your wife hereafter. Keep yourself pure for her. When you are married, all that you have and all that you are you will hold for the good of the woman you love. And there will be one woman the less in our land to fill an early grave, or have her constitution broken for life by having her children faster than her strength can bear, or than her means can feed, and clothe, and educate."

" Then to you will be fulfilled the highest promise, 'Blessed are the pure in heart for they shall see

God.' Then to the woman, the weakness and ang-
uish and degradation of the ages will be passed away,
for through the power of the Cross she will have
redeemed the man."

Manly Conduct.

"Whomsoever else you deceive," says Ruskin,
"whomsoever you injure, whomsoever you leave unaided, you must not deceive or injure, nor leave
unaided according to your power, any woman whatever, of whatever rank. Believe me, every virtue of
the highest phase of manly character begins and ends
in this—in truth and modesty before the face of all
maidens, in truth and reverence, or truth and pity, to
all womanhood."

Ellice Hopkins, who quotes these noble words in
that touching tract, entitled " My Little Sister," further declares :

"On this matter the whole tone of your character
depends. Take, first of all, the attitude of the True
Man toward women—He who came quite as much
to reveal man as to reveal God, the real man beneath
the false perishable man with which it is so often
overlaid ; the man that is in you if you will only come
to Him to work it out. See how high He placed
women, aye, even Eastern women, who had not been
ennobled by centuries of Christian freedom, and recognized equality of the sexes.

"See how instantly they rose to the touch of the
True Man, just as they will rise, the women of to-day,
to your touch, if you will clothe yourself with your
true manhood and be to them such men as Jesus
Christ was. His deepest earthly tie was to a woman,

to His blessed mother. He made women his friends.
It was a woman, aye, even a degraded woman, who
by her kisses and her tears won for the world the
word that 'He that has been forgiven much loveth
much.' Nothing in the life of the true Man on earth
stands out in more marked features than, if I may
venture to use the words, His faith in women; as if
to stamp it forever as an attribute of all true manhood, as that without which a man cannot be a man.

"Men are beginning to see that when they set small
store by a woman's virtue, when they set no store at
all on their own purity, by which alone reverence for
all womanhood is possible, they have to pay for it by
an ever-lessening hold on those virtues which all ac-
knowledge no man should be without; an ever-lessening hold on all truth, and justice, and generosity;
on all power of divine vision of love and goodness in
others, of all high seeing of duty and self-sacrifice in
themselves. The man who has lost faith in woman
has lost all power of living faith in his God. Impure
in heart, he cannot 'see God' in the humblest of His
redeemed creatures; the divinity shown even in the
weakness of women and little children touches him
with no reverence, and awakens in him no sense of
sacredness; he responds to no trust, he answers to
no sacred claim."

The One Unfailing Rule

*for a young man's conduct toward all young girls and all
women is to treat them in word, look and act, with that
consideration which he would desire shown by another to
his sister if she were placed in like circumstances.* This
test alone will enable him to refrain alike from awk-

ward restraint, undue familiarity or overt acts of wrong. It is worth volumes of etiquette, for it enters with the greatest delicacy into all situations, however unexpected.

An Instructive Illustration.

A young man of mature years traveling by rail in the far West, toward night shared his seat in the crowded car with a young girl who had entered the train at a country station. She exchanged a few remarks with him, but soon became drowsy. Overcome by sleep she laid her head upon his shoulder and fell into a sound slumber. The young man made her as comfortable as possible and acted the brother's part through the night. After she had awakened in the morning he made kind inquiries as to her comfort, and then took occasion to give her the advice and instruction which she so evidently needed. He told her that while she had, in this case, made no mistake in trusting to the honor of an entire stranger, it was extremely inadvisable that she should ever again approach a stranger with such freedom. Many men would have presumed upon such conduct to count her as a girl of doubtful morality, and would have taken advantage of her ignorance. The girl—she was scarcely more than a child, was greatly overcome by this brotherly talk. She had been entirely uninstructed hitherto, as to the dangers about her, and the necessity for circumspection and reserve in her intercourse with strangers, and was deeply touched by the kindness of this young man who had thus nobly shielded her from the results of her own imprudence. His faith in her true womanliness was rewarded.

That young women are largely entering into business life and thus mingling much more freely than formerly in business circles, is no occasion for letting down the barriers of courtesy and consideration which should mark intercourse with them. Rather is it demanded that thoughtful young men create on these new lines yet higher standards of demeanor. A noble young business man of pure heart and life, and of princely bearing, said recently, "All of my young lady friends are girls who are self-supporting, and I am proud of them. I do not desire as my friends any other kind."

"*I Write unto You Young Men, Because You are Strong.*"

To quote again from Ellice Hopkins:

" If a young girl's foolish feet have slipped ever so little, then she is, by many, considered fair game. 'She gave him encouragement; what else could she expect? It was all her own fault.' To expect that every man with an ounce of true manhood in him would at once say, 'It is my little sister! such a silly, inexperienced little sister! she doesn't in the least realize the danger she is in, and I must get between her and the edge of the precipice, and see she comes to no harm;' is this to expect the wildly impossible? Have faith in the truer woman that exists beneath all that levity and apparent lightness, and insist on treating 'your little sister' with respect till you impel her to respect herself. You will be surprised to see how quickly women will rise to your faith in them as they rose to the touch of the Christ of old. And you will find that, assuming your true attitude to them, training yourself in little daily acts of knightly service will be a priceless help to you in preserving yourself from temptation.

"So shall your manhood be cut out of one solid chrysolite, and the bright beams of God's Spirit be able to strike through and through you. So shall you win a perfect love from the woman you will care for in your after life, as one who has kept himself pure and unspotted for her, and done service to all women for her sake.

"Then, indeed, you will find that in 'giving yourself for the woman,' in being true to God's idea, in fighting with the strong temptations that would lead you to lower and degrade her, in consecrating all the strongest and holiest forces of your nature to the good, body and soul, of the woman you love, in this highest of battles, this noblest of all conflicts, you will find you have worked out the divine possibilities of your own manhood. You will find that in reverencing her you have learned to reverence yourself; that in losing your life for her, you have gained a deeper, fuller, purer life for yourself; a life with no shameful secrets in it, and no miserable, quenchless thirst of unsatisfied desires.

> ' My strength is as the strength of ten,
> Because my heart is pure.' "

PHYSICAL CULTURE.

SPECIAL EXERCISES

ADAPTED TO

PERSONS OF SEDENTARY HABITS

FOR THE

ATTAINMENT OF HEALTH, STRENGTH, LONGEVITY

AND POWER OF ENDURANCE.

Exercise of the body gives the best external aid to self-control and the harmonious development of the individual. That athletic sports are encouraged in schools and colleges portends good for the future citizen and the future state.

Health, strength, longevity and power of endurance depend mainly upon lung capacity.

The A, B, C of health lessons is in *deep natural respiration*. To accomplish this the lungs must be

(292)

filled to the bottom, and the involuntary muscles of breathing brought into action. The most eminent vocal teacher of this country asserts that in breathing, "The main action should be at the waist and below the waist." Animals and children have this natural breathing. Men and women lose it from lack of exercise and through constrictions of dress.

The curious structure of the lungs, admirably adapted to the work they have to do, renders them also keenly susceptible to abuse and neglect. Their expansive power is immense, and they can thus appropriate great quantities of pure air; being permitted to do this they become the bulwarks of the body, defending it against encroachment and attack of each and every disease.

General and habitual exercise is essential to promote this complete respiration as well as good circulation, a healthy nervous tone, and power and elasticity of the muscles.

Dr. Taylor, in Health by Exercise, says: "It is a curious and interesting fact that children and young animals, whose desire for motion is inherent, are inclined chiefly to those exercises, and those positions which necessarily affect the central region of the body.

"It is in such exercises as *climbing, rolling, crawling, jumping* and *playing* generally that these parts are most disturbed. We are convinced that the means prescribed by nature will secure healthful development and power in these most essential portions of the system. As if to insure these healthful effects, nature has ordained that by *respiration*, as an efficient and constant means, these motions shall be secured."

Deep breathing, using the diaphragm and abdom·
inal muscles, gives the most efficient exercise to the
digestive tract. Hence, its importance, for it is thus
shown to be an aid in the digestive process, as well as
the great blood purifier.

To aid in acquiring and maintaining a proper habit
of breathing, one should first know and practice the

Military Position.

1.   Heels in line, and together.
2.   Feet turned equally outward, forming an angle
of forty-five degrees.
3.   Knees straight.
4.   Body square to the front.
5.   Chest expanded and advanced, but without
constraint.
6.   Arms hung easily to the side. (Swing them out
and let them drop like a pendulum).
7.   Shoulders equal height.
8.   Shoulder blades flat.
9.   Head erect, raised at the crown (as if suspended
by a cord), not tipped in any direction.
10.   Chin *slightly* drawn in.
11.   Form raised to full height.
12.   Body poised slightly forward, so that the
weight bears mainly on the ball of the foot.
13.   Eyes straight to the front.
14.   Whole figure in such a position that a line will
pass through ear, shoulder, hip, knee and ankle.

Get this position before a glass and practice it, until
it can *always* be maintained. It gives ease, grace and
strength.

GYMNASTICS

requiring little or no apparatus, will be found valuable to people of sedentary habits. Many of them are also well adapted to the use of invalids.

Special Exercises for Deep Breathing.

1. Horizontal position on back, flex the knees and elevate the hips, resting the body on shoulders and feet. Move slowly up and down ten times. Hold each time to count ten, and then rest to count the same. Lungs had better be inflated. No exercise is more valuable for developing deep breathing. Sick and well would be benefited by taking this exercise morning and night.

2. Horizontal position on back; hands clasped over the head; raise both feet and head at same time making the body as-

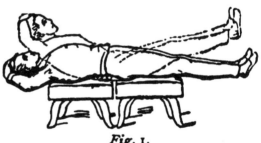

Fig. 1.

sume a curved shape; (Fig. 1.) hold to count ten; repeat this only five or six times at first. This is a powerful exercise, affecting the abdominal viscera and general circulation.

3. Stand with toes at angle of 45°, knees together, hands crossed upon the back. Bend the knees. The body is kept perpendicular and slowly descends until sitting upon the heels. Then slowly straightened, keeping trunk in same position. Count four with each movement, and from four to ten with the rest.

4. Stand as before. Palms of hands placed over lower ribs, fiugers forward. Inhale through the nostrils and expand the waist as if to burst the belt. Expel the breath slowly and assist it by pressing with the palms against the ribs.

5. Lie in the horizontal position; hands clasped over the head, the head and heels only resting on supports, as

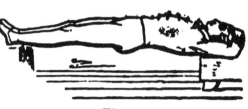

Fig. 2.

two stools, while the body is quite free; (Fig.2.) hold in this position from five to ten minutes, according to strength, practicing waist breathing; at first one might place the stools nearer together.

6. Erect position. Inhale. Finger tips to shoulders. Hold the breath to count twenty, then with clenched fist strike downward and forward. Stop suddenly as if striking an object. Expel breath forcibly with the motion. If the motion is decisive the breath will naturally be expelled by the diaphragm.

7. Same position; inhale through the nostrils; retain, to count twenty; expel through the mouth as whispering the syllable Hool to a person forty feet away.

8. Kneel with one

Fig. 3.

leg, place the other forward with the foot firm upon the floor; arms parallel, stretched upward to the side of the head; (Fig. 3.)move backward and forward slowly, while counting four to each movement, and for rest; repeat three or four times, and change to the other knee.

9. Sit on the floor; limbs horizontal and parallel; lungs inflated; hands joined over the head; move backward and forward slowly as far as possible; rest; same position, move sideways.

10. Upon both knees wide apart, hands on hips, fingers forward. (Fig. 4). Move quickly from right to left, and back as far as possible.

The following exercises will be found invaluable to promote natural breathing, increasing the number and time devoted to them as ability is gained.

11. Kneel on a cushion, knees far apart, stretch arms upwards, parallel

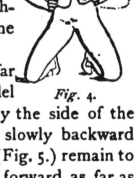

Fig. 4.

with each other by the side of the head, bend trunk slowly backward as far as possible; (Fig. 5.) remain to count four; return forward as far as possible, keeping knees and feet firm. This is one of the best exercises for strengthening the muscles of the back and pelvis.

Fig 5.

12. Same position, hands clasped on top of head, move the body from side to side slowly, count four with each movement and then rest. In the same position twist the body from right to left.

13. Same position, arms extended horizontally forward, throw them backward in a direct line as far as possible. (Fig. 6.) This may be practiced quickly, or slowly as if carrying a weight.

GOING UP AND DOWN STAIRS

takes the place of many other exercises, providing one observes the following conditions:

Fig. 6.

1. Keep the mouth closed.
2. Fill the lungs with air, holding the breath until the top is reached, and then expel slowly.
3. Maintain the erect position.
4. Step upon the entire sole of the foot.

Notice what has been accomplished. The diaphragm and abdominal muscles have been brought into action by the deep breath, while the muscles of the thigh, pelvis, perineum and groin are all engaged in elevating the body. Each time the thigh is raised, pressure is made upon the abdominal viscera, which are pushed outward and upward, and with the opposite movement resume their place.

Going up stairs is the best way to get desired exercise in a short time. A successful, self-educated man of this city said that, when studying, and his brain became weary and stupid, he left his books and ran up and down stairs three or four times, accomplishing more for himself than by half an hour's walk, or by gymnastics. For him it was both rest and recreation. The whole secret of being able to run and defy all competitors is to *keep the mouth closed.* Why? Simply because it *forces deep breathing*, and compels the use of the diaphragm. Any one can prove this. So with any exercise, but especially in climbing hills or stairs, *keep the mouth closed.*

In many people the muscles of the chest, trunk and abdomen, are weak and atrophied. " They have not been trained to life's occasions."

The following exercises will produce vigor of muscle, accelerate the circulation, increase the action of all the digestive organs, and also correct any tendency to hernia.

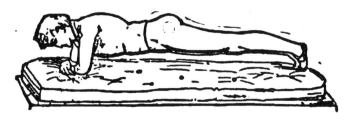

Fig. 7.

14. Horizontal position, face dowward. Elevate the body slowly five times, resting only on toes and elbows (Fig. 7). Hold to count ten.

15. Kneel face downward, gradually raise the hips until the whole weight rests upon the shoulders. Remain in this position for five minutes. One may get the position more readily by sliding off from a bed or lounge head first; relatively, standing on one's head.

16. Sit upon a stool, feet firmly upon the floor, hands upon sides, hips firm ; sway body from side to side as far as possible.

17. Same position, hands clasped over the head; sway body backward and forward.

18. Same position ; combine Nos. 16 and 17 in a

twisting motion of the body. The effect of the three last can be varied by holding one or both hands perpendicularly over the head.

19, 20, 21. Same as 16, 17 and 18, only standing position.

The beneficial effects are increased in the six last by inflating the lungs.

Occupations are tending more and more each year to specialties. This is in many respects a benefit, for a man learns to do one thing well, giving him a greater chance to excel in his line. But physically this may be unfortunate. It does not conduce to an all-round development. Some muscles are unduly exercised, to the detriment of others which are seldom used. There is greater need, therefore, for thought and action in the direction of systematic, healthful exercise.

A little attention to the subject, with careful experimenting, will enable a young man to decide which special movements are most restful and invigorating.

Experience and observation prove that so nicely has Nature fitted in one part to another, that no one portion of our being can be exclusively cultivated or trained without detriment to the others. To attain a perfect manhood, the mental, moral and physical should be co-educated. This is also true of the various members, nerves and muscles of the body.

The joyousness of physical well-being is the privilege and duty of every man. But how can the enjoyment of living come to one whose unduly stimulated nerves are never relieved by wholesome and thorough-going exercise, whose system is subject only to one-sided and partial development ?

Office Gymnastics.

Some exercises taken in a sitting position are especially beneficial in the line of developing the muscles and equalizing the circulation. Their practical value is great in that they can be used during the noon interval in shop or office, when one is weary with sitting or standing.

22. Sit on the edge of a chair, with thighs at right-angles, arms extended vertically above the head and parallel to each other,

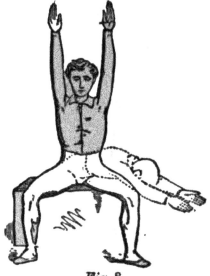

Fig. 8.

(Fig. 8). The trunk falls slowly forward in a line over one thigh, bringing the breast close to the knee. Resume the first position. Repeat five times, alternating beween the right and left sides.

23. Same position, except that it may be necessary to secure the feet by placing them under some firm object. Trunk falls slowly backward (Fig. 9), then slowly regains first position. Repeat five times.

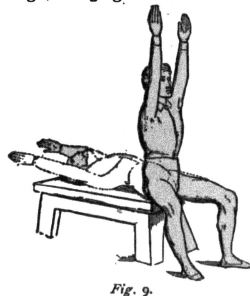

Fig. 9.

24. Position as before, one hand placed upon the hip, the other stretched perpendicularly upward (Fig. 10). The trunk remains perpendicular; neither bending nor swaying in any direction, but *twists* on its own axis, while the seat remains immovable on the chair.

25. Standing position, leaning backward, elbows flexed, upper arm close to the body, one leg placed

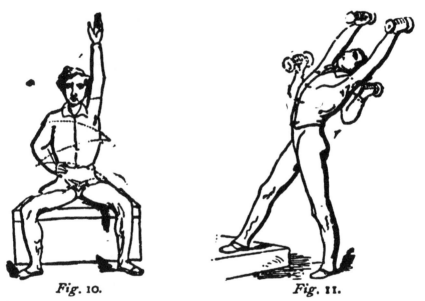

Fig. 10.   Fig. 11.

forward on stool, weight of the body mainly upon the other leg (Fig. 11). The arms slowly rise, till they become straight and parallel, with head thrown back. Retain this position for a few moments. The arms then *slowly* resume the first position. Repeat four times. Reverse position of legs and repeat.

Noon Stretch.

For busy people who can have little time for recreation or systematic gymnastics, the following exercise can be made to supplant the need of most all others: Inflate the lungs slowly—at the same time rise upon the tiptoes (Fig. 12) lifting the arms and reach as high as possible. Then slowly expel the air, at the same time stoop and touch the floor, still reaching out.

This one exercise involves nearly every muscle of the body, and repeated four or five times will give the same benefits as a run. of half a mile. It is especially recommended to book - keepers, stenographers, telegraphers and others of sedentary habits. Although we have named it the *noon stretch*, it will be found a valuable morning stretch as well, for it awakens every fibre and faculty, and if accompanied by the strong mental demand for health and strength, will be an efficacious tonic or stimulus upon which to begin the most arduous day's work.

Fig. 12.

In taking any of the foregoing exercises, especially those to develop lung power, always carry with it the declaration of health. Many an acute attack, such as cold, headache, neuralgia, etc., can be warded off, if one understands how to do this. Fill the lungs and hold the breath; during this time mentally protest against the encroachment or presence of disease; the essential point is to hold to the *positive principle of health*.

One can think this:—" If breath is life, life is health; with this breath I claim health," or with the breath, deny the power of sickness over the body. Some claim

that they can control disease, or banish it entirely by
thought alone.   If this is true, one can educate himself
to do this much more readily through the process of
breathing, for the breath is the emblem of life, strength
and vitality.   *The more breath the more life.*

INDIAN CLUBS

square the shoulders and strengthen the chest, back
and arms, besides conducing to graceful movements
and easy manners.   They are the gymnast's specific
for pulmonary complaints, and are particularly useful
to counteract the injurious effects of sedentary life.

Clubs should be selected with discrimination, being
careful not to get them too heavy.   A club about
eighteen inches long and three or four inches in diameter, is suitable for most persons.

In practicing, stand erect, expand the chest, square
the shoulders and slightly elevate the chin, look
straight to the front, lean a little forward so as to have
the weight center on the balls of the feet, have the
heels two inches apart, with the toes spread at an
angle of forty-five degrees.

No skill can be acquired when the movements are
done in a careless or awkward manner.

In Fig. 1 the black spots represent the handle of
the club and the centre of the circle made by the
other end of the club, the hand being held nearly
stationary.

All club-swinging may be resolved into THREE distinct movements: the Straight-arm, the Bent-arm and
the Wrist movements.   All combinations of move-

CLUB SWINGING.

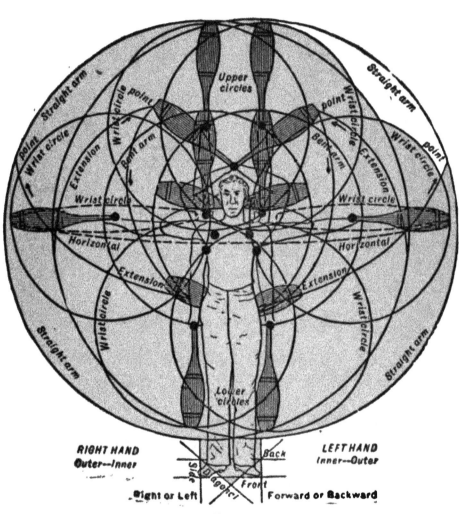

Fig. 1.

ments are made by variations of these, holding the arm in different positions while the club is made to describe the circles.

Any circle done in one direction can be reversed and made in the opposite direction.

Any circle done with the hand in any one of the nine positions can be done with the hand in any of the other positions.

Thus the pupil will be able to invent combinations.

Position.

First bring the club to the starting position, (Fig. 2.) with the hand opposite the breast, the elbow closely pressed to the side, the knuckles turned out and the club extended vertically.

Fig. 2.

Straight-Arm and Wrist Positions.

1. Arm extended vertically, making a wrist circle.
2. Arm extended horizontally, making a wrist circle.
3. Arm down, making wrist circle in front.
4. Arm down, making wrist circle at the back.

Bent-Arm Positions.

5. Back of the shoulder.
6. Front of the shoulder.
7. Over the opposite shoulder.
8. Front of the opposite shoulder.
9. Under the opposite arm.

Rules.

1st. Start every circle or movement from this position.

2d. Let every movement be done in perfect time.

3d. Exercise the greatest precision.

Remember that horizontal means exactly horizontal, and perpendicular means no deviation. By the persevering observance of these three rules, grace and elegance, as well as health and strength will be attained. Describe all the circles squarely to the side or front, and do not move too rapidly. ·

Let it not be forgotten that in every exercise where it is possible, the right arm performs the feat first, then the left, then the two arms alternately, and last of all simultaneously. In each case the feat is to be executed five times.

Inner Movement. Fig. 3.

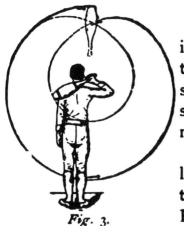

Fig. 3.

This movement combines the inner bent-arm circle, back of the shoulder and the plain straight-arm movement or sweep in front of the body, thus making a circle within a circle.

Execute the same with the left hand, carrying the club to the right instead of the left. Reverse for outer movement.

The only difference between the inner and outer circles is the direction of swinging them. With the right hand you drop the club to the right for the outer circle, and to the left for the inner circle, and the reverse of both these with the left hand.

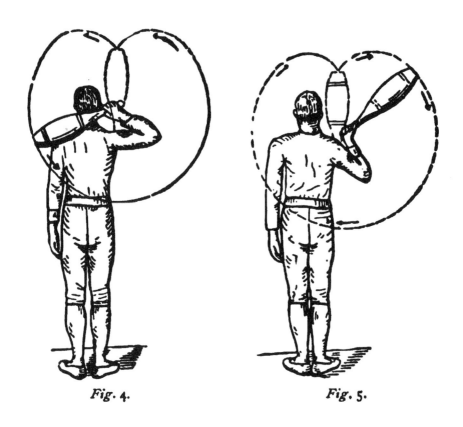

Fig. 4.   *Fig. 5.*

Bent-Arm Circles, Back. Figs. 4 and 5.

Hold the club in the starting position, raise the arm and drop the club over the shoulder, make a complete circle behind the back, and repeat. Allow the wrist perfect freedom, do not hold the club too tight, as it will make the movement awkward. In the inner circle let the hand pass from the top of the head to the back of the neck.

Side Movement. Fig. 6.

From the starting position, drop the club forward or back, letting it turn loosely in the hand, finish the bent-arm circle with a straight-arm circle, both being complete. Repeat with the left hand.

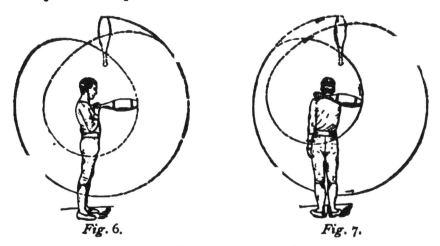

Fig. 6.   *Fig. 7.*

Over-Arm Movement. Fig. 7.

From the starting position raise the arm and extend it across to the opposite shoulder. Drop the club over it and make it describe a complete circle behind the back. Throw the head back to allow the arm to go over the shoulder as far as possible.

Finish with a straight-arm circle and repeat. Execute the same with the left hand. Reverse to the inner movement.

Under-Arm Movement. Fig. 8.

Extend horizontally the arm not in use. Drop the club, reaching as far as possible, turn the knuckles out and describe the circle behind the back, with the hand close up under the opposite arm.

In this movement combine the straight-arm with the under-arm circle. Reverse to outer-circle. Execute in the same manner with the left hand.

Extended-Arm Wrist-Circles. Fig. 9.

Turn the club in the hand, horizontal, to the right or left above or under the arm, or forward or backward on either side of it.

Fig. 8.　　　　　　　　　Fig. 9.

Let the club roll in the hand and endeavor to keep it perfectly horizontal or vertical. When swung in front fiuish with a straight-arm circle. Keep the arm stationary.

Front Bent-Arm Circle. Fig. 10.

Bring the shoulder forward, hold the hand in front of the opposite shoulder, turn the palm out, carry the club around for a complete circle and finish with a straight-arm circle. This circle is made principally by the action of the hand and wrist. Reverse, swinging with the other hand,

Double Movements.

The best method for learning these is as follows: Hold the clubs in the starting position, go through the movement several times with the right hand, then do the same with the left. Repeat, making one circle less with each hand and continue, making one less each time, until the movement is done once with each hand. Then count the circles and proceed.

Parallel Movement. Fig. 11.

This movement is a combination of the Inner and

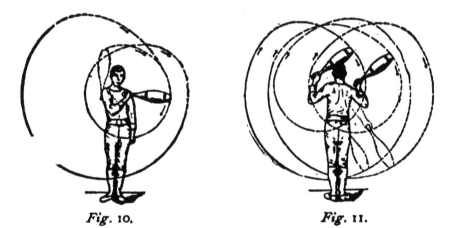

Fig. 10.   Fig. 11.

Outer circles, the clubs moving parallel for a complete circle.

It is of great importance to thoroughly understand that the descriptions of double movements are not only for the Straight-arm circles, but also for every circle described in the Single circles. They can all be done in the ways described, and any two or more can be combined.

All of the double movements can be varied into

parallel movements by making the clubs follow each other like the wings of a windmill, retaining the same relative distances.

Cross Movements, Inner or Outer.   Fig. 12.

For the Inner Cross-circle, start by crossing the arms or clubs at the top of the circle and separating them at the bottom, coming together and crossing as before at the top.

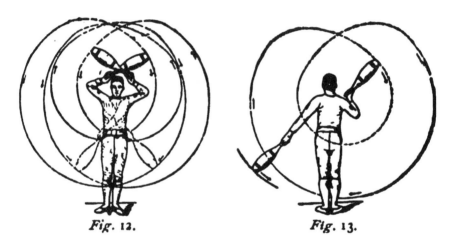

Fig. 12.　　　　　　　　　*Fig.* 13.

For the Outer Cross-circle, start by separating the arms or clubs at the top and crossing them at the bottom.

Combined with the Lower Back or Front circles this movement is very pretty.

Outer Reverse Movement.   Fig. 13.

The Outer Reverse movement is the Outer Straight and Bent-Arm circles combined, the arms or clubs crossing and separating at the sides of the circles. Start by swinging one half of a circle with one hand before moving the other; then move both toward each other passing at the outermost part of the circle, repassing at the opposite side.

To combine the Straight and Bent-Arm circles, as in the figure, start both clubs in opposite directions at the same time, make the right hand club describe a complete Outer Bent-Arm circle, while the left describes an Outer Straight-Arm circle, the clubs regaining the starting position together. Then repeat, making the left hand club describe the Bent-Arm circle, and the right, the Straight-Arm circle.

First Exercise for Heavy Club. Fig. 14.

Stand with the feet well braced, as in the figure. From the Starting Position raise the club and drop it over the head and let it hang behind the back, then reverse the movement, passing the club with arm extended, around in front and up to a horizontal position behind the back.

Fig. 14.

Vary the movement by passing the club to the right or left of the body.

Second Exercise for Heavy Club. Fig. 15.

Raise the club, drop it over the shoulder, extend the arms to full height, pass the club in a full sweep in front of the body and as far up behind as possible.

Reverse the movement, carrying the club to the Starting Position. Make the movement over the head principally with the wrist.

Straight-Arm Exercise. Fig. 16.

Extend the arms full length, pass the clubs in opposite directions describing full circles. Reverse the movements. Vary the movements by swinging both

Fig. 15.   *Fig.* 16.

clubs in the same direction but having them at opposite sides of the circle.

Turn the body from side to side to assist the movement of the arms.

None of the manly sports is more fascinating than the use of the Indian clubs. Interest constantly grows more intense, and ambition is stimulated to excel, especially in the line of invention. To produce new figures and evolutions is an absorbing diversion, of which the enthusiast never wearies.

The mind and body are gently and healthfully stim ulated together, thus securing an ideal recreation.

THE HORIZONTAL BAR .

is, taking all things into consideration, the most useful
of all the appointments of the gymnasium.   It brings
into play and thus benefits the muscles of the arms,
wrists, hands, chest, spine, loins, hips, legs and abdomen; in a word, it exercises nearly all the muscles of
the body.   It is a convenient substitute for the trapeze
or swinging bar.

The Horizontal Bar should be made of ash or hick-
ory, turned perfectly round, one and three-fourths inches
in diameter, except at the ends, where the shoulders
should be formed to slide up and down in the grooves
between the standards.   These latter should be seven
feet apart and seven feet high, formed in two pieces
with a space or continuous groove of one and three-
fourths inches between them to receive the shoulder
at the end of the bar.   If the standard is pierced
with holes two inches apart, through which movable wrought iron pins are inserted for it to rest
on, the bar may be adjusted to any required height.
In order to fix the proper height for the bar, stand on
tiptoe and reach up so as to merely touch it with the
outstretched fingers of both hands.   At this height
the gymnast can just swing clear of the ground when
hanging by the hands.

EXERCISES.

1. *Hanging by the Hands.*

1.   Spring from the ground, grasping the bar, with
the arms stretched straight forward, thumb and fingers
together, trunk upright, the legs straight, legs and feet
together and toes pointed to the ground.   (Fig. 17.)

Fig. 17.

2. Remain hanging in this way as long as possible without over-fatigue. This exercise may be varied by hanging by each hand alternately, also by raising the body and lowering it alternately with the right or left hand. The use of one hand only should not be practiced, however, unless the muscles have sufficient strength and elasticity to sustain the weight of the body coming upon one arm alone.

II. *To Swing by the Arms.*

1. As in first exercise.

2. Swing the legs and body a little in front, then suddenly dropping them, swing forward again, endeavoring to gain sufficient impetus on the return oscillation to almost describe a semi-circle and carry the body back and beyond the bar. Similar motions given to the legs and body on the return forward swing will cause them to rise higher to the front than before. These efforts repeated will soon enable the learner to swing the body forward and backward *above* the level of the bar. Avoid *jerking* the legs.

Do not be afraid of swinging too high. Swing backward and forward five or six times, and when the feet have risen to a level with the face, leave the bar, in the forward swing. A slight *forward* impetus should be given, by a spring from the wrists, just before releasing the hand from the bar. This will enable the learner to alight on the toes, in a graceful manner, at some distance forward from the bar.

Or, watch for the exact point of equipoise at the end of a backward swing; then let go of the bar and drop easily to the ground. The point of equipose is reached when the swing assumes a direction somewhat above the horizontal line of the bar.

III. *To Rise Above the Bar.*

Stand with shoulders at right-angles to the bar. Spring from the ground and grasp the bar with both hands, the left in advance, thumb and fiugers meeting.

2. Bend the arms, lift the legs, separating the feet as they rise, pass the left leg over the bar, flexing the knee, pass the right leg under the bar and over the left leg, resting the calf of the right on the instep of the left, the head held back and trunk sustained.

3. Letting go with the right hand, pass it under the bar to the opposite side and grasping the bar, rest the fore-arm on it. Then straighten the left leg, and swing it rapidly under the bar, with a momentum sufficient to enable the body to rise above it. Press strongly with both hands, extend the arms, advance the left leg, and rest on the bar. In descending, rebend the right arm, draw back the left leg, lower the body, and again place the right leg over the left. Detach the legs from the bar, straighten the arms and descend with heels raised, knees bent, and whole frame relaxed, thus breaking the shock of the fall.

IV. *To Turn Round the Bar.*

1. Take position as in first exercise, having the thumb and fingers meet around the bar.

2. Lift the lower limbs to the front, flexing at the hips, until the feet are as high as the bar, keeping the arms straight. Bend the arms, carry the feet and lower limbs over the bar, letting the hips pass up the side of the bar and over it. While the head and shoulders ascend, straighten the legs from the hips, until the whole body has cleared the bar, and rests in a perfectly vertical line on the hands, on the bar, with arms extended (Fig. 18).

Fig. 18.

To descend, flex the elbows, letting the body down, straighten the arms and descend as in exercise III.

V. *To Turn Round the Bar, the Hands Reversed.*

1. As in preceding exercise, but with the grasp of the hands reversed, that is, with the palm turned in toward the face:

2. As in preceding exercise. In descending, bring the elbows close in by the sides, tighten the grasp of the hands, slowly incline the head and shoulders to the

Fig. 19.

front, elevate the lower limbs to the rear, support the body upon the fore-arms (Fig. 19), return over the bar, passing the body again under it, bring the lower limbs to the vertical line, and descend as before.

VI. *To Rise to the Bar.*

1. As in exercise IV.

Fig. 20.

2. Flex the elbows, raising the body until the chin rises above the bar, (Fig. 20.), sink again to the full extension of the arms, quit the grasp and descend as before.

This exercise may be repeated with the legs flexed at hips and extended horizontally in front.

Repeat three, six, nine or twelve times, according to ability of learner. Repeat with grasp reversed.

VII. *To Rise Above the Bar by the Fore-Arm, Right and Left.*

1. As in exercise IV.
2. Bend the arms until the chin rises above the bar; then raise the right elbow and extend the fore-arm along the bar, then the left elbow; pressing strongly with the hands, straighten the right arm to its full extension, then the left, and remain sustained by the hands, in a vertical position above the bar. (Fig. 18.) To descend, return the left fore-arm first to the bar, then the right; pass the left fore-arm beneath the bar, the right following, quit the grasp and descend gently.

VIII. *To Rise Above the Bar, Right and Left.*

1. As in exercise IV.
2. Flex the arms until the chin rises above the bar; raise the right elbow vertically above the bar, the left following. Straighten both and rise above the bar in the vertical line. (Fig. 18.) .

To descend, re-bend the left arm, the right following, then let the left arm sink below the bar, the right following, straighten the arms and descend easily.

This exercise may be repeated left hand leading.

IX. *To Rise Above the Bar, Both Hands at Once.*

1. As in exercise IV.

2. Flex both arms until the chin rises above the bar, and without pause press strongly upon the bar with both hands at once; continue the upward movement and rise above it, sustaining the body on the hands, in the vertical position above the bar. (Fig. 18.)

These movements must be completed without any pause and at an even pace.

To descend, slowly re-bend the arms, sink beneath the bar, quit the grasp and descend gently.

X. *To Rise Above the Bar Backwards, Right and Left.*

1. As in exercise IV, but the grasp of right hand reversed.

2. Raise the lower limbs in front until the feet are as high as the bar, pass the feet under the bar, between

Fig. 21.

the hands, straighten the lower limbs, letting them descend (Fig. 21); elevate the right side of the body, bringing it close up by the bar, and pressing strongly with the right hand until the fore-arm is straight above the bar, slackening but not quitting the grasp of the left hand; then rest the weight of the whole body on the right arm, quit the grasp of the left hand, and re-grasp the bar *beyond* the right, thus turning the breast fully round to the bar, and rest again equally on both hands.

To descend, reverse the movements, or descend, as in Exercise IX.

This exercise should be repeated left and right.

XI. *To Rise Above the Bar Backwards, Both Hands at Once.*

1. As in Exercise IV, but with grasp of both hands reversed.

2. As in Exercise X, to the point where the grasp of the left hand is quitted. Instead of doing this, elevate the left side and raise the forearm above the bar; press strongly from both hands and rise, seated on the bar.

In descending reverse the movements.

XII. *To Sit on The Bar.*

1. Rise above the bar, as in Exercise IX.

2. Throw the left leg over the bar, grasp the bar outside the left thigh with the left hand; then throw the right leg over the bar, grasp the bar outside the right thigh with the right hand, and assume an upright sitting position.

XIII. *To Sit on the Bar. Slow Movement.*

1. As in first exercise.

2. Throw the head and body back, bring the legs up under the bar between the arms, then *over* the bar, the head back far as possible, so that the face is parallel with the ground (Fig. 22), shorten the arms with

Fig. 22.

an effort, pulling the body up, so that the seat is a little over the bar; *bend* the legs backward over the bar as much as possible; then lengthen the arms, bringing the body into a sitting posture. When the position shown in Fig. 22 is gained, the body can be drawn up so as to bring the center of gravity above the bar; when this is accomplished, the bending of the legs easily brings the body up into a sitting position.

XIV. *To Sit on the Bar and Swing Round Forward.*

1. Sit on the bar as in exercise XIII.

Fig. 23.

2. With reversed grasp seize bar with both hands, support the weight of body on straightened arms (Fig. 23); raise the body as far above the bar as possible, chest out, head back, legs straight. Clasp the bar firmly, swing forward the body with impetus, keeping the arms straight and make a complete turn forward around the bar.

XV. *The Short Swing or Circle, Backwards.*

1. Rise above the bar as in exercise IX (Fig. 18).

2. Rest the pit of the stomach against the bar, move gently but determinedly the lower limbs, to and fro; throw the head back, the legs forward and upward.

Fig. 24.

This movement, greatly assisted by the wrists, will (if done properly) give sufficient impetus to enable the body to revolve around the bar and return to the original position. (Fig. 18).

It will take considerable practice to go around without allowing the body to touch the bar, yet it can in time be done, though the wrists will then have all the work to do. (Fig. 24).

XVI. *To Hang by the Legs.*

1. As in first exercise, but hands wider apart.

2. As in exercise XIII as far as where the legs are brought up under the bar between the arms.

3. Flex the knees over the bar, clasping firmly; letting go with the hands at the same time; hang by the knees with the arms folded across the chest.

Remain for a short time in this position, then raise the body, grasp bar with both hands, remove the right leg and, passing it under the bar, rest it on the instep of the left foot. Let go with the hands and hang by the left leg. Alternate, hanging by the right leg. Continuous practice in this exercise is exceedingly strengthening to the knee joint, and will be found a great advantage to those who would climb mountains.

XVII. *To Swing by the Legs.*

1. Hang by the legs, as in preceding exercise with feet pointing toward the ground.

2. Drawing up the body in the forward movement, and carrying the arms as far back as possible in the backward swing, move the body to and fro.

XVIII. *To Pass Through the Arms.*

1. As in first exercise.

2. Bring the feet up and pass them through between the hands, without touching the bar with them; then drop them until they nearly touch the ground. (Fig. 25). This may be repeated several times.

These exercises cover the principal evolutions on the Horizontal Bar. A young man who has fully mastered them has attained sufficient proficiency for all practical purposes.

Constant practice will enable the learner to reduce the severe strain

Fig. 25.

put upon the muscles, to a considerable degree, by discovering the point in each where the severest exertion is needed, and then concentrating his energies upon that point.

WHEELING,

Or bicycle riding has come to be very popular, as shown by the numerous clubs all over the country. Many use the wheel in going to and from business, while for a vacation nothing can be better than a tour on wheels through the country, roughing it on the way. One summer, six boys of Jacksonville, Ill.,

spent three weeks of their vacation in this way, traveling over 1,000 miles, sleeping at farm houses, in barns,
or wherever night found them, returning at the end of
the time, brown and dusty and travel stained, but full
of health and vigor, with a stock of vitality laid in,
to carry them prosperously through the coming winter
of college life.

The consciousness of strength and agility makes a
man courageous. He is like a soldier with his armor
on, ready for battle. In time of danger he is cool and
ready for action; his nerves are under his control and
quick to carry the messages of the brain to the muscles, which are equally quick to respond.

APPENDIX.

THE WHITE CROSS.

ITS ORIGIN AND PROGRESS.

BY B. F. DE COSTA, D. D.

The White Cross Movement owes its existence to an instinctive sympathy for increasing good. To judge otherwise is to labor under a popular misapprehension as to the growth of evil. Its founders are not pessimists. They do not believe that the world is growing worse, even though specific evils, proportionally, may be on the increase. The origin of the White Cross was essentially unlike that of various existing societies for the purpose of combating evil. These, in the main, represent a negative work. This negative work is one of long standing in the history of the English-speaking world. Its development in England was coincident with the Great Reformation, when there was a joint crusade against false morals and false theology.

The enormity of prostitution three hundred years ago pressed upon the soul of Wat Tyler, firing his heart to such a degree, as to turn him aside, while on his march to London, to destroy in Surrey those

dens of vice which flourished there with the conniv-
ance and consent of many of the nobility and others
high in social life:

About the year 1870 a movement was begun for
the abolition of the laws for the State Regulation of
Vice, which had been enacted by the British Parlia-
ment. Mrs. Josephine Butler, with great ability
and courage, has devoted the better portion of her
life to this monstrous evil as it existed in Great
Britain. She is still doing heroic service for the general cause of purity, in which many women of Great
Britain are actively engaged.

Work was undertaken in 1877 to destroy the system
of exporting girls from England to the Continent for
the purposes of vice. This work is still going on, and
in parts of the Continent, effort in this direction is
needed more than ever before. In our own country
this traffic is conducted with more or less impunity,
and the evil, if possible, is on the inerease, demanding
even now perhaps, a special agency to counteract the
efforts of bad men.

During the summer of 1885, Mr. William Stead, in
the "Pall Mall Gazette," struck the finishing blow
at state regulation of vice in England, though the
crusade is still being carried on in the British colonies,
in some of which, as in India, the application of State
Regulation now shocks the moral sense of both Hindoo
and European. Thus we see that in the generations
all along, most of the attempts in the interest of morals
have assumed a suppressive or negative character,
purposing to strike down the evil rather than to build
up the good. The White Cross aims indeed to over-

come evil, but it seeks to act positively, overcoming evil by presenting the good. When any one in his heart accepts and comes into full understanding of the power of good, evil cannot enter, any more than darkness can affect a room already flooded with light. Therefore, we have said that the movement took its origin out of sympathy for good and for the *increasing* good. This point should be distinctly understood, if we wish to avoid error respecting the principles, methods and general expectations of the White Cross Society. The White Cross Crusade must not be accepted as a sign of increasing moral failure in the world at large. It exists, because the world is becoming *better* instead of becoming worse. It forms a declaration of the fact, that men and women are no longer willing to tolerate the low moral tone that was so long one of the marked characteristics of society. It points to the encouraging reality that a higher, nobler and purer life is coming in. Hence it is declared again and again that this movement was not born of the sewer but of the fountain. It has come out of the growing love of purity, not out of pollution. It draws its vitality from the River of Life. Like Siloa's Brook, it flows fast by the Oracles of God.

ORGANIZATION.

The organization of the White Cross began February 14, 1883, at Bishop-Aucland, Durham, England, under the guidance and direction of that distinguished scholar, Bishop Lightfoot. Miss Ellice Hopkins was present, and took part in the deliberations. This was done, it will be seen, before Mr.

Stead's work at London began. The White Cross
movement, therefore, had no connection with the
great work of Mr. Stead, and should never be con-
founded with it; nor with any of those numerous
undertakings that have been devised for combating
evil. At the same time this movement is in sympathy
with every wisely ordered plan for the moral improvement of mankind. Dr. Lightfoot indicates some of his
reasons for undertaking the White Cross Crusade in
a letter which he addressed to the people for whose
moral improvement he was the more particularly
responsible. In the course of the letter, he said:
"The visit of Miss Ellice Hopkins to these northern
counties has awakened in many consciences the sense
of a strong responsibility, unrealized hitherto, on a
question affecting more nearly than any other the
physical, moral, and spiritual well-being of England.
Those who have heard her appeal on behalf of her
wronged and degraded sisters—her sisters and ours
—feel that they cannot any longer let the matter rest
where it is." It is to Miss Hopkins that we owe so
much in connection with this movement, her life, her
talents and her inspiring eloquence being consecrated
to the growth and support of the White Cross. Under
this most distinguished advocacy and combined leadership, the movement at once took its way through
the world. Its symbolic color declares its nature,
linking it with the purity of Alpine snows, the spotless lily and the enduring marble; while its cross
teaches "the truth that the whole movement is
based on the perfect manhood of our Lord, and on
self-giving as the root of all true manhood, as of all
true womanhood."

WATCHWORD AND PLEDGE.

For its motto the founders took the words of the spotless Knight, Sir Galahad :

> "My strength is as the strength of ten,
> Because my heart is pure."

For its platform these five Principles were adopted :

1.—To treat all women with respect, and endeavor to protect them from wrong and degradation.
2.—To endeavor to put down all indecent language and coarse jests.
3.—To maintain the law of purity as equally binding upon men and women.
4.—To endeavor to spread these principles among my companions and to try to help my younger brothers.
5.—To use every possible means to fulfil the command, "Keep THY-SELF pure."

The authorship of these grand principles is credited to Colonel Everett Poole, who in them has furnished the basis of a moral creed destined to prove as extended as the human race, demanding a single standard of purity for man and woman.

The movement soon began to spread, and in due time it reached Scotland and Ireland. It has taken a strong hold in such seats of learning as Oxford, Cambridge, Edinburgh and Dublin, and is making rapid progress in India, Africa, Australia and Canada, as well as in other portions of the world under English rule.

In the United States the work was first undertaken by the young men of the Church of St. John the Evangelist, in New York City. They organized Branch No. 1, which observed its first anniversary

February 8, 1885. Since then the work has spread over the United States and Territories. Young Men's Christian Associations in many localities have taken a leading part in its introduction. A work of great magnitude and value has also been accomplished by the National Woman's Christian Temperance Union, under the able leadership of Miss Frances E. Willard. This, the largest and most useful society ever organized by women, is now successfully managing a department of Social Purity, co-operating with the White Cross. One can hardly exaggerate the value of woman's participation in this work. For while the White Cross is a society composed exclusively of men, and seeks by saving men to save women, yet women exert a peculiar influence which men cannot command, and secure thereby a degree of attention which otherwise the work might fail to receive.

THE OUTLOOK FOR THE FUTURE.

No recent movement has been so favorably received as this. Though critics have not been wanting, it has nevertheless been styled by a high authority "the greatest Crusade of the Nineteenth Century." What, therefore, of the future? Of this movement it may truly be said that it has no ambitions, and is animated by no spirit of rivalry. It is co-operative in its principles and policy, being ready to work with, or operate independently of other organizations. It is ready, as occasion demands, to enter any open door, and to fill any place, large or small.

It holds out its helping hand to Churches, Pastors, Teachers, Publishers, Temperance Societies, Societies of Christian Endeavor, Sunday Schools, Bible Classes and all the varied agencies now in operation for the improvement of humanity. It has only one desire, namely, to see the work of purity everywhere advancing. Coming with such large and beneficent aims, and in such a generous spirit, it cannot be otherwise than that a career of usefulness should lie before it in the future. The movement is every way flexible and fitted to go with every other good movement of moral and spiritual aims. The times call imperatively for action. The condition of things demands instant and unceasing activity, from both pulpit and press. Though the White Cross has been called into existence by the growing love of what is pure, one must not forget that the mission of purity is to overcome impurity. The work is lofty and arduous, and calls for the consecration of all that is highest and best. It is not a work for weak hearts or feeble hands. It calls us to a struggle with an evil far more widely spread, and more deeply implanted than the evil of intemperance. There are Eastern nations, comprising hundreds of millions of people, deeming it a sin to touch a drop of wine, who are nevertheless sunk in the deepest sensuality. Men may doubt about the ultimate success of the White Cross, but do not men likewise question the whole future of Christianity? They tell us that human nature, being what it is, we must not hope for any complete and permanent victory. Even Christian men are heard to say these things, regardless of the fact that in so saying they embrace one of two doubtful positions,—either that humanity being what it is, indulgence in vice, is not, upon the whole, very criminal, perhaps not criminal at all; or else, in the second place, that God has made the nature of man such as to render the regeneration and purification of the social system impossible. These doubts proceed on the theory that in the struggle for purity man's nature is wholly against him, and consequently, though they would refuse, in this connection, to avow it, that the very constitution of his nature is wholly and hopelessly bad, and altogether beyond the reach of the ordinary operations of Divine grace. This sad view of the situation is entirely unchristian, and does not recognize the innate good in man. The advantage lies to-day with the friends of social purity. Man's nature, if we could only understand it, is on that side. God is on that side. Man was formed for holiness. If one desires to know what is possible in the future, let him consider what has been accomplished in the past, and realize the radical change that has been effected in society.

A BACKWARD GLANCE.

Eighteen hundred years ago, when the Apostle to the Gentiles went out to his work, he found vice, not only universally practiced, but protected as a lawful traffic by the State, and forming a part of its religion. The whole weight of society was thrown in its favor. The worship of the Cyprian goddess was the orthodox worship, and mothers proudly devoted their daughters to the foul service of the Temple. The priestess was a profligate, and pollution was esteemed a virtue, all classes of people being unblushing devotees. Against this state of society, St. Paul was called to array a pure religion. Men sneeringly said that human nature being what it was, the case was hopeless, and that no change could be accomplished. Yet the preacher of Christ's religion wrought until the estimate was changed, and what had been pronounced pure and right came to be recognized as foul and wrong. The Goddess of the Temple was revealed in her true character as a fury in disguise, plotting to madden and destroy mankind. Thus, this false theory of what was called "human nature" gave way. To-day we are entering upon a still higher phase of the struggle, in which we are to prove that the physical system is not the despotic thing generally supposed, and that it is possible to keep the body in sujection, rendering it what it was intended to be, the Temple of the Holy Ghost. Returning to the general subject of this paper, let us proceed to notice that

THE OBJECT

of the White Cross Society is to elevate opinion respecting the Nature and Claims of Morality, with its equal obligation upon Man and Woman, and to secure a proper, practical recognition of its precepts and authority on the part of the Individual, the Family, and the Nation.

METHODS.

As the work went on, it was deemed needful to take some further action with respect to methods that might prove particularly useful in the prosecution of the work here in America. Hence the following form was drawn up and presented in various quarters for approval, having been signed, first, by nearly all the Bishops of the Protestant Episcopal Church; yet it should be said here that though this movement originated in the Church of England and has had the especial attention of Episcopalians in this country, it is in no sense denominational. It has been formally approved by thousands of clergymen of all denominations, and by numerous and large bodies representing Temperance work, which goes hand in hand with the White Cross.

The White Cross Society seeks to carry out its object by the use of the following methods:

1. By the full presentation of those spiritual truths which form distinguishing characteristics of Christr anity, and demonstrate its unalterable hostility to every form of impurity.

2. By securing the delivery of Discourses and Appeals addressed to men only, together with such public teaching of a more general character as may be desirable for both sexes.

3. By the dissemination of Literature specially adapted to shape a high type of manly and chival- rous character, and by a more careful attention to the moral and domestic environment of the poor.

4. By the discouragement and condemnation of whatever may be impure in Literature, Amusements and Art.

5. By encouraging the proposition to enact a National Marriage Law; by the promotion of legis- lation particularly designed to protect the virtue of women; and by seeking so to guard them in their

industrial pursuits that penury may not become a temptation to sin.

6. By the organization of local branches where it may be deemed desirable to carry out the Object of the Society, and by presenting the claims made by the Movement upon Temperance Societies.

7. By hearty co-operation, so far as circumstances admit and justify, with approved Societies, Guilds, and Brotherhoods, that conduct their work in accordance with one or more of the foregoing methods.

A glance at these methods will serve to prove that they are at once legitimate, wise, and far-reaching. They summon both religion and law to aid in advancing a pure morality in accordance with spiritual laws. They reveal the work, not as human, but as Divine, the person assuming the White Cross obligation promising, "by the help of God," to keep his vow. The White Cross work, in all its methods, honors Christ and His Gospel, and seeks to find its true strength in the grace of God. The methods may be described, upon the whole, as old-fashioned, the aim being to do plain, practical work for purity, based upon Gospel lines. It does not seek to act as a Society for the Suppression of Vice, important and indispensable as such societies may be, but it seeks to employ existing agencies, and summon the Church in all its branches to press upon the consciences of the people the necessity of leading pure lives. The methods suppose, not the superseding of the churches, but the full employment of all existing religious agencies as moral factors. The body to which Christ delegated the work of spreading the

Gospel, is asked by the White Cross Society to rise
to a full sense of its duty and privilege, and stand
forth anew with all the early apostolic fervor as the
moral teacher of the world.

"THE TEMPLE OF THE HOLY GHOST."

Under the head of methods, however, something
needs to be said with respect to the White Cross
teachings regarding the human body. St. Paul
taught the first Christians that the body was the
temple of the Holy Ghost, and the White Cross fails
essentially where it neglects to set forth this truth.
That the body is the temple of the Holy Ghost, is
one of those truths hard to be received by a considerable class of excellent men and women. To the
pure all things are pure, and yet there are men and
women, apparently models in society, to whom much
seems impure. Impurity, for instance, is found in
connection with the body, and especially with sex.
We have indeed been taught the importance of reverencing the body, but how often has reverence for
the body taken on the form of war against the body.
On the same principle reverence for the soul would
be shown by suppressing the aspirations of the soul;
while reverence for the mind would exhibit itself in
the suppression of thought. We must remember,
however, that every faculty of the body and mind
has been created for a purpose. Still there is this
unreasonable distrust of the body, while marriage
itself is often looked upon as impure, or at least as
forming an inferior state. This false reasoning has
cost many a noble man and woman health of body

and peace of mind. The truth, if better known, would afford an explanation of much of the prevailing invalidism. The White Cross Movement, nevertheless, concerns itself fearlessly, but reverently, with the question of the body, and seeks to bring the soul into rational agreement with the tabernacle which temporarily forms its home. The White Cross teaches that

ALL THE CREATIONS OF GOD ARE GOOD,

and that the revolt against sex is a war against that which is no enemy; for the body, when rightly understood, is the friend of the soul. The White Cross calls us to be at peace with the natures that God has given, to study them, and to comprehend them. Successful methods, then, must include due attention to physiology, which must be studied as a part of the science of Christianity. Without a proper understanding of the body, and a correct appreciation of what is natural and what is unnatural, we shall be troubled by that skepticism, already pointed out, with respect to the possibility of curing popular vices. The White Cross teaches what the apostle taught, namely, that vice is unnatural, and that in reality, in this struggle against the evils of the day, both God and our own physical natures are on the side of the soul.

ITS RELATION TO OTHER MOVEMENTS.

The White Cross occupies a peculiar relation to many other philanthropic movements, and in order to succeed, there must be a study of its relation to them. It does not stand out in the attitude of soli-tariness, neither does it offer itself as a panacea. In presenting its methods its friends recognize the claims of other efforts. It is connected, indeed, with all good works. Notably, as already indicated, must its methods be urged with reference to the temperance reform. It is also intimately associated with the subjects of work and wages, for womanly purity is maintained with difficulty while thousands, as at the present time, cannot earn a reasonable livelihood. The present development of woman's activities in benevolent and industrial enterprises is tending greatly to her moral elevation. She is prov-ing herself successful and capable, both in philan-thropic and in business relations. The purity issue is likewise closely related to female suffrage, since it is becoming more and more evident that if woman is ever truly protected, it will be when she has the fullest opportunity of protecting herself by the ballot.

In the organization of White Cross Societies, men are banded together on the platform that has already been presented, the leader being a Christian man of wisdom and experience. For the benefit of those into whose hands this paper may fall, and who may desire to form organizations, we give a set of Rules and Regulations which will be found ample for all purposes, notwithstanding their simplicity and brevity.

ORGANIZATION.

1. This Association shall be called —— Branch of the White Cross Society.

2. The management of the branch shall be intrusted to a committee of not more than ten members, including the president, vice-president, recording secretary, corresponding secretary and treasurer, all of whom shall be elected annually by the members. Any vacancy occurring may be filled by election at the next following meeting.

3. The branch shall consist of male " members," not less than eighteen years of age, and " associates," not less than sixteen years of age. The latter shall be admitted to such meetings only as the committee shall deem advisable.

4. The members and associates shall be admitted after being proposed in writing by a member of the branch, and approved by the committee. Every person so admitted, on signing the five-fold promise, shall receive a copy of the Object, Methods, and Rules of the Society, with a card of membership.

5. The committee shall have full power to suspend or dismiss from the branch any member or associate for reasons which shall appear to them to be sufficient, and to erase his name from the books.

6. The general work of the branch shall be carried on under the guidance of the central association.

7. All expenses shall be defrayed by voluntary contributions.

8. The regular meetings shall be held quarterly, and special meetings at such other times as may be deemed expedient by the committee.

9. All meetings held in connection with this association shall be opened and closed with prayer,

FURTHER METHODS.

While the White Cross Society is exclusively for men, its interests include women, girls and boys. A special department has been created for women, which is generally known as "The White Shield."

THE WHITE SHIELD PLEDGE.

I promise, by the help of God,

1.   To uphold the law of purity as equally binding upon men and women.

2.   To be modest in language, behavior and dress.

3.   To avoid all conversation, reading, art and amusements, which may put impure thoughts into my mind.

4.   To guard the purity of others, especially of my companions and friends.

5.   To strive after the special blessing promised to the PURE IN HEART.

As this card may be used in connection with other associations, no special society for women need be formed. The pledge, for instance, is in general use among the branches of the National Woman's Christian Temperance Union.

The difficulty of working for young girls is apparent. This is a task especially for mothers, and the White Cross societies interest themselves as far as possible in helping mothers to do their duty by their daughters. But it is sad to think that thousands of mothers have neither the disposition nor the ability to teach their daughters as they need to be taught. For young girls a card has therefore been formulated, and in many instances, under the guidance of discreet and experienced Christian women, they have been associated for mutual help in societies or guilds, called "The Daughters of the Temple." This work may, where convenient, be attached to temperance and other societies, having for their object increased purity of life.

PLEDGE FOR THE DAUGHTERS OF THE TEMPLE.

I promise, by the help of God,

1. To reverence all sacred things, and to be modest in language, behavior, and dress.
2. To repress all thoughts, words and deeds which I should be ashamed to have my parents know.
3. To avoid all conversation, reading, pictures, and amusements, which may put wrong thoughts into my mind.
4. To guard the purity and good name of my companions and friends; and never needlessly to speak evil of any, especially when they are absent.
5. To strive after the special blessing promised to the PURE IN HEART.

It will be seen by comparison that the subject is brought forward in a simpler way than in the White Shield card.

The greatest difficulty is met when we come to consider the best methods of dealing with boys. Sixteen being the age of "associate members," and eighteen of "active members" of the White Cross, there has been devised the Guild of "The Silver Cross," for younger boys. This may shape its own particular organization, while accepting the common platform.

PLEDGE OF THE SILVER CROSS.

I promise, by the help of God,

1. To treat all women with courtesy and respect, and to be specially kind to all persons who are poorer or weaker or younger than myself.
2. To be modest in word and deed, and to discourage profane and

impure language, never doing or saying anything I should be unwilling
to have known by my father or mother.

3. To avoid all conversation, reading, pictures, and amusements,
which may put impure thoughts into my mind.

4. To guard the purity of others, especially of companions and
friends, and avoid speaking or thinking evil.

5. To keep my body in temperance, soberness and chastity.

Here we have an excellent basis for action., How
beautiful would the lives of our boys be, and how
soon would the whole constitution of society be
changed, if the noble and chivalrous thoughts here
set forth were given a practical shape in daily conduct. But it is not enough that we lay down valuable rules for the guidance of the young. We must
teach them what the rules really mean, since the
plainest language needs illustration. This is especially the work of the elders, who, in the White
Cross societies, are pledged to help their "younger
brothers." The boy of to-day needs the greatest care
of all, and for the reason, among others, that he is
exposed to peculiar temptations. The case of the
girl is indeed one that awakens the most painful
solicitude. Danger constantly lurks around her, and
a thousand eyes are upon her, and a thousand brains
are plotting her fall. Yet, notwithstanding this, the
girl lives a comparatively secluded and sheltered
life. She has a protection that the boy can never
enjoy. Soon, of necessity, the latter goes forth from
the family circle to make his way in the world. He
is found in every public place, exposed to many bad
influences.

Then, too, the strength of passion in the boy is
greater. He has special need of discipline and power

of self restraint. At a certain period of his life he becomes conscious of a change in his entire system, and he feels himself swayed by a mysterious power which, unless he has been duly instructed, he cannot understand. Then, if unprepared to meet new and strange impulses, he may be borne away on the tide of ungovernable and ruinous passion, and in a few years become a moral and physical wreck. A great responsibility, therefore, rests upon parents, guardians, teachers, and, in fact, upon all who in any way have the oversight of boys. The White Cross realizes its own share of the responsibility. It recognizes the fact that some parents are incapable of teaching boys, that others are careless and indifferent with respect to their duty and, therefore, that it must act in at least one of three ways: First, by securing the attention of parents and persuading them to fulfill their obligations; or, second, by directing the attention of pastors and teachers to the dangers and the needs of boys; or, in the third place, by seeking to set in motion such general machinery as in one way or another may reach and educate the rising generation, preparing them to meet evils and temptations which they are certain to encounter.

OBJECTIONS.

We are all, no doubt, familiar with the objection which is often urged, to the effect, that the course suggested involves "the putting of things in the minds of the young." Things are certain to be put in the minds of the young. The only question is, by whom shall things be put, and what shall the things

themselves be? It is absolutely certain that, sooner
or later, the boy will learn; therefore we ask what
shall he learn, and how shall he learn it? Shall he
learn truth or falsehood? Shall he learn it from his
father and mother, from his pastor or medical ad-
viser, or from the stable boy or some chance companion on the street? Shall he be taught that chastity is perfectly consistent with sound health, or that,
to enjoy health, he must violate the laws of God and
man? To-day these are some of the questions with
which we are brought face to face, and the White
Cross answers them without flinching, declaring that
the boy of the rising generation must be properly
instructed in relation to the mysteries of his nature
and being. The boy, above all, not only needs to
know the truth, but to receive it from the properly
accredited person in the right spirit, and in the right
way. Everything depends upon the manner in
which the truth is lodged in the mind. Every truth
in relation to his nature should be so set before the
boy's mind as to secure a sober and reverent reception, and never in such a way as to excite either
merriment or disgust. The boy should be taught in
the simplest and most solemn manner that the body
was designed to be the temple of the Holy Ghost,
and that he who defiles the temple will be judged at
last; while, for the time being, nature will follow any
violation with a stern and unrelenting retribution.
The youth must know *in season* that when nature is
assaulted and invaded, she will turn upon the ag-
gressor, and that when struck she will strike back.
The sin of the boy or the man will find him out in

time, and follow him into eternity. Whatsoever a man soweth that shall he also reap. This is a terrible truth, and one of which the conductors of the White Cross Crusade are fully conscious. They would therefore spare no wise means of teaching and informing the young in season to save themselves from the awful consequences that almost invariably follow ignorance and neglect. Many a lad, when too late, has demanded in piteous but unavailing terms: Why did you not tell me?

LITERATURE.

Besides faithful oral teaching by authorized and qualified instructors, who naturally should be the parents of the lad, we have the silent instruction of the printed page. But in the choice of reading there is encountered a difficulty of the very gravest kind. The production of the proper purity literature for the youth of this country is no easy task. Comparatively little literature adapted to boys has as .yet been produced. That now accessible is mainly the work of foreign authors. With regard to the merits of these productions there is a great diversity of opinion. The White Cross papers for men, however, are quite abundant, and there is no reasonable ground for doubt with respect to the value of the work. The great need at the present time, therefore, is printed instruction for boys, instruction too, that is scientific, that is to say, based upon a thorough physiology. There is a great deal of a certain kind of instruction already, yet it is generally deficient in connection with those aspects of the science which need the most earnest and emphatic treatment. What is generally *avoided,* both in books and in oral teaching, is the one thing most imperatively needed. The incapacity of teachers and writers for treating the " Avoided Subject " forms one excuse for this neglect. It is however, to a false delicacy and downright prudery that the greater part of the avoidance is to be attributed. This prudery needs to be put aside. This result cannot be accomplished too soon. Nothing can take the place of plain and faithful teaching. It is one thing for parents to love their offspring, but quite another to deal with them honestly and candidly, helping them to become acquainted with the secret of their being at the right time, and in the right way. Thousands of precious lives are annually sacrificed and the graveyards are made populous through false delicacy and parental neglect. The pitfalls lie all around us and the boys will stumble in and be lost, if they are not faithfully warned. The mysteries of life must be taught, if we do not wish the young to profane and wreck their bodies, which means the wreck of the soul. We can accomplish the needed work only by the employment of a sound Christian physiology, teaching the supreme importance of personal purity based on the Scripture teaching that the body is the temple of the Holy Ghost.

The White Cross Societies everywhere must, therefore, welcome and heartily encourage publishers and publications in the interest of this great educational work. Without special fundamental instruction, something going deeper than a mere literary expression of the moralities, the best intentioned precepts may eventually fail. What we need in this connection is to carry physiology into religion, and religion into physiology. In thorough White Cross teaching these things must know no divorce, and we must never allow ourselves to become weary of repeating that the *body* is the temple of the Holy Ghost.

In the choice of books, of course, one cannot be too careful. Yet it would be unreasonable to expect to find many works or even a single one that will answer every demand. Whatever book we choose, however, must be written from the Christian view point and recognize the fact that man is endowed with an immortal soul.

A single book of the right kind may bring untold blessing into a family of boys. A single White Cross paper, at the beginning of the movement in this country, saved a brilliant young man, the son of a clergyman, from throwing himself away and entering upon a life of sin. To this course he had been recommended by an ignorant and immoral physician who taught, in opposition to the highest medical authorities of England and America,—that chastity was incompatible with health. We need therefore, to spread the light, by every possible agency, through a rational physiology, persuading the youth of this land, that the road on which the White Cross army marches is the road of the soul's safety and of bodily health.

GLOSSARY.

Absorbents—The vessels and glands which perform the function of absorption.

Absorption—The taking up of liquid substances.

Alchemy—The transmutation of metals.

Alimentary Canal—The entire passage (from the mouth to the anus) through which the food passes.

Alvine—Belonging to the bowels.

Anatomy—A description of the different organs or parts of the body.

Anus—Circular opening or outlet of the bowels.

Aorta—The main artery of the body.

Arachnoid Membrane—The second covering of the brain.

Arterial Blood—Blood purified by oxygen.

Assimilation—The transforming of foreign materials into living substance.

Atrophy—Wasting or emaciation, with loss of strength.

Automatic—Functions or motions performed without the will.

Bile—The liver secretion.

Blastema—Organic matter in the process of formation.

Bronchial—Belonging to the bronchia—the two main branches of the windpipe.

Calcium—The basis of lime.

Canaliculi—Little channels.

Capillaries—Hair-like vessels conveying fluids in the body.

Cartilage—Gristle.

Cartilaginous—Of the nature of cartilage.

Castration—Removal of the testicles.

Castrato—One who has been castrated.

Celibacy—The unmarried state.

Cerebellum—The smaller or lower brain.

Cerebro-spinal—Pertaining to the brain and the spine.

Cerebrum—The upper or larger brain.

351

Chastity—Purity; freedom from unlawful sexual intercourse.

Chyle—Chyme transformed into a milk-like liquid from which blood is formed.

Chyme—The pulpy mass formed from food in its first change in the process of digestion.

Circulation—The regular vital action by which the blood passes through heart, arteries, capillaries and veins.

Coagulation—The thickening of certain fluids by application of acids or heat.

Coition—The sexual act.

Colon—That part of the large intestine above the rectum.

Congress—Sexual intercourse.

Constipation—Torpid action of the bowels.

Continence—Abstinence from sexual intercourse, except for the purpose of procreation; self command.

Continent—Restrained; limited; chaste.

Copulation—Congress; sexual act.

Corpora Cavernosa—Cavernous or hollow bodies.

Corporeal—Bodily.

Corpuscles—Cells; atoms.

Corpus Spongiosum—The spongy portion of the penis.

Cowper's Gland—Two small glands joined to the urethra near the bladder.

Cremaster Muscle—A muscle supporting the testicle.

Cuticle—The outer skin.

Debris—Rubbish.

Deltoid—A large muscle covering the shoulder joint.

Duct—Canal or tube.

Duodenum—The first portion of the small intestines.

Dura Mater—The external membrane of the brain.

Effete—Dead; useless.

Ejaculatory Duct—A tube conveying semen into the urethra.

Eliminated—Expelled.

Emaciation—The state of becoming lean.

Emasculated—Deprived of virility.

Emissions—That which is thrown out.

Emollient—A softening or soothing application.

Epididymis—Flattened bodies lying upon the back of the testes.

Erection—Enlargement of the penis.

Erotic—Pertaining to sexual desires.

Eunuch—A man who has been castrated.

Excretion—The rejection from the body of useless matter.

Excretory—Pertaining to excretion.

Expiration—Expelling air from the lungs.

Fecal—From the bowels.

Femur—The thigh.

Fibril—Extremely minute parts of a muscle.

Fibrillæ—Fibrils.

Fibrine—An organic ingredient of the blood and chyle. Coagulates spontaneously.

Flaccid—Weak and soft.

Foreskin—The prepuce.

Fornication—Unlawful sexual intercourse.

Gall-bladder—The reservoir containing bile from the liver.

Gamut—The musical scale.

Ganglia—Nerve centers in the sympathetic system.

Gastric—Pertaining to the stomach.

Generative—Relating to reproduction.

Genital—Generative.

Gland—An organ for secreting some fluid from the blood.

Glandular—Pertaining to a gland.

Glans—The head of the penis.

Granule—A little grain.

Hepatic Veins—The liver veins.

Hieroglyphic—A sacred symbolic character.

Histologist—One who is learned in the minute structure of tissues.

Hygiene—The art of preserving health.

Hygienic—Pertaining to hygiene.

Impotence—Incapacity for procreating.

Inspiration—Taking air into the lungs.

Instinct—Natural intelligence.

Integument—Skin; covering.

Intestines—The bowels.

Iris—The colored part of the eye.

Kidneys—The glands which secrete urine.

Lachrymal—Pertaining to tears.

Lacteal—Pertaining to milk.

Larva—The grub; the first condition of insect life.

Larynx—The upper part of the trachea or windpipe.

Lascivious—Lewd; gross.

Libidinous—Lewd; lustful.

Licentiousness—Dissoluteness; immorality.

Lobe—A round projecting part of an organ.
Lobule—A little lobe.
Lymph—Colorless, transparent fluid in the body.
Lymphatics—The vessels which contain lymph.
Mammary—Pertaining to the breast.
Masturbation—Self-abuse of the sexual organs.
Meatus Urinarius—The orifice of the urethra.
Medullary—Pertaining to the marrow.
Membranous—Composed of membrane.
Microcosm—A world in miniature.
Motor—Pertaining to motion.
Mucous Membrane—The membrane which lines the cavities communicating with the open air.
Nitrogenous—Rich in nitrogen.
Nocturnal—In the night.
Nucleus—A central point.
Nuclei—More than one nucleus.
Nutrition—That which provides food for repair and growth.
Œsophagus—The gullet.
Oleaginous—Oily; fatty.
Olfactory—Pertaining to the sense of smell.
Omosis—The passage of liquids through thin membranes.
Ossification—The hardening of cartilage into bone.
Ova—More than one ovum; eggs.
Ovaria—More than one ovarium or ovary.
Ovaries—Ovaria.
Ovarium—The organ containing the ova.
Ovary—Ovarium.
Ovum—An egg.
Ovules—A little egg.
Pancreatic—Pertaining to the pancreas.
Pancreas—A gland lying near the stomach.
Paternity—Fatherhood.
Pelvis—The bony cavity in the lower part of the trunk.
Penis—The male organ of copulation.
Periosteum—The membrane covering the bones.
Physiology—A description of the organs and parts of the body.
Pia Mater—The inner membrane of the brain.
Plasma—The liquor in which the blood corpuscles float.
Plexus—A network of minute vessels and nerves.
Pores—Minute openings in the surface of the body.

Portal Veins—Veins conveying blood from digestive organs to the liver.
Post-natal—After birth.
Pregnant—Being with child.
Pre-natal—Before birth.
Prepuce—The membranous fold which covers the glans penis.
Priapism—Continual erection.
Procreation—Reproduction.
Prostate Gland—A gland situated near the bladder.
Protoplasm—Cell contents, from which also all cells are formed.
Prurient—Uneasy with base desires; illicit.
Puberty—The earliest age at which persons have the power of reproduction.
Pubes—External part of the organs of generation, covered with hair.
Pulmonary—Pertaining to the lungs.
Quickening—The first motion of the unborn child.
Quintessence—Pure, concentrated essence.
Raphe—A division wall between the two testicles.
Recapitulation—A concise statement of points or facts; a review.
Reproductive—Adapted to reproduction.
Residuum—That which is left; the residue.
Respiration—The act of breathing.
Rete Testis—The network of seminal tubes.
Salacious—Lustful.
Saliva—Spittle.
Salivary—Pertaining to saliva.
Salts—Compounds of an acid and a base.
Sebaceous—Secreting fatty matter.
Scrotum—The bag which contains the testicles.
Secretion—A substance separated from the blood by various organs of the body.
Sedentary—Accustomed to sit much; inactive.
Self-abuse—Masturbation.
Segments—Divisions.
Semen—Secretion of the testes.
Seminal—Pertaining to seed.
Seminal Tubes—The fine tubes which compose the body of the testicle.
Serous—The lining of cavities having no external opening.
Serum—The liquid portion of the blood after coagulation.
Sexual—Pertaining to sex.
Silicon—The base of flint and quartz.
Smegma—The soap-like substance which exudes around the glans penis.

19

Sperm—Animal seed.

Spermatic—Relating to semen; seminal.

Spermatorrhœa—Involuntary emission of semen.

Spermatozoa—The living principle of semen.

Spleen—A gland situated in the left side of the body.

Stricture—Contraction of a canal or duct.

Sub-clavian—An artery situated under the collar bone.

Synovia—The secretion which lubricates the joints.

Tendons—The white fibrous cords which unite muscles with bones.

Testes—Glands which secrete semen.

Testicles—Testes.

Therapeutic—The treatment of disease; curative.

Thoracic Duct—The chief duct of the absorbents. It empties into
  sub-clavian vein.

Tortuous—Wreathed; twisted.

Trachea—Windpipe.

Transude—To pass through the pores of a substance.

Tubule--A little tube.

Tubuli Seminiferi—Seminal tubes.

Tunica Albuginea—The dense white coat forming the inner covering
  the testicles.

Turgid—Swelled; bloated.

Ureters—The membranous tube conveying the urine from the kidr
  to the bladder.

Urethra—The membranous tube conveying the urine from the hlac
  to the external surface.

Uterus—Womb.

Vagina—Passage leading from the womb.

Vas Aberrans—Winding tubes in the testis.

Vasa Efferentia—Tubes that bear away semen from the lobules.

Vasa Recta - Straight tubes in the testes.

Vas Deferens—Tubes that bear the semen out of the testes.

Vena Cava— The large vein communicating with the heart.

Venous—Pertaining to veins.

Vermiform—Worm shaped.

Vesiculæ Seminales—Receptacles for the semen.

Villi—More than one villus.

Villus—A minute absorbent.

Vito-chemical· Life force.

Virile—Manly.

Virility—Manhood.

Volitional—By power of the will.

Womb—The uterus; the organ in which the fœtus is developed.

Zoosperms—Spermatozoa.

INDEX.

CPSIA information can be obtained
at www.ICGtesting.com
Printed in the USA
LVHW031910271118
598385LV00002B/224/P